My Eighty Years in Texas

Personal Narratives of the West

Fred Gipson, General Editor

(FORMERLY EDITED BY J. FRANK DOBIE)

William Physick Zuber. Oil portrait by Jenkins, 1910.

MY EIGHTY YEARS
IN TEXAS

by William Physick Zuber

Edited by JANIS BOYLE MAYFIELD

With Notes and an Introduction by
LLERENA FRIEND

UNIVERSITY OF TEXAS PRESS, AUSTIN

Requests for permission to reproduce material from this work should be
sent to:
    Permissions
    University of Texas Press
    P.O. Box 7819
    Austin, TX 78713-7819
    https://utpress.utexas.edu/book-permissions/

Library of Congress Catalog Number 73-161971

ISBN 978-0-292-75022-7, paperback
ISBN 978-0-292-76953-3, PDF e-book
ISBN 978-0-292-76954-0, ePub e-book

EDITOR'S FOREWORD

I first learned of William P. Zuber and his manuscript, Eighty Years in Texas: Reminiscences of a Texas Veteran from 1830 to 1910, from his niece, Virginia Lee Edwards Mayfield, who was my husband's mother. The youngest of six children, Jennie, as she was called, grew up in the loving companionship of her grandmother, Mary Ann Zuber, who often told her granddaughter of the old days in Texas and of the adventures of her son William.

Years later I read Zuber's manuscript in the Texas State Archives, Austin. I was astonished that such a treasure could have gone unnoticed for its own narrative value, although earnest students of Texas history have poured through the lengthy handwritten pages and it is frequently cited by writers as reference material. I decided to carry through to publication work already started by Mr. Zuber and his daughter, Mrs. Rachel Zuber Mize, so that others could share my pleasure.

The manuscript is comprised of over eight hundred pages of large handwriting and ninety-five generally short chapters. This published version has been somewhat condensed by eliminating, with no indication of ellipses, some of Zuber's repetitions and redundancies, some of his recurrent moralizing, and some digressive background reviews of events and of such figures as Stephen F. Austin, the accounts of which are well known and play no part in his immediate story. Certain portions have been placed in chronological sequence. The subtitles generally correspond to Zuber's chapter titles in the manuscript. I have attempted to edit the writing itself only for the sake of economy and clarity.

With gratitude I acknowledge the assistance of members of the Texas State Archives staff for helping to make the original manuscript available. A special "thank you" goes to Dr. Llerena Friend for her invaluable work in preparing the introduction, footnotes, bibliography, and the historiography of the Rose account.

Finally, I wish to acknowledge the loving encouragement given me by my late husband, Walton, and to express my joy for the privilege of peaceful days and nights spent on the old Zuber homestead near Shiro, where William Zuber spent his most impressionable years.

JANIS BOYLE MAYFIELD

CONTENTS

CONTENTS

INTRODUCTION

What has been called one of the most pathetic days in time—and certainly in Texas history—derives much of its fame from an account based solely upon one man's total recall of the narration of an incident known only to the narrator, or upon the fertile imagination of the raconteur.

The man who related the story of that memorable day, March 3, 1836, was W. P. Zuber, who had heard from his parents of the escape of their friend Moses Rose from the Alamo. Rose left the mission after William B. Travis called together his small force and gave them a choice—to attempt to escape or to remain with him in the old mission, to meet certain death. Rose chose the first. When their son William returned from the San Jacinto campaign, the Abraham Zubers told him of Rose's experience and related Rose's account of his last hours with the doomed defenders of the Alamo. Again and again young Zuber questioned his mother as to the details. But he was fifty-one years old before he wrote the story, substantially, he said, as Rose had related it. When the Zuber account was published in the *Texas Almanac* in 1873 as "An Escape from the Alamo" —a third-hand story—it was thirty-five years after the fact.

In 1901, at a time when critical historians were expressing doubts about the credibility of this story, William P. Zuber wrote as follows to the chairman of the history department of The University of Texas to state his concept of the duty of historians: "I hold that we, as contributors to history, ought first, to write only true and interesting facts; secondly, to search out and correct as many as practicable of our own mistakes; thirdly, to correct mistakes of others, as delicately as we can; and fourthly, to thank others for correcting us, if they do so justly and courteously."[1]

Zuber's *My Eighty Years in Texas* is Texas history. It consists of his autobiography and his reminiscences, as compiled by the wife of his grandnephew from the original manuscript, Eighty Years in Texas: Reminiscences of a Texas Veteran from 1830 to 1910, in the Texas State Archives. The story of the Rose escape is not a part of that manuscript, but it has been added as an appendix, and perhaps it is well that the writing by which Zuber has been best known should be included.

The publication of *My Eighty Years in Texas* is a case of the last being first. It represents the labor of the last three years of Zuber's life. Its manuscript preface calls it a "substitute for my former work on the lives of Texas Veterans." At the age of ninety, he still hoped that he could complete and publish the "more important work." Zuber had started the manuscript on the lives of the veterans in 1886 and had worked on it constantly until his wife's death in 1904 and his subsequent removal from Grimes County to Austin in 1906.

Zuber's adult years, until he reached about the age of fifty, were spent in soldiering, farming, and teaching school—with the Methodist church as a background. After 1870, Texas history and the veterans who contributed to that history absorbed most of his attention. He began to write articles about early incidents of the Texas Revolution and from 1886 on he wrote voluminously on the biographies of early Texans, many of whom he had known. Once he estimated that he had written over a thousand letters of inquiry concerning them. As he prepared some 130 biographies, he used for his sketches his own knowledge, the letters he had accumulated, and the printed sources available at the time, footnoting his material to point out inconsistencies and inaccuracies. This material, written legibly in ink on lined paper, is compiled in ten hand-bound volumes. Volume I has a Table of Contents. Their covers are stitched in a sort of diamond-shaped pattern through two or three sheets of manila paper; the edges are buttonholed and each volume is tied together with the same heavy

[1] W. P. Zuber to G. P. Garrison, December 10, 1901, Garrison Papers, The University of Texas Archives, Austin.

lined thread used for the stitching. Zuber may have prepared the binding, or it may have been the work of his daughter Rachel, Mrs. S. P. Mize.

There is some indication that the manuscript of Eighty Years in Texas in the State Archives may once have had a similar binding. After Zuber's death, his daughter added her father's biography to the compilation of Texas veterans. She stated that he had prepared another sketch, which was to be published, but that she felt he "deserved space among the lives of the Texas Veterans."[2]

Periodically Zuber would think his work was ready for the press. So it is ever with authors! As early as 1891 he was culling letters in preparation for printing. By 1894 he was still working, although he had decided to confine his work to "first class veterans." Later he was disappointed that the Daughters of the Republic of Texas could not assist in financing the publication.[3] Indications are that some of the articles appeared in Texas newspapers. One correspondent wrote, for instance: "Your article on Stephen F. Austin was read by us with the greatest interest and pleasure. Every word of it is true; and I am glad that you wrote it and had it published."[4]

Despite failing eyesight and attacks of vertigo, Zuber continued to accumulate material and to write. He must have found real satisfaction in the *Houston Post*'s publication of a series of his articles, early in 1904. In March, 1904, came the death of his wife and the disruption of his life.

While he was still living in Grimes County, Zuber did some writing in two other areas: on behalf of the Texas Veterans Association for pensions or land for its members, and for the early volumes of the *Quarterly of the Texas State Historical Association*, which association was organized in 1897.

For twenty years after 1870, the subject of pensions for veterans of the Texas Revolution was of periodic concern to the Texas Legislature. In Eighty Years, Zuber tells of his experience in validating

---

[2] Biographies of Texas Veterans, Zuber Papers, IX, 1535–1536, The University of Texas Archives, Austin.

[3] Zuber to Guy M. Bryan, September 2, 1891, April 14, 1894, and June 8, 1898, Zuber Papers.

[4] John Jenkins, Sr., to Zuber, July 30, 1890, Zuber Papers.

his claim to his pension. The first pension law was passed on August 13, 1870. On January 1, 1874, Zuber wrote an impressive memorial to the upcoming legislature on the justification of and the necessity for the pensions. San Jacinto Day of 1874 was appropriately the date for passage of the next Pension Act, one which granted annual pensions to the surviving veterans and provided for the liquidation and settlement of all arrearages due the veterans under the 1870 act. The 1874 law was repealed on March 13, 1875, but the new Texas Constitution of 1876 stated that the legislature might provide annual pensions of not over $150 to indigent veterans. That constitutional provision was implemented by a law of July 28, 1876, providing for an annual pension but stipulating that four times a year the state comptroller must have proof that the veteran pensioner still survived and was indigent. In 1879 the Legislature further provided that each veteran enrolled under the act of 1876 should be granted a land certificate for 640 acres of public land.[5]

By the time the 1879 law was passed, most of the state's land had already been filed upon. One area where there was perhaps a possibility of securing titles lay between the north and south forks of the Red River in Greer County. Ignoring action of the United States government, which also claimed the area, the Texas legislature in 1879 reserved Greer County land from location and appropriated one half of any income therefrom for educational purposes and one half for payment of the public debt. John M. Swisher, representing the veterans, memorialized the United States Congress to cede all right to Greer County to the state of Texas, one half to be used for educational purposes and the other half to go to the Texas veterans of 1836. Swisher also memorialized the Texas legislature, in April, 1882, and January, 1883, concerning the location of veterans' certificates in Greer County. Patents were secured, but they were contested by speculators.[6]

[5] H. P. N. Gammel, ed., *The Laws of Texas, 1822–1897*, VIII, 116, 485, 833, 897, 1475; Memorial of William P. Zuber on the Subject of Pensions to the Honorable Legislature of the State of Texas (1874), Texas State Archives, Austin.

[6] John M. Swisher, *Address of John M. Swisher in Behalf of the Texas Veterans, to the Legislature of the State of Texas upon the Subject of Greer County* (Austin, 1882).

Zuber also memorialized the legislature. He considered the requirement that the old and decrepit veterans had to incur the trouble and expense of proving their identity and continued existence four times a year both "burdensome and unnecessary." "If," he said, "some of them die soon enough to save their funeral expenses, the State should consider that this is their last straw. None of them will purposely die to make a clear profit off their last pension."[7]

In March of 1882 the legislature broadened the appropriations to include pensions not only for the surviving veterans or surviving wives of veterans, but also for the surviving signers of the (Texas) Declaration of Independence, and a similar law was passed in March, 1885. Up to 1889 Swisher continued the struggle to get land for the veterans; Zuber contributed his part when he prepared "An Address to the People of Texas in Relation to Greer County Matters," which was printed in the *Dallas Herald*, October 8, 1885. Some of the veterans had their original land patents canceled and received new certificates; some held on to the old patents and hoped; Zuber was among the considerable number who turned their certificates over to Swisher for location, agreeing to give him half of the land involved if he could secure patents in Greer County. In 1889 Swisher again memorialized the Texas government for relief—to compensate him for six years of labor and $30,000 in expenses and to fulfill the obligations to the veterans.[8] In 1896 the battle was lost. The United States Supreme Court ruled that Greer County was a part of the United States.

Besides his interest in veterans' pensions, Zuber participated in the Texas Veterans Association from the organizational meeting at Corsicana in 1872 until he had his picture made with the last five survivors at the Goliad meeting in 1906. It was at the Dallas reunion in 1886 that he was inspired to begin his veterans' biographies. In

[7] Memorial of William P. Zuber, a Texas Veteran, on the Subject of Pensions. To the Honorable Legislature of the State of Texas Soon to Assemble, Texas State Archives, Austin.

[8] Gammel, ed., *Laws of Texas*, IX, 342, 714, 1071; John M. Swisher, *To the Honorable Executive and Legislative Departments of the Government of the State of Texas* (Austin, 1889), p. 10.

1890, at Fort Worth, he delivered the response to the mayor's address of welcome and announced at the business session that those biographies were to be published. He was appointed one of the supervisors of the organization and served on the Committee on Resolutions and the Committee on Membership. At the 1901 meeting in Austin he read, at his own request, his "Escape of Rose from the Alamo," and the article was printed in the *Quarterly of the Texas State Historical Association.*

Zuber corresponded with Lester C. Bugbee of the *Quarterly* staff and with George P. Garrison, its editor. He made three contributions to Volumes I and II and supplied a note for Volume V. Four contributions to Volumes V and VI concerned Rose and Travis at the Alamo.

The years in Austin (1906–1913) brought new experiences. Zuber was the only surviving veteran, so that correspondence was no longer possible, but as a guide in the Senate Chamber he could point to the pictures of Texas heroes and heroic events. His salary was forty dollars a month, and he loved his work. When the monument to Hood's Texas Brigade was erected on the Capitol grounds and dedicated with services in the Senate Chamber, October 28, 1910, Zuber was introduced. He thanked the audience for the honor done him and said that he received it as a proxy for those who had preceded him "across the river." On his ninetieth birthday, in July, 1910, he had begun his book of "recollections of the State from its infancy to its prime." He worked on the book steadily until he suffered a stroke before his death. He died on May 22, 1913—a Methodist, a Mason, and a member of the John Bell Hood Camp of Confederate Veterans. He was buried with Masonic honors in the state cemetery. The obituary in the *Austin Statesman,* September 23, 1913, stated that his book was not quite finished, but would be published in its incomplete form. That was more than half a century ago.

For 1913 or for 1971, the publication of this book is appropriate. As is so often the case with those who have reached the allotted three score and ten, not to mention the more than four score and ten years that were Zuber's, the events of early life are much more vivid than those of the later days. Thus his stories of the Texas Revolution are more graphic than the depiction of post-1865 Texas, although there are some memorable paragraphs on Reconstruction events. His political history after 1865 is hazy.

The account of the disintegration of the Twenty-first Regiment is particularly poignant. Those old soldiers didn't die; they just lagged behind for a while—or took the way toward home when they came to the proper crossroad.

I know not what the reaction of the true Civil War buff will be, but considering the apparent dearth of material on the Confederate unit to which Zuber belonged, this naming of the personnel and description of a private soldier's experiences in four states (including the brief foray into Missouri) may be a unique contribution to history.

LLERENA FRIEND

My Eighty Years in Texas

The End Came Too Soon

You will see, kind reader, that my dear father did not quite complete his work as he wished. Had he lived, he yet would have years to add to his continued experience. Most of his eighty years that he could call to mind is ready for the press, and at his earnest request that I should have it published as he left it, I present the work just as he dictated.

He was born July 6, 1820, and died September 22, 1913, aged ninety-three years, two months, and sixteen days. He was blessed with many years of good faculties and a wonderful memory. He read his Bible and wrote constantly up to the twenty-fifth of May, at which time he was stricken with paralysis and was void of reason till the last.

I find among his library an Indian story. Though not a part of his written eighty-years' experience, I add it in the last pages.

His daughter,
MRS. RACHEL ZUBER MIZE

Preface

On this the sixth day of July, 1910, on which day I become ninety years old, I commence this substitute for my former work on the lives of Texas Veterans, which I planned long ago, hoping this will interest the public, and I may yet have the pleasure of completing and publishing the more important work.

The design of the present work is to state consecutively such events in the history of Texas as were known to me when they occurred, or soon thereafter, including my own biography for sake of connection. I design to include a considerable part of the history of my state, and to award due honor to many persons, mainly private citizens and soldiers, and some of our noble women. I pray God our Heavenly Father that he will so direct my pen that this book shall be interesting and profitable to all Texians.

W. P. ZUBER

1

Ancestry

I, William Physick Zuber, was born in Twiggs County, Georgia, July 6, 1820.[1]

My parents were Abraham Zuber, Jr., and Mary Ann Mann.

My maternal grandparents were Thomas Mann and Ann Deshazo.

My mother's maternal grandparents were Robert Deshazo and Mary Trevelian. She was called Mollie.

Mollie Trevelian was born in Virginia, about the year 1732. One of her parents, I know not which, was a native of Scotland, the other of Ireland. While young, they migrated from their respective native countries to Virginia, where they were married. Later, with their daughter Mollie and other children, they moved to North Carolina. There Mollie married Robert Deshazo.

---

[1] The account of Zuber's ancestry appears also in *Ancestry and Kindred of W. P. Zuber, Texas Veteran* (1905). Zuber's "delineation of my ancestry on all lines, so far as I can trace it" is addressed "To My Near Relatives and Personal Friends."

Mollie Trevelian Deshazo had an elder brother, John Trevelian, who suffered much in the Old French War, 1755, and later. As a volunteer in the Virginia Militia, he participated in the campaign against Fort Duquesne, in 1755. He fought in the battle of Monongahela, remembered as General Braddock's Defeat, on July 8 of that year. In that battle, he was captured by the French and conducted, prisoner, to Canada. How long he was held a prisoner, I am not informed; but he was finally set at liberty—penniless, in a strange country, among a strange people whose language he did not understand.

There were only two ways by which he could return home. One was through a wilderness infested by savages, who would surely kill him if he should try to traverse it alone; and he could not learn of any body of adventurers whom he could accompany on such a trip. The other way was to go by sea. Money was needful for either route, yet he had none. He could obtain employment only at low wages and for short terms, but he worked when he could, wages however low, hoping by rigid economy to save money enough to pay his way. Finally, after an absence of four or five years, he made the trip to Virginia.

He owned a good home, well-furnished for that period, which his friends had not disposed of, though they believed he had been killed in the battle in which he had been captured. He sold his possessions in Virginia and went to North Carolina, whither his parents had already gone.

He never married, but, by industry and economy, he amassed a fortune. He was a very pious member of the religious society called Methodists.

At the beginning of the revolutionary war, he enlisted in the rebel army, in which he served till the end of the war.

He resided in North Carolina till he was past ninety years old. Then he sold his property, went to South Carolina, and during the rest of his life resided with his brother-in-law and sister, Robert and Mollie Deshazo. There he related his history to his little grandniece, Mary Ann Mann, and many years later, she, my mother, repeated the same to me. He died at the Deshazo residence, in Edgefield District, South Carolina, at the age of ninety-six years.

My mother's maternal grandfather, Robert Deshazo, was born in Virginia about 1730. He was the son of Nathaniel Deshazo, who was a native of France. His mother also was of French descent, for Robert often boasted that he was "a full-blooded Frenchman," though he never learned the French language.

When Robert was twenty years old, his father sent him to North Carolina with money to purchase land and build a home in that colony. He found a suitable place and bought it. Then, with hired help he built houses, cleared and enclosed land, and made a crop. He also purchased a fine lot of livestock. All this he accomplished in one year. Then he returned to Virginia to move his father's family to North Carolina.

There being no mail at that time, Robert had not heard from his family since his departure. Upon arriving home, he found that his father had died and that his mother and brothers were averse to moving. Therefore, his father's heirs amicably effected a partition and distribution of the estate, and Robert took for his part the property which he had procured and improved in North Carolina. Then he returned to North Carolina, where he married Mollie Trevelian and took her to his home. During this time, he participated in battles against hostile Indians.

Robert Deshazo raised livestock and was an adept tobacco farmer, and he acquired wealth rapidly. At the beginning of the revolutionary war he owned thirteen Negroes, all grown-up Africans. He had sixteen head of valuable horses and plenty of other livestock. He was a pious member of the Baptist Church, highly esteemed by his neighbors, and his servants loved and served him faithfully.

At the beginning of hostilities, Robert's eldest son, Lewis Deshazo, then sixteen years old, enlisted in the rebel army, and served till the end of the war. But Robert stayed at home to care for his family and property. Frequently, however, he served for short terms as a volunteer soldier for the rebel cause and sometimes participated in battles.

A large majority of Robert's near neighbors were Tories. At first they tried to persuade him to join them. Next, they threatened to kill him, and, finally, they robbed him of much property and hunted him as if he were a wild beast. Then he spent much time hiding from them in the swamps.

After driving away all his horses and cattle, the Tories surprised his Negroes in the field, cut off their retreat, and drove away twelve of the thirteen, whom they sold in some distant locality. Only one, a woman named Genie, escaped into a swamp. The Tories never captured her. Once she saved her master's life by warning him of approaching danger.

Another time, a body of British and Tories surrounded Robert's dwelling, entered it, cursed his wife, and threatened to kill her unless she would tell them where her husband was. But Mollie withstood them for hours, and they finally departed, no wiser for their dastardly conduct.

When the war ended, Robert Deshazo's Tory neighbors, having lost their cause, tried to recover their former friendly relations with him. But their presence was a torture to him, and he resolved to leave North Carolina.

When peace was restored, Robert sold his home and moved to Edgefield District, South Carolina. There he established a new home and again acquired wealth, though not so rapidly as he had done before the war. Here he and Mollie lived till 1814, when their respective ages were eighty-four and eighty-two years. In 1814, notwithstanding the advanced ages of himself and his wife, he sold his home and moved to Twiggs County, Georgia, whither two of his sons had preceded him. There he died in 1815. Soon after his death, his widow returned to Edgefield District, South Carolina where she lived during the rest of her life with her son-in-law and daughter, Nathan and Mary Norris. She died there in 1830, at the age of ninety-eight years.

My maternal grandmother, Ann Deshazo, daughter of Robert and Mollie Deshazo, was born in North Carolina, about the year 1765. With her parents, she moved to Edgefield District, South Carolina. There she married Thomas Mann, about the year 1792.

My maternal grandfather, Thomas Mann, was a son of John Watts Mann, who was born in France of Welsh parents. Thomas was born in North Carolina, about the year 1760. From there, he moved to South Carolina, where he married Ann Deshazo. His wife died in her father's house in 1800, aged thirty-five years. Thomas then moved from South Carolina to Florida, where he married again. Thence he moved to Georgia, and thence to Alabama. He died in Pickens County, Alabama, in 1840, aged eighty-five years.

My mother, Mary Ann Mann, was born in Edgefield District, South Carolina, September 18, 1793. She was a little girl when her mother died, and she was brought up by her grandparents, Robert and Mollie Deshazo. In 1814, she moved with them to Twiggs County, Georgia, and resided with them till January, 1815, when her grandfather died. Then she resided with her uncle, William Deshazo, in the same vicinity, till her marriage in his house to Abraham Zuber, Jr., February 16, 1816.

My father, Abraham Zuber, Jr., was a son of Abraham Zuber, Sr., and Mary Bartling. Mary was a daughter of a physician and had always lived in towns or cities. She was born in Denmark, about 1745 or 1750. When she was nine years old, she moved with her parents to London, England, and thence when she was fifteen years old, to Philadelphia, Pennsylvania, where she married Abraham Zuber.

My paternal grandfather, Abraham Zuber, Sr., was a son of Daniel and Elizabeth Zuber, both of whom were of German descent and spoke German. Abraham was born in Lancaster County, Pennsylvania, probably between the years 1740 and 1745, and raised among people called "Pennsylvania Dutch." He was brought up to speak German, which he called his "mother tongue," though he was educated in both German and English. Soon after reaching his majority, he married Mary Bartling of Philadelphia and brought her home to Lancaster County. He and his wife used German as their family language. They both were members of the Lutheran Church, and each had a Lutheran Bible, which they kept and used while they lived.

At the beginning of the revolutionary war, Abraham Zuber enlisted in the rebel army, and he served therein continuously except while at home on furlough. He participated in many battles, one instance being the siege of Yorktown, Virginia, in 1781. At the close of that battle, he witnessed the surrender of Lord Cornwallis' sword to General Washington. He then received an honorable discharge for service during the entire term.

Records of this service were destroyed when the federal capitol was burned by the British during the War of 1812. However, a certificate under seal of office, by Luther R. Kelker, custodian of public records, Pennsylvania State Library, Harrisburg, Pennsylvania, dated September 28, 1905, refers to page 368, Volume Thirteen, Pennsylvania Archives, Second Series, 1896 Edition, which reads: "Abraham Zuber was Lieutenant of Fifth Company, Fifth Battalion, Lancaster County Associators; . . . in service, August 26, 1780." Those who are acquainted with the manner of some military reports in early times will understand why this record shows his service of only one day. On that day, and perhaps only then, a list of the Pennsylvania troops was returned to the state authorities.

In 1786 Abraham Zuber moved from Lancaster County, Pennsylvania, to Oglethorpe County, Georgia. There he purchased land and established a farm, on which he lived during the rest of his life.

He and his wife, Mary Bartling Zuber, were the parents of thirteen children, twelve of whom lived to maturity. About half of these were born in Pennsylvania, the others in Georgia. Those who were born in Pennsylvania spoke only German while they remained in that state, but after they moved, having no German neighbors in Georgia, they learned to speak English and abandoned the use of German. Those who were born in Georgia never learned to speak German.

Abraham Zuber, Sr., died at his home in Oglethorpe County, about the year 1802, being probably between fifty-seven and sixty-two years old. His widow, Mary, resided on his homestead till her youngest children had grown up. Then she abandoned housekeeping and lived with some of her children. She died at the residence of one of her children in Georgia in 1820, probably about seventy-two years old.

My father, Abraham Zuber, Jr., was born in Lancaster County, Pennsylvania, November 14, 1780. He was six years old when, with his parents, he moved to Oglethorpe County, Georgia. He was brought up a farmer, but on reaching his majority in 1801 he engaged in the carpenter's trade, at which he worked several years. Then he became a merchant. In 1816 he was merchandizing in the town of Marion, Twiggs County, Georgia. On February 16 of that year he married Mary Ann Mann. A year later he purchased a farm near Marion, where in 1820 I was born.

Childhood And Youth

Dixon Manac, a Half-Breed Creek Indian

In the fall of 1822, my father removed from Triggs County, Georgia, to that part of the old county of Montgomery, Alabama, which is now Lowndes County, and settled and improved upon a tract of public land. That country was then new and thinly settled. We had no neighbors, and sometimes several days elapsed during which we saw no person excepting our own family and our Negroes.

While we were there, an Indian, called Dixon, visited us frequently, bringing presents of venison and wild turkeys.[1] My parents said that at first he was shy, but by degrees he became quite friendly.

---

[1] The material included here on Dixon Manac is bound in Book IX, pp. 839–851, Zuber Collection, Texas State Archives, Austin. (As Mrs. Mize stated in her preface, she found the Indian story among her father's library and added it to the last pages of his Eighty Years manuscript. It is here placed in chronological sequence. JBM.)

According to them, he was a bright young half-breed, of slender form, dressed in the usual Indian costume of blue calico hunting gown, leather belt, and buckskin leggings. He wore his hair hanging in a long plait on his back, and on his head was a red cotton kerchief instead of a hat. His speech generally was the short imitation of English used by most Indians, but sometimes he spoke fluently, for a few minutes, in good English. Then, as if correcting himself, he would lapse back into his Indian lingo. He sold deerskins, venison, and wild turkeys in Montgomery, and with the proceeds thereof purchased the few articles that he needed. The kind feeling he manifested toward us was returned by my parents, and they became good friends.

For a considerable time, however, my parents knew nothing of Dixon's history or his character, except what they saw during his visits. But one day my father called at a store to trade and there witnessed an incident that caused him to make inquiries concerning the young half-breed.

His full name was Dixon Manac. His father was a respectable half-breed of the Creek Nation, and his mother a sister of the Grand Chief Weatherford.[2] Both Weatherford and the elder Manac were three-fourths white, as was Dixon's mother. His father and his uncle were fair English scholars, but the younger Manac was quite illiterate. The elder Manac dressed as a white man and spoke good English, generally using it in preference to the Indian language, and so did Dixon, before the Creek War. But after that, he was ambitious to be as much as possible like the Indians.

It is known that during the Creek War of 1812 many Creeks sided with the white people and fought their own people. They were called Friendlies, while those Creeks who fought the whites were called Hostiles. Many families were divided, with members fighting each other. Weatherford was the Grand Chief of the Hostiles, but his brother-in-law, Manac, was a Friendly. Dixon Manac, though scarcely old enough to bear arms, joined the Hostiles under his uncle Weatherford, and was said to have "fought like a tiger."

---

[2] William Weatherford (Lamochattee or Red Eagle) was a half-breed Creek chief (F. W. Hodge, ed., *Handbook of American Indians North of Mexico*, II, 927–928).

In one of the battles of that war, a body of Friendlies, including Manac, charged to within about twenty steps of the Hostile line and halted for a few minutes while sharp firing ensued. This movement brought Manac almost directly in front of his brother-in-law and son, who were about six feet apart, each sheltered by a tree. They both recognized the elder Manac, and Weatherford said that he could easily have shot him, but refrained because he was his brother-in-law. But Dixon was not so conscientious. He drew a bead upon his father and was about to draw trigger, when Weatherford stormed, "Hold, Dixon! You rascal! You must not kill your father!"

Dixon lowered the muzzle of his gun and replied, "*He* is the rascal, and ought to be killed for fighting his own people."

"Let another man kill him," said Weatherford. "He is *your father*. Sneak out of sight and never show your face again." Dixon slipped back to the rear and disappeared, and he and his father never met again till some ten or twelve years later, on the day my father went to trade at the store.

The store faced the bank of a small river, flowing through Montgomery County. This bank was a low, steep bluff, and the storekeeper had dug steps from the top of the bluff down about six feet to the water. The root of a tree formed the lowest step, and his custom was to descend to this root, where he could stoop to fill a bucket with water for the store. At this point, the water was some seven or eight feet deep.

On this day, my father met about a dozen citizens of the county at the store. A stranger was also present, and was introduced as Mr. Manac. He was Dixon's father. While they sat in the shade of a tree in front of the store, they saw Dixon approaching on foot. When he got within a few steps of the men, he recognized his father, started, and shied away. He walked slowly toward the steps of the bluff. His father arose and followed him in a brisk walk. The others also followed, to see what he would do to his son.

Dixon, furtively looking back at his father, halted nearly on the brink of the bluff and looked down at the ground. The elder Manac was a large, strong man, while his son was slender and light. Neither of them spoke a word, but suddenly the father took hold of his son's long plait of hair and dragged him down the steps to the root at the surface of the water. Dixon offered no resistance. Then Manac plunged his son into the water and pushed his head under the surface, still holding him by the hair. When Dixon was considerably strangled, his father drew his head above the water and held him till he had cleared his throat of water by coughing. Still holding him by his plait, he ducked him a second time, and a third. Then he dragged him by his hair to the top of the bluff and laid him down on the ground.

When Dixon had sufficiently recovered to understand what was said to him, his father, who till now had not uttered a word, said, "Now! you dirty puppy! Try to kill your father again!" Then the old man walked away, and did not look toward him again.

Dixon lay there for some time after his father left. Then, raising himself to a sitting position, he wept aloud for a long time, after which he sat in sullen silence. Late in the afternoon, the men all left him, still there on the bluff, looking down at the ground.

After my parents learned that Dixon had been a Hostile Indian, and had tried to kill his father, their kind feeling toward him was much diminished. Yet, considering the meekness with which he had submitted to the punishment, they decided that, if he should ever visit them again, they would continue to treat him kindly.

A considerable time elapsed before Dixon again visited our home, and on his first visit he was shy. But finally he recovered his usual composure. As soon as my father thought it prudent to mention the incident to him, he said, "Dixon, you are young and active. Why didn't you run from your father and escape that ducking? We all thought he intended to drown you, and I have no doubt that you thought so too."

"Me rascal," Dixon replied. "Me deserve my father kill me. Me let him kill me if he wish."

My mother then asked Dixon why he had fought the white people during the war. At first he made no reply. She asked him again, but he only shook his head. When she inquired a third time, he said, "Me no like talk about it."

But my mother persisted, and finally he dropped his Indian lingo and in good, fluent English gave her a statement of his experience.

Dixon remembered when his father had been a prosperous farmer, owning a plantation, with Negroes to cultivate it and a white man hired as an overseer. Manac wished to give Dixon a liberal English education, so he employed a private tutor for him. But the boy was too lazy to study, so he said, and never learned to read or write.

After a time, some white men established themselves in the Nation as licensed traders and solicited the elder Manac to become their partner. Accordingly, he sold his plantation and Negroes for money which he invested in their store. Manac entrusted the entire management of the business to his white partners, but examined the books often and kept himself fully posted on their trade. They prospered wonderfully and enlarged their business accordingly, but when they learned that an early war between the Creeks and the white people was almost certain, they agreed to make no more purchases, and to sell out the goods on hand and close their business.

After selling their most salable goods, the white partners departed secretly, taking all the firm's money with them and leaving their red partner nothing but a small remnant of unsalable goods. Thus was Manac suddenly subjected to poverty. The impending war made it impracticable for him to apply immediately to the courts for redress. Whether he had ever done so Dixon did not know, since, from the beginning of that war, he had known nothing of his father's affairs.

"Had not those white men robbed my father," Dixon said bitterly, "I should now be a rich man, instead of the poor vagabond that I am. I then believed, and I yet know, that the Creeks were morally justified in that war. The white people were plotting to take their country from them by fraud and intimidation, and, but for the war, they would have done it all before this day. The Indians fought for their homes, and, had not a large proportion of them treacherously fought for the whites, I believe they would have been quite successful. But two-thirds of the Indians could not whip all the white people with the other third of the Indians to help them. The Hostiles preserved part of their country for a time, but *only* for a time. Twenty years from today, there will not be one Indian in Alabama."

Still smarting from the robbery of his father, Dixon had condemned all white men as robbers and had joined the Hostiles, under his uncle Weatherford.

"I now know that I was mistaken," he said, "for some white people, as well as some Indians, are good, though most people of all colors are bad."

Dixon Manac hated those Indians who fought for the white people more bitterly than he hated the whites themselves, for he regarded them as traitors. When he learned that his father had enlisted in the white men's cause, he believed him to be the vilest man on earth and hated him more than all other men, because he thought that he, as a special victim of white men's avarice, ought more than any other man, to fight to redress his people's wrongs. Indulging in this extreme hatred against his father, he resolved that if he should ever meet him again, he would kill him.

But when that time came, his uncle's rebuke, administered just in time to prevent the execution of his purpose, convinced him of his error. Then, for the first time, he felt the horror of his proposed crime and it overpowered him. After that moment, he was always wretched.

In 1814 the war terminated, but its close brought no peace to Dixon's troubled mind. Even his former comrades-in-arms hated him as a parricide and hissed him from them. And the white people, whom he had fought, hated him for the same reason. Hence, he was an outcast from all people, and he acknowledged that he was justly such. He spent most of his time in solitude, hunting game for a scanty support and camping out alone. I think that his friendship for my parents resulted from their great kindness, which doubtless would have been withheld had they at first known that he had been a Hostile and had tried to kill his father.

When my mother asked him if, in case of another war, he would again fight the white people, he said, "No, it would effect no good. The white people are destined to supplant the Indians and do as they please to them. I have no idea what the end will be, but resistance would be in vain."

Then she asked him if he would fight *for* the white people. "No," said he, "I would not do that either, for, though my people hate me,

I love them and will never fight them. In case of another war, I would take no part, on either side."

My mother suggested that he go to his father, confess his sorrow for his crime, and beg his pardon. But Dixon shook his head, and resuming his lingo replied, "Me shamed to see him."

Early Religious Impressions

I was four years old when my parents left Montgomery County, Alabama. We moved to Louisiana, where we settled first in East Feliciana Parish. There, on April 15, 1826, my only sister, Mary Ann, was born. In December of that year we moved to St. Helena Parish, where we lived for about three and a half years.

Some of my earlier religious lessons were that God made all mankind, including myself, and the world and all things therein; that we all must die; that I must reverence Him and never call His name, but speak of Him as "the Good Man"; that it is profane to call the Devil and Hell by their popular names, and that I must speak of them as "the Old Hairy Cap Man" and "the Bad Place." I was also told that, if I told lies, swore, or took or claimed anything that was not my own, the Old Hairy Cap Man would catch me, take me to the Bad Place, and burn me forever; but if I always spoke reverently of the Good Man, said nothing but the truth, and restored everything that I found to the loser as soon as possible after learning who lost it, the Good Man would take me to Heaven when I die, and I would be happy forever.

I was not thus early taught that I ought not to become angry, or to hate an enemy, or to seek revenge for an injury or insult. Hence I was easily provoked to anger or revenge, and hated such persons as were offensive to me. I thought I was very religious, but, being ignorant of genuine conversion, my religion consisted in formal imitation of adult members of the church, some of whom were enthusiastic and noisy.

When I was about seven years old, my mother and I visited a wealthy family who owned a very pious black woman called "Aunt Nelly." Aunt Nelly's husband was a very pious old preacher called "Uncle Arthur," who could not read or write. He belonged on another plantation, but, one Sunday night, Uncle Arthur was to preach in Aunt Nelly's cabin, and the landlady proposed that my mother and I go with her to hear him.

A small congregation of Negroes was present and they tendered to us the choicest seats. I now remember only so much of the sermon as was addressed to the young men, but I think I give it just as Uncle Arthur spoke it:

"Young men, you is widout scuse for your sins. You can read, an' you has de Bible. Go an' read it, an' it will tell you what to do. I tell you, go an' read. Read de fust, second, an' third epistle of Mathie, Mark, Luke, an' John."

Uncle Arthur professed to be a Baptist preacher, but I understand that, on one occasion, he christened some children, that is, baptized them by sprinkling water upon their heads.

In the Redlands

In June, 1830, we moved to the District of Aes, now San Augustine County, Texas, which was to be our temporary home while my father made preparations to move us into Austin's Colony. While crossing the Sabine River into Texas, I knelt in the boat and washed my hands and face in the river water. While I was doing so my mother said, "William, don't drink any of that water." Later I heard a popular saying that "when a man drinks Sabine water, he becomes a thief."

We arrived in the District of Aes on the nineteenth of June. My mother and I were total strangers, but my father knew many of the men of that section. He had visited Texas in 1827, 1828, and 1829 and had become extensively acquainted with settlers in the districts of Teneha (now Shelby County), Sabine, Aes, and Nacogdoches. From them he had learned of the early settlers and events of that part of Texas, which he later repeated to me.[3]

[3] The accepted history of San Augustine County is George Louis Crocket, *Two Centuries in East Texas*. In his bibliography, Crocket credits his information on Martin Parmer (also spelled Palmer) to Zuber. Crocket used a typescript loaned by R. E. McFarland, the original being "property of members of the Parmer family, at whose request they were written. Mr. Zuber, an old resident of Texas, was quite intimate with the Parmer family. He lived to a great age, and

We were in the heart of the "Redlands," the country between the Sabine and Attoyac rivers. It took its name from the redness of the soil, which is highly impregnated with iron ore and very productive. Here in the Redlands many people ignored their Creator, saying that "there is no God in Texas." Horse racing and other gambling were extensively practiced, mostly on the Sabbath day. Homicides were so frequent that they attracted but little attention outside the families of the men who were killed, and manslayers were seldom or never prosecuted at law. The inhabitants of that section were called "Redlanders," a name which implied the worst type of wickedness.

Nearly all of the white inhabitants were immigrants from the "Neutral Ground," a part of Louisiana that borders on the Sabine River, which had been settled mostly by outlaws. Some of these immigrants came to the Redlands while Texas was subject to Spain, and others came after Mexico had become independent of that kingdom. They had not come as invited immigrants by either Spain or Mexico, but were intruders. They had brought with them the principles of the outlawry which they had practiced in the Neutral Ground and were disregardful of human rights. Yet the Mexican authorities recognized them as citizens, because they had joined the filibusters under Augustus William, who, in 1812, invaded Texas, ostensibly to assist in achieving Mexican independence of Spain. Many honest persons had settled among them, but the men from the Neutral Ground were the majority in 1830.

One practice of those desperadoes was to steal horses, convey them into Louisiana, and sell them. They did not steal from one another, and, as a prudent measure, they respected the property of their honest near neighbors. Instead, they went a considerable distance from home to perpetuate their thefts. Then, by agreement, two of them would meet at some public place and, in the presence of witnesses, would swap their stolen horses, after which each would sell the horse he had received. Thus, when one of them was detected possessing or selling

his memory was extraordinary until his declining years. The MS. differs in some respects from the account given by Frank W. Johnson, but in the main I judge that is quite veracious and is a valuable document." (Parmer was Mrs. Zuber's grandfather.)

a stolen horse, he could prove that he had obtained it by honest exchange from another man, and he could not be punished by law.

Sometimes two or three of them would collect a drove of fifteen or twenty horses and deliver them to some colleagues, who would drive them by night to others who would do likewise. The last drivers would sell the horses in Louisiana or Arkansas, and the money was divided among the original thieves and the drivers. Thus each relay of operators generally avoided detecting by being absent from home only a day or two at a time.

The desperadoes, in large companies, often engaged in broils with Mexicans in Nacogdoches. The Mexicans frequently held fandangoes, that is, Mexican dancing parties. On such occasions, twenty or thirty Redlanders would sometimes attend in a body and join in the dance. Some of the Mexican women were partial to the Americans and danced with them rather than with men of their own race. This excited the Mexican men's jealousy. Further, the women who preferred not to dance with Americans, or were already engaged to dance with others, were sometimes forcibly pulled upon the floor and compelled to dance with Americans. To this indignity, some women submitted from fear. Such violence to female friends excited the resentment of the Mexican men, and they sometimes attacked the Redlanders with knives. Then a general row ensued until the company dispersed.

As these rows occurred frequently and as many Redlanders participated in them, the Mexicans could not always distinguish between the guilty and the innocent, and they became disgusted with all Americans as a race. Thus these rows produced and sustained a mutual hatred between the two races.

Some of the Redlanders who had immigrated from the Neutral Ground engaged in manufacturing bogus money and operated what they called the "Owl Creek Bank." Of course there was no such a bank, but they printed and signed fictitious names to papers which resembled bank bills, on each of which was a promise to pay to the bearer a certain sum when it should be presented at the bank. During a short time, they used those papers in the purchase of property and often offered them on sale at discount.

Profanity was practiced so extensively that some men seemed un-

able to speak without swearing. Such language was also extensively
used by our schoolboys, but not in the presence of their teacher. I first
attended school in the District of Aes. Our teacher, Dr. Brownrigg,
seemed to be a good moral man, and he was a noble instructor. But
my fellow schoolboys, when not in his presence, were quite profane.
At first they treated me with due courtesy, but soon ridiculed me for
not swearing as they did. I disregarded their ridicule. They took to
cursing me outrageously. But I had been taught that it was wrong to
quarrel and fight, so I paid as little attention as possible to their
bullying.

Misconstruing my meekness for cowardice, one of them finally
began striking me with his fists. But I astonished him and the other
boys who were present by defending myself. We worried each other
for several minutes. My antagonist was older and stronger than I, and
I was probably the worse hurt, but when he tried and tried to retire,
I pursued him and compelled him to renew the combat. This convinced my schoolmates that it was dangerous to provoke me too far,
and they relaxed their persecution.

During our six months of residence in the District of Aes, I heard
three sermons preached by the Reverend Henry Stephenson, the first
Protestant to preach in Texas. Being in charge of a circuit in Louisiana, bordering on the Sabine River, he had visited the district of Aes
in 1829 and had preached at the residences of George Teal and
Thomas Spencer. Again, in 1830, he visited the same neighborhood
and preached at the same places, this time including my father's residence. A large congregation, including our family, heard him at Mr.
Teal's on Sunday, and then he accompanied us to our home where
he stayed till Tuesday morning.

On Sunday afternoon some of our neighbors called to see him and
requested him to preach that night. He promised to do so, if a congregation would come to hear him. Accordingly, my father sent
messengers to other neighbors announcing the promised service. That
night a small congregation assembled in our house and heard Mr.
Stephenson. On Tuesday morning my father and I accompanied
him to Mr. Spencer's, where he again preached to a large congregation. Soon afterward he returned to his circuit in Louisiana.

The laws of Mexico forbade any religious worship but that of the Roman Catholic Church. But Mexican authorities permitted the Texas colonists to adopt temporarily the laws under which they had lived before immigrating, until the Mexican laws should be translated for their benefit. Mr. Stephenson believed that this privilege embraced their right to worship God as they had done in their native country and that he was not acting unlawfully.

At Harrisburgh, 1831

In December, 1830, we commenced a removal from the District of Aes to Austin's Colony, but, the weather being excessively inclement, and the roads almost impassable, our arrival at Harrisburgh on Buffalo Bayou was delayed till about the fourth day of February, 1831.

This town had been surveyed and settled by John R., William P., and David Harris in 1823.[4] Being great-grandsons of John Harris, who was the first settler of the city of Harrisburgh, Pennsylvania, they gave to their town the same name. The original spelling of the name of the city was *Harrisburgh*, including the final *h*, and they so spelled the name of their town in Texas. William P. Harris told my father that he and his brother John wished that it should always be so spelled, but custom has dropped the final *h*. In respect to their wish, I yet so spell it when treating of the town historically.

The town, as it stood in 1831, was on the west bank of Buffalo Bayou, at the mouth of Bray's Bayou, and on both sides of the latter, with a bridge connecting the parts north and south of Bray's Bayou. Only two residences stood north of Bray's Bayou, and the part south of that stream consisted in two irregular rows of log houses, extending a little more than half a mile from Bray's down Buffalo Bayou. One row was in a narrow valley, generally about a hundred yards wide, on the bank of the bayou; the other was on the brow of the hill, near the edge of the valley. The whole number of white inhabitants did not exceed forty persons.

[4] Details concerning the Harris family are given also in W. P. Zuber, "The Story of John R. Harris," *Houston Post*, April 3, 1904.

There were only two small commercial houses in the town, operated respectively by John W. Moore and George F. Richardson. In
1831 Harrisburgh was believed to be at the head of navigation in
Buffalo Bayou, but in 1836 steamboats began to ply the stream eight
miles farther, to the city of Houston. The Harrises had built a saw-
mill and gristmill, combined as one. It was propelled by steam and
drove two saws, which worked perpendicularly, like whipsaws worked
by hand. This was the first steam mill that I ever saw—the first built
east of the Sabine River, and, in 1831, the only one in Texas.

Much of the land owned by the Harris brothers was a forest of
noble pines growing within two hundred yards of Bray's Bayou.
These were cut down for saw stocks, hauled to the bayou, floated
to the mill, and sawed into lumber. The Harrises boarded their employees, the number of whom, including choppers, haulers, floaters,
sawyers, and cooks, was generally twenty men. John and William
Harris were the head bosses of their enterprise, and David Harris
was generally employed on a twenty-five–ton schooner, shipping
lumber to Tampico, Mexico, where it was sold at fabulous prices.

In 1832, when the Mexican garrison evacuated Anahuac, Captain David Harris conveyed about two hundred soldiers on his
schooner [*The Rights of Man*], to Tampico. On the day of departure, the Mexican colonel marched his soldiers aboard, uninvited,
before the captain was ready to receive them. Then he ordered Captain Harris to hoist anchor and sail. Captain Harris told him that
he had not yet received supplies for the voyage and that to sail without them would be suicidal. The colonel then said that if the captain
would not obey, he would cut his cable. And he chopped it in two
parts with a hatchet. The vessel drifted away from the anchor and
the anchor could not be found. Captain Harris then cabled the vessel to a post on the shore and sent six miles away to a schooner that
was lying up and borrowed an anchor. Thus the colonel, by his
tyrannical haste to sail, delayed his departure for several hours.

Captain Harris had no further trouble till he arrived in sight of
the port of Tampico. Here the colonel assumed command, put the
crew in the hatch, filled their places with soldiers who were not sailors, and headed for the landing. The vessel was badly managed,

missed the landing, was driven onto the beach and wrecked. No lives were lost, but I do not know what became of the crew.

Captain Harris, shipwrecked, penniless, and on foot, managed by some means to travel from Tampico to Matamoros. Thence he traversed the uninhabited and pathless prairie region to San Antonio. He made the trip without accident, but was subjected to great weariness, hunger and thirst. From San Antonio he easily found his way home.

John R. Harris had married in New York and became the father of several children. Since the people of Texas were in an unsettled condition, he left his family in New York, intending to bring them to Texas after preparing a home for them. He subsequently died aboard ship en route for New Orleans, and perhaps for New York and his family.

His widow, Jane Harris, did not come to Texas till about 1834 or 1835. Her eldest son, DeWitt Clinton Harris, had preceded her, and her younger children came with her. She settled in Harrisburgh and erected a commodious boardinghouse which she operated and which in 1836 became historic.

After the adjournment of the Constitutional Convention in March, 1836, the President, Vice-President, and Cabinet of the government *ad interim* removed from Washington-on-the-Brazos to Harrisburgh, a port to which supplies could be easily shipped from New Orleans. The President and Cabinet boarded in Mrs. Harris's house, using the rooms of the building as offices in which to perform their respective official duties. Hence her house was, for the time, practically the capitol of the Republic of Texas.

Our schoolteacher in Harrisburgh was Mr. Hayden Boyden, a native of Connecticut. He had been a druggist in New Orleans, as well as a volunteer nurse for hospital patients who were afflicted with yellow fever in that city. He was also an excellent educator.

Here in Harrisburgh I first became acquainted with seafaring men and saw marine sailing vessels. These were old things, but new to me, as was the idea of traveling on land by steam.

Two of my schoolmates, Erastes and Harvey Lytle, had a brother-in-law, Thomas Farmer, who received a weekly paper published in

New Orleans. During a recess at school one day, one of them said
to me, "William, they are now running a wagon by steam in the
north."

"No," said I, "that is impossible."

"Yes," said they, "the newspaper says so. We heard Farmer read
it yesterday."

"The newspaper lies," said I.

"No," said they, "all that a newspaper says is true."

"Just think," said I, "how can they steer it?"

"By a rudder."

"A rudder cannot be used on land."

"Yes it can, just as well as in water."

I proposed that we ask our teacher to explain the mystery, and they
agreed to do so. We went to the teacher and I said, "Mr. Boyden,
Erastes and Harvey say that Mr. Farmer's newspaper says that they
are running a wagon by steam in the North. But I say that they cannot steer it. We want to know what you think of it."

"Well, boys," replied Mr. Boyden, "it's a mystery which I cannot
solve. I have a paper which makes the same statement, published in
the town from which the wagon is said to run five miles and return.
I know the gentlemen who publish the paper, and they are honorable
and truthful men. But the statement does seem to be unreasonable.
As William says, it could not be steered. Nevertheless, if the road
were straight and level, it could be easily run. But I am well-ac-
quainted with that country, and I know that the roads pass over high,
steep hills and deep hollows. When going down a hill, its great weight
would make it run so fast that it would break into pieces. On ascending a hill, it would not rise, and the rolling of the wheels would
simply rub trenches in the ground. So, for the present time, we must
remain ignorant of the subject. If the statement is true, we will know
more about it after a while."

Mr. Boyden's prediction was verified. A few years later a railroad
was built from Washington, D.C., to Baltimore, Maryland. Loco-
motives—*veritable steam wagons*—plied each way, 150 miles, between the two cities, each locomotive drawing a train of cars after

it, and now, all parts of North America are connected by a network of railroads.

In June, 1831, the yellow fever visited Harrisburgh. There was no physician in that town, the nearest being in San Felipe de Austin, which was sixty miles distant. Therefore, we were fortunate in having Mr. Boyden, our teacher, who had nursed yellow-fever patients in New Orleans.

The first patient in Harrisburgh was Mrs. Perry, a native of Mississippi and wife of Mr. Daniel Perry. Her case was not recognized as yellow fever till her death, immediately after which her face became spotted with black gangrene. Mr. Perry requested Captain William Harris to select ground for a public graveyard, and Mrs. Perry was the first person buried in it. But during that summer about thirty other persons, all strangers, were also buried there. My mother, who was a voluntary nurse to Mrs. Perry during her illness, was the second patient, but the kind attention of our schoolteacher, Mr. Boyden, saved her life and restored her to health. I was the third patient, and my only sister the fourth, but the vigilance and skill of our teacher also preserved us. My father was the only member of our family who escaped. The disease spread, and nearly every white person in the valley was prostrated by it. But Mr. Boyden successfully treated them all.

The families who lived on the hill and all the Negroes in the town escaped the disease. But just at that time there happened to be more strangers—that is, sailors, recent immigrants, and prospective explorers—than citizens in the town, and they were the ones who filled the graveyard.

While convalescing from yellow fever, I was fretful and peevish and fell into the habit of swearing. Thus I became aware that I was a great sinner. Yet laboring under the mistake that I had been converted in Louisiana, I thought myself a backslider, but hoped that I would some day be reclaimed. But for the next six years the habit grew as I grew, so that in the beginning of the year 1837 I was notoriously profane.

In spite of my profanity, however, I never lost my strict regard for the truth. One day Mr. Boyden told his pupils to lay by their books for a few minutes and hear him read a description of life in Hindoostan. While he was reading, my attention was attracted to something else, and I ceased to listen. He threw his hickory switch at me, striking me, and then ordered me to bring it to him, which I did. He then paddled my hand with a little slat which he used in ruling straight lines on writing paper and which he called his rule. This treatment angered me, and when school was dismissed for the day, I lingered inside till the teacher and all the pupils had gone away. Then I took the switch and the rule, went to the bayou (the schoolhouse was near the bank of Buffalo Bayou), broke the switch into short pieces, and threw it and the rule into the water.

On the next morning, when Mr. Boyden could not find his rule, he inquired of each pupil if he knew what had become of it. All except myself replied in the negative. I felt sure that if he learned what I had done, he would whip me severely, so I played dumb.

Lastly he said to me, "William, I left the rule on my table, and it ought to be here yet."

Then I told him what I had done. He replied, "I thought that you had tried to avenge yourself in some way." Thus ended the investigation. I had acknowledged my offense and was not whipped. Mr. Boyden never again mentioned the affair to me, but I afterward learned that he called me a "truthful boy, who, like George Washington, would not tell a lie to escape punishment."

This experience strengthened me and led me to resolve never to tell a lie, *under any circumstance*. In later years and another locality, my fellow schoolboys ridiculed my truthfulness, saying that I had not sense enough to tell a lie. But I deemed it better to be called a truthful fool than a skillful liar. During all my life, those who know me best have taken my assertions as clear proof of any fact.

One rainy day my mother stood in the door of our cabin, looking toward the road, which was about eighty yards distant (there was no street in the town, and only one road, extending up and down Buffalo Bayou). Mother said, "I wonder who that man is, sitting on his horse yonder in the rain."

I went to the door and saw the man looking up the road toward the steam mill. My father also came to the door and answered my mother's inquiry: "That is Colonel Austin. He came over from San Felipe yesterday and is on his way to Anahuac to transact some public business with Colonel Bradburn. Doubtless he is waiting for someone whom he expects to accompany him."

I was very curious to have a fair view of the man who was settling a great colony of immigrants in Texas, and who was the most influential man in the country. So I went through the rain to the road and took a good look at him.

He was small of stature. He wore a sealskin cap, with the reflex edges turned down to protect his ears, and a drab overcoat which covered him from head to foot, the collar being turned up to protect his neck, leaving his face exposed to view. We looked at each other, but neither of us spoke. After viewing him for about three minutes, I returned to the house, glad to get out of the rain. Though I knew that this man was much admired by many persons, I had no idea of the magnitude of his character, nor dreamed of the sufferings which he was to endure for his country.[5]

In the District of Brazoria, 1832

In January, 1832, we moved to a farm which my father rented on the edge of the Brazos bottom. It was east of the river, in the District of Brazoria (now Brazoria County), twenty-five miles above the town of Brazoria. Our nearest neighbor, Mrs. Bradley, was about two miles north of us in a direct line through the bottom, but by the road, through the prairie, winding around points of timber, it was three miles. Our second nearest neighbor, Mr. William Hall, was three miles south of us. Our nearest neighbor west of us was on the river, five miles distant by a road that led through the bottom. Our nearest neighbors east of us lived in the narrow skirt of timber on Chocolate Bayou, ten miles distant. With this exception, the country between us and Galveston Bay was all unsettled prairie.

[5] In 1889, 1890, 1891 and through 1894, Zuber and Guy M. Bryan, nephew of Austin, engaged in a brisk correspondence concerning Austin and his proper place in Texas history. See letters in Zuber Papers, The University of Texas Archives, Austin.

Here I did my first work on a farm, our crop being Indian corn and tobacco. And here we had a bitter experience with mosquitoes. We could not sleep without mosquito bars, and once I saw a three-month-old colt covered so completely by those insects that his color could not be seen. But the colt lived to become a good horse.

During this year I did not attend school, because the locality was too sparsely settled to support one. But I used my leisure hours in general reading. Here I did my first historical reading, Horry and Weems's *Life of General Francis Marion, of South Carolina.* General Marion served with the American army during the revolutionary war. When my mother informed me that my ancestors had participated in that war, I became very proud of them and wished that I had lived in that day that I might have participated in it.

As I read, I was struck with the cool courage and prompt action of Guinn, a fourteen-year-old boy, who saved the life of Major Horry by shooting a Tory captain as he was about to shoot the Major. I also admired the heroism of Sergeant McDonald, who performed many feats of valor in battles and skirmishes. From this reading, I got my first impression of patriotism, but unfortunately, it gave me a thirst for military life, which, I fear, poisons the minds of many of our boys.

War is just and honorable only when prosecuted in defense of life, property, and self-government, but, for any other purpose, it is unjust and murderous. Every man slain in battle is basely murdered, but not always by the man by whose hand he dies. The moral responsibility of the murder rests upon the nation or party that provokes or necessitates the war, and every person who causes, encourages, or willingly participates in an unjust war is, to the extent of his acts or influence, guilty of every murder committed therein. But those who fight for their country's rights are blameless. Also, those who prosecute or encourage an unjust war are, both generally and personally, morally responsible for all the suffering and death inflicted or endured in that war. Thus the British government and soldiery were morally guilty of all the murders, robbery, and vandalism perpetrated in the revolutionary war, and the Tories not only were equally responsible with the British, but were blemished by fighting against their own country and rights.

In June of this year, 1832, the Mexican colonel Juan Davis Bradburn, who commanded a garrison at Anahuac, perpetrated some shameful acts of tyranny, violating the laws, suspending civil authority, and imprisoning citizens, in some instances without accusing them of any known crime.[6]

These outrages were too great and many for the people to bear, and many citizens, commanded by Col. Francis W. Johnson, besieged Bradburn's fort, demanding release of the prisoners. But Bradburn refused. John Austin, a personal friend of Stephen F. Austin but not related to him, was dispatched to the settlement on the Brazos for reinforcements and a cannon. He intended to sail down the Brazos and reach Anahuac by way of the Gulf of Mexico and Galveston Bay, but the Mexican colonel Ugartechea, commanding a fort at Velasco, which is at the mouth of the Brazos, refused to let the schooner past that point. Austin then assaulted Ugartechea's fort. After a fierce battle, the Mexican garrison surrendered.

The men of Austin's Colony seem to have all been minutemen, ready to enter service at any moment when called upon. When John Austin called for them, all responded immediately. Before I knew of the call, all our neighbors who were able to bear arms departed for either Anahuac or Velasco. Remembering the examples of Guinn, McDonald, and others of whom I had read in *The Life of General Francis Marion*, I implored my father to procure for me a gun and some ammunition and let me follow our neighbors to the seat of war.

He said that I was too little. I replied that, though only twelve years old, I was nearly as large as a certain one of our neighbors, a little man, who had gone to the war. He then said that I was too young, but I replied that I was only two years younger than Guinn was when he saved Major Horry's life. He admonished me that I might be killed, but I said that no victory could be achieved without

[6] For more on the garrison at Anahuac, see Edna Rowe, "The Disturbances at Anahuac in 1832," *Quarterly of the Texas Historical Association*, 6 (1902/1903).

the risk of life and I wished the honor of taking my chance. Then he said that if I should kill an enemy in battle I would be guilty of murder, but I said, "No, the Mexicans have provoked the war and the responsibility is theirs." Finally, he said that I *should not go*. Now the fiat was uttered, and I was grieved because I was not permitted to participate in the deliverance of my people from oppression. My patriotism was commendable, but my thirst for military achievement was foolish.

Removal to My Father's Headright, 1833

In 1832 my father explored the northeastern part of Austin's Colony in search of a location for his headright of a league of land. He was shown an excellent body of land on Lake Creek, in what is now the eastern part of Grimes County. He employed a surveyor to survey his headright thereon and then returned to our temporary home in the District of Brazoria. Early in December he conveyed most of our household goods to Harrisburgh and left them there till he could prepare a home on the place which he had selected. Later that month he commenced our removal to his intended permanent home.

Because of the bad conditions of the road, caused by heavy rains, we did not reach our destination till January, 1833. Then my father learned that the surveyor had surveyed a league of land for him as per contract, but it included most of another man's headright, previously located.

Weary from many removals, especially the present one, my father's courage was exhausted, and he was disposed to locate almost anywhere. A settler then told him of an abandoned Indian village, also in Lake Creek bottom, in the present county of Grimes. The village had been inhabited two years previously by a wandering tribe of Kickapoos, and it still contained comfortable cabins and patches on which corn had been raised. Here my father located his headright league.

On moving to the abandoned Indian village, we found that only two sod cabins were standing. They were each sixteen feet long and twelve feet wide, with Mother Earth for floors. My father, my mother, my little sister, Mary Ann, and I occupied one, and our small family of Negroes occupied the other. Our cabin was just large enough to contain the few household goods we had brought with us, and we occupied it till we built log cabins a year later. Then we brought our effects which we had left at Harrisburgh.

Briars had grown thick over the Indian corn patches, and we had to clear them again and enclose them with a rail fence. About one-fourth of the league was excellent land, with about 150 acres of arable prairie. But the rest was woodland, with dense thickets of pine and post-oak trees.

When we settled here, our nearest neighbors were west of us, respectively four, six, and eight miles distant; the nearest east of us was eighteen miles away, the nearest south twenty miles, and the nearest north indefinite. The nearest mercantile houses were at San Felipe de Austin, sixty-five miles distant, and the nearest physician was at the same place. Physicians being too far away to be called speedily, every family kept a supply of medicines (not patent medicines), and treated their own sick. The prevailing disease was intermittent fever. Also, the nearest market for cotton was at Harrisburgh, about seventy miles distant. Consequently, it was difficult to get supplies. In the season for hauling cotton to market, the road to Harrisburgh was almost impassable, so that raising cotton was unprofitable and therefore neglected. The only means of securing money by the farm was the sale of corn to immigrants. But during several years no immigrants settled near us, so such sale was impracticable. During that first year we had no cattle and, of course, no beef, butter or milk.[7]

Small parties of Kickapoos and Coushatta Indians frequently camped near us, with whom we bartered corn and sweet potatoes for moccasins, dressed deerskins, venison, and slain wild turkeys. While on their hunting excursions it was the custom of these Indians to encamp just two and a half days at a place, removing every third day. The women and children kept the camp while the men hunted for

---

[7] Further descriptions of living conditions on the headright are in a letter from W. P. Zuber to Mrs. J. S. Anderson of Orange, post-marked Iola, Grimes County, December 14, 1899 (published by *Zest Magazine, Houston Chronicle,* April 2, 1961, as presented by Garland Roark).

game. When removing from a camp, they set the grass on fire for a considerable distance to the right and left of their route, thus killing the grass on the ground on which they had last hunted and driving the remaining deer in the direction in which they traveled. Thus herding the deer with fire, they kept plenty of them conveniently near their camp.

Once each fortnight during the years 1833 and 1834 I went twenty miles to Robinson's water gristmill, the nearest mill to our residence. I rode on horseback, seated on a sack containing two bushels of corn. My custom was to stay all night, sleeping in the millhouse, while Mr. Robinson's son, Washington, sat up and ground my grist. Sometimes half a dozen boys, some residing thirty miles distant, would be waiting during the same night to have their grist ground, and the miller would be kept up all night. But he enjoyed the time, singing songs and thus amusing us boys. On the next day, I would return home with my meal. If the weather was bad and I could not go to the mill, we would beat our grist in a mortar with a pestle and later grind it on a steel handmill, which we used for many years.

In 1834 my father purchased a small stock of cattle. Then we enjoyed the luxury of milk and butter. That same year my father raised his first crop of cotton on his headright, which he hauled twenty-five miles to the nearest gin to be ginned and baled, and then forty-five miles farther to Harrisburgh to be sold. Both the ginner's fee and that of the teamsters were enormously high, and the cotton brought only eight cents per pound.

My Education

When I was four years old, my mother began to teach the alphabet to me, and she was my diligent teacher during four years. I soon learned to repeat the alphabet from *a* to *z*, but I could not remember the mechanical forms of the letters. When eight years old, I knew only two letters by sight, *i* and *o*. Almost despairing of teaching me anything from a book, my mother consulted some friends, who advised her to put me to spelling. This she did, and I began to spell words or syllables of two letters. After repeated trials and the exercise of much patience, she finally taught me to know all the letters by sight. Then, after learning to spell words of three letters, I voluntarily began to read.

Soon after this I was sent to school. During the first three months of my school life, I used Noah Webster's Spelling Book, 1824 edition, which contained lessons in reading, corresponding with those in spelling. Its spelling lessons were graduated from the simple syllables to the most compound polysyllables, and the spelling was interspersed with reading lessons. Near the end were tables of words spelled alike but pronounced differently, and tables of words spelled differently and pronounced alike. Then followed a moral catechism, in the style of the old Authorized Version of the Bible. The whole was easily learned and contained valuable information.

During my first three months at school this was my only book, and I spelled and read it through more than once. I could then read in the Bible or in almost any book printed in English.

Next, I took lessons in writing, but my want of proper ability to retain the idea of shape, and my consequent want of mechanical skill, rendered me slow in learning. My letters were unduly large and ugly, but very plain. I practiced writing letters on imaginary subjects to imaginary people. In 1836, when I was in the Texas army, I frequently wrote letters to my parents at home. These were my first letters to real persons, on real subjects, but were useful practice for writing articles. During this time I kept a diary of the proceedings of the army, so far as I knew them, and this also was a helpful practice in composition. In 1845, I attended a writing school, taught by one J. K. Lockwood, a native of New Jersey. His hand was peculiar and easily learned, and, by practice, I acquired a beautiful chirography and could write rapidly. However, as I grew old, I lost my ability to write a good-looking hand, or rapidly, and now, in 1912, I write slowly, and my handwriting is homely but still very plain.

During my first experience at school, I saw other boys ciphering on the slate. I did not understand the principle on which they worked, nor for what purpose their art could be used, but once this was explained, I found ciphering easy. My first arithmetic book was Thomas F. Smiley's *New Federal Calculator*, now long out of use.

During the year we lived in Brazoria District, and until two years after we removed to my father's headright in Lake Creek, I was not able to attend school. My great desire was to obtain a good education, and so my only chance was to study at home. Necessity compelled me, however, to perform manual labor during every weekday, except two hours at noon, about thirty minutes of which were occupied in taking dinner. This opportunity to study being limited, I resorted to Sabbath-breaking. Each Sunday I retired to the shade of a red-haw thicket near our dwelling, where I sat and studied most of the day, often not returning home to dinner.

My opportunity not yet being adequate to my necessity, I resorted to night study. Our house room was very small, and my parents sat up late, engaged in loud conversation (my father's hearing being very dull, my mother was obliged to talk loudly to him), I could not study until they retired to bed. So I sat up while they did, and, after they had retired, prosecuted my studies by artificial light. Though wearied from work during the day, I often studied past midnight.

Since my father did not yet have slaughter beeves from which to extract tallow for candles, I devised another means of light. In clearing some new ground, we had made many brush heaps of the bushes that we had cut down. Exposed to the hot sunshine, the sap had evaporated and the brush had become very combustible, so as to produce a bright blaze when lighted. I cut up some of the brush and piled it in the house near the fireplace. When my parents had retired, I kept throwing handfuls of brush upon the fire each two or three minutes, thus keeping it blazing and giving light. I had to lean very low, scorching my forehead by the fire; yet I learned well.

In a short time I found a better way of procuring light. Our frontier people had already invented a homemade lamp, which was a saucer, with a stiff wick set upright in its center—the saucer filled with lard instead of oil, and the wick lighted. A saucerful of lard would burn and give light during a whole night. But I did not have access to lard, so I found a substitute for it. The surrounding forest abounded in raccoons. With our dog, Patch, I hunted them and rendered oil from their fat. I then filled a saucer with raccoon oil. For a wick I enfolded a metal button in a scrap of thin cotton cloth, the borders of which I drew together and tightly enwrapped with a cotton thread. The button held the wick in place in the saucer, and the enwrapped part of the wick stood up through the oil and its top was ignited. A saucerful of oil and the wick were sufficient to give light during an entire night.

While engaged in night study, I learned well each night till I felt a peculiar uneasiness in my head. Then, if I did not immediately suspend my study, I forgot all that I had learned during that night. This method of educating myself was laborious and prevented me from enjoying many of the pleasures which young people generally enjoy. It sometimes exposed me to ridicule. But it was interesting and pleasant, besides being my only chance to escape being an ignorant and worthless animal.

By 1834, after my father had purchased cattle, I used candles made of beef tallow. Some years later, I used star candles, which were made in Tallow Town, an annex to the city of Houston. They were made of lard or tallow, hardened by some chemical process until nearly as hard as wood. They gave an excellent light and melted very slowly, and one of them was sufficient to give light during about two-thirds of a night.

In 1835, Samuel Millett, originally from Maine, taught school for six months in Kennard's Prairie, five miles from our home. I was one of his pupils and boarded with the teacher. This was the longest term of my schooling. During this time I studied only English grammar and geography with short lessons in John Walker's Dictionary. I used Lindley Murray's *English Grammar* and John Adams' *Geography*. These two books were doubtless the best of their kind that had ever been published. The geography and its accompanying atlas were separate volumes, and the maps, showing the natural division by watercourses, were far preferable to those now published, which nearly obliterate the courses of streams by giving the chief prominence to railroad lines. Geography, as then taught, was an indispensible adjunct to the study of history.

Murray's *Grammar* was systematic, and a most complete and accurate explanation and demonstration of good language. During this time, I became so charmed with the study of English grammar that I made it my principal study for the next twenty or more years.

Another source of mental improvement that I enjoyed, along with other pioneer boys, was conversation with intelligent persons. As our facilities for obtaining information by mail were very meager, few of our people were blessed with the opportunity of reading newspapers. Consequently, the more studious of our youth learned much by conversing with travelers from the United States. Most of these were explorers of the country, seeking localities for their future homes, and many of them were of the most intelligent class of men. They, like all such men, took especial interest in young persons who were studious and took pleasure in conversing and in imparting such knowledge as they possessed. And I took delight in conversing with them. Though I learned but little from each, snatching short conversations with them as they halted for short times where I happened to be, the total of what I thus learned amounted to much.

Late in the year 1835 Joseph Baker, also called "Don José," and Gail and Thomas Borden established a weekly newspaper at San Felipe, which they named the *Telegraph and Texas Register*. This was immediately after the skirmish known as the "Battle of Gonzales," or "the Lexington of Texas." The paper was ably edited, and it promptly and faithfully related all events of the battle that had just occurred and of the proceedings of the "Consultation," which met at San Felipe about the same time. Its successive numbers embraced an excellent history of the important events then occurring in Texas.

One of the *Telegraph*'s patrons was Isaac Lafayette Hill. My father had known some of his relatives in Georgia, which circumstance caused an intimate friendship between Mr. Hill and our family. Mr. Hill then had no permanent home, so he had the newspapers mailed to our post office in care of my father. Thus I was able to read the *Telegraph* every week during its publication at San Felipe and I became familiar with Texas history for that period.

3

Fighting for Texas Independence

Opposition to Army Service

My early reading of Horry and Weems's *Life of General Francis Marion* and of Weems's *Life of Washington* inspired me with a spirit of patriotism, and I wanted to imitate these men in the performance of military feats. When [Gen. Martín Perfecto de] Cós and [Col. Domingo de] Ugartechea invaded Texas in 1835, I longed to become one of those brave volunteers who marched to the seat of war to expel the invaders. This desire was intensified by the fact that my father was too infirm to participate in such service.

But my parents vehemently opposed my aspirations. In this they acted inconsistently, for they ardently sympathized with those volunteers for risking their lives in defense of their country, but argued *with me* that such expeditions were unnecessary. They especially praised such boys of my age as participated in our country's defense, but said that *I* was too young for such service. They even said that there were enough men to fight our country's battles without my help and that many men older than I were staying at home for such simpletons as I to fight their battles.

When I told them that I might win honor in such service, they said that my grandfather, in the old revolutionary war, had won all the honor that I could reasonably desire. When I replied that my grandfather's honor was not mine, they said that I had inherited it. When I argued that to inherit my grandfather's honor I must prove myself worthy of him by following the example he had set, they became impatient. They even told me of the hardships of war—difficult marches by night and day, and exposure to all sorts of weather—as if I did not already know of them. Further, they said that there was danger of being killed in battle; but I was more than willing to encounter that danger. They urged another objection, saying that I had not courage to fight in battle and would disgrace myself by turning my back to the enemy and running from him. Then I was even more determined to go, that I might demonstrate this objection to be a mistake. But their sorest blow to my self-respect was when my mother, in my presence, remarked to my father that George Washington was a surveyor when only sixteen years old (I was then fifteen years old). Father said, "Humph! William could not be a surveyor one year from now." Mother replied, "But you must remember that your son is not a George Washington."

In addition to these verbal arguments, my father used the more potent one of neglecting to provide for me the usual supply of winter clothes, lest I should wear them in the army. Thus, the opposition of my parents kept me out of service during the siege of San Antonio, the Battle of Concepción, the Grass Fight, and the storming of San Antonio, all in 1835.

After the repulsion of General Cós and his army, by which Texas was, for a brief period, relieved of the presence of the invaders, I believed that the war had ceased. I was much ashamed of my nonparticipation in my country's deliverance and resolved not to live in a country which others had saved. Thus I left home about the middle of December, 1835, intending to return to Louisiana, where I had friends.

I had borrowed some books of Capt. Joseph L. Bennett, who resided ten miles from our residence, on the road to Louisiana. Taking the books with me, I called upon him to return them. In answer to his inquiries, I told him of my purpose—to go to Louisiana—and why I was doing so.

Captain Bennett had commanded a company in the Battle of Concepción. He assured me that the war had *not* ended, but that Santa Anna was enlisting and equipping ten thousand soldiers with whom to invade Texas during the spring. He also said that he expected to raise another company for service at that time. He advised me to return home and promised to accept me in his company and to supply me with clothes and a gun if my father would not do so, as he could draw the articles from the public stores.

I consented to do so, providing that he permit me to occupy the most dangerous positions in battle. He assured me that, when he could go into danger, he would take me with him. Relying upon his promises, I returned home to my parents. I told them what the Captain had said and assured them of my resolve to go with his company to the war. I did not afterward remind them of it, and they seemed to think that I had forgotten it.

Late in February, 1836, we learned that the enemy had arrived at San Antonio and had invested the Alamo. In the meantime, Captain Bennett had succeeded in raising a squad of eleven men, including myself, and had set the first day of March as the time for us to rendezvous at Mr. A. D. Kennard's, four miles from our home. It was understood that our destination was the Alamo.

As I had not said anything for many days about my proposed service in the army, I reminded my parents of it. They seemed astonished that I yet adhered to my resolve and reminded me that I had no gun, or any clothes suitable to a campaign. But I reminded them of Captain Bennett's promise. They then said that I *should not go*. Finding me determined, my father immediately visited Captain Bennett and bluntly ordered him not to receive me into his company or to permit me to go with him.

But Bennett replied, "Mr. Zuber, you are doing your son a great wrong by stifling his patriotism. I have promised him that I will accept him in my company and draw an outfit for him from the public stores if you will not provide it for him. And I shall do so. But you can go to San Felipe and purchase material for his clothes, and your wife can call in help and make his garments by Sunday, the sixth of March. If you promise that you will do so, I will defer the rendezvous to that day."

Finding Bennett inflexible, my father made the promise and went home. On the next day he departed for San Felipe. On the third day he returned with the desired goods, and my mother, with help, had the garments ready by the day of rendezvous.

At San Felipe, a man of very bad character, a reputed thief, had tried to sell a rifle to my father, demanding twenty-five dollars for it. But my father learned that the gun was worthless and did not buy it. So I yet had no gun, but relied on Captain Bennett to draw a musket for me from the public stores. My father also gave me about thirteen dollars in money.

Off for the Army, March, 1836

On Sabbath morning, March 6, 1836, our family took breakfast by candlelight, and, at early daylight, I departed for the rendezvous. To my grief, my parents went with me. On reaching Mr. Kennard's, the place of rendezvous, I found only six or eight men, including the Captain, the others having arranged to fall in with us on our march.

I saw my mother weeping and going from one to another of our men, talking with them. At first I thought that she was trying to influence them to induce me to stay at home, but, I soon learned that, having despaired of keeping me out of the army, she was begging them to keep me out of danger. They all promised to do so, including Captain Bennett. This wounded my self-respect more than her efforts to keep me out of the army, for this was an effort to make me worthless as a soldier. I was indignant at Captain Bennett; however, I decided that his sympathy for my mother had forced him to reply as he did to her but that he would faithfully keep his promise to me.

My mother then requested a friend, a *young man* who was going with us, to see the man who had tried to sell a gun to my father, and if it should be a good one, to buy it for me, on time. But she instructed him not to buy it unless Captain Bennett should approve it.

Two of the men who wished to join our company, Thomas Webb and Benjamin Johnson, were not supplied with clothes to wear on a campaign. Therefore several women who had assembled to see us depart for war, having material on hand, promised to prepare clothes for them by the ninth, if we would wait. Accordingly, Captain Bennett deferred marching till the ninth of the month.

My parents then proposed that I should return home with them and wait till that time. But, by doing so, I should have subjected myself to a renewal of the difficulties which I had already overcome in leaving home. Much to my disappointment, they then determined to stay on at Mr. Kennard's till I should leave.

On the morning of the eighth Dr. Anson Jones, of Brazoria County, arrived at Mr. Kennard's for breakfast. He had lodged during the preceding night at Mr. Fanthorp's, nine miles distant. He said that on the seventh he had passed through Washington-on-the-Brazos and had learned that a courier from the Alamo had arrived there on the sixth, bearing a dispatch dated March 3, from Colonel Travis, calling on the Convention to send him help.

This was Colonel Travis' last dispatch, and the courier who bore it was Capt. John W. Smith of San Antonio.[1] According to Dr. Jones, Captain Smith told members of the Convention that the enemy had advanced several times to the walls of the Alamo, doubtless meaning *to the ditches surrounding the walls,* that is, as near the walls as they could approach.

On this morning, March 8, 1836, I heard Dr. Anson Jones read the Texas Declaration of Independence, which the Convention at Washington had adopted and signed on the second day of that month, and which had been printed in handbill form. By it, I first learned that Texas had relieved herself of allegiance to Mexico.

Captain Bennett's company was now a squad of twelve men, of whom eight had horses to ride. Samuel Millett, Richard Chadduck, William E. Kennard, and I were footmen. Yet we all were to be infantry. This arrangement, though unmilitary, was practiced in the

[1] "March 5, 1836 . . . William B. Travis dispatched him [James L. Allen] as a courier to go to Goliad to ask James W. Fannin for aid" (*The Handbook of Texas,* I, 30).

army when we all came together. Then we had three companies of
volunteer cavalry, all mounted; three companies of regulars, all infantry and all on foot; and twenty-odd companies of volunteer infantry, with from half to three-fourths of each company mounted. All
the volunteer infantry mustered and fought on foot, but, when
marching, the mounted men rode by companies, like the cavalry, and
the footmen walked by companies, infantry style.

Though a footman, William Kennard led a three-year-old filly, too
weak to carry a rider, which he used as a pack-horse for the baggage
of his mess, of which I was a member. Both he and I were July colts,
he in his twentieth year and I in my sixteenth.

After taking breakfast, William Kennard and I left Mr. Kennard's
and went to Mr. Fanthorp's which was on our way to Washington.[2]
At this time my father was sick and not able to travel, but, if he had
been well, doubtless he and my mother would have accompanied us
to Mr. Fanthorp's.

Early on the morning of the ninth, Kennard and I left Mr. Fanthorp's and took the road for Washington. On the way, we were
overtaken by other members of our company, but we kept ahead, and
sometimes beyond sight of them. Our road led us through the ground
on which the town of Navasota now stands, and then through a thick
bottom, four miles wide, to the Brazos River. We passed only one
house in the Brazos bottom, the residence of Mr. James Whitesides.
This house and its proprietors were generally known to travelers who
passed this way. Mr. and Mrs. Whitesides were very hospitable and
were called by the fond names of "Uncle Jimmie" and "Aunt
Betsy."

As Kennard and I were passing, an elderly lady came out and
saluted us. I had never seen her previously and I think Kennard had
not; yet we immediately recognized her to be Aunt Betsy.

She inquired where we "children" were going. (Kennard was six
feet high, but looked young in the face.)

---

[2] "In 1834 [Henry] Fanthorp married Rachael Kennard and built her a home
at the intersection of the Houston and Springfield and Nacogdoches and San
Felipe de Austin mail routes. The home grew into the Fanthrop Inn" (ibid.,
p. 584).

We answered that we were going to the army.

"Good Lord!" said she. "Our people must be in a bad straits when even the children must go to the war and fight."

We answered that we were going at our own option and coveted all the hardships and dangers that lay before us.

"God bless you," she said. "My prayers shall follow you, and I will pray for you till you return."

We bade her goodbye and proceeded, feeling encouraged by our short conversation with her.

At Washington-on-the-Brazos

Having arrived at the Brazos River, we ferried to the west side, crossed a low bottom, less than a hundred yards wide, and ascended a tall, steep hill. Now we were at the edge of Washington.

There were only three good houses in the town, all frame and all in a row on the south side of Main Street. John Lott's hotel was the first from the river;[3] the second was one built for a commercial house, in which the Convention was sitting;[4] and the third S. R. Roberts' hotel. Besides these, there were only a few pole cabins.

But what a beautiful site for a town!—an inclined plain, gently rising and extending westward more than half a mile, crowned with an open forest of splendid shade trees.

Our little company took quarters in the Lott Hotel, its proprietor, Mr. John Moore, being a commissary, whose duty was to feed and lodge volunteers en route for the army. We remained in and near Washington during two days, waiting for the Convention to prepare a commission for Captain Bennett.

On the tenth day of March, I visited the Convention. The house in which they sat was a two-story frame, but they occupied only the first floor. It fronted on the south side of Main Street about twenty

[3] William Fairfax Gray had also been at Lott's. He wrote, on March 5, 1836, "changed my boarding house. Paid Lott 7.50" (William Fairfax Gray, *From Virginia to Texas, 1835*, p. 124).

[4] For more on the building in which the Convention met see L. W. Kemp, *The Signers of the Texas Declaration of Independence*, pp. xxii–xxvi.

feet and extended south about forty feet. It had two doors, one in
the middle of the front end, and the other, which was kept closed, in
the east side near the southeast corner. I entered at the front door
and met several visitors coming out. The doorkeeper admitted me
and requested that I not come in touch with the delegates as they
sat.

I found myself the only visitor present. A long improvised table,
covered with writings and stationery, extended north and south
nearly the whole length of the floor. The delegates sat around it on
chairs, the chairman occupying a seat at the south end. There were
no seats for visitors and no bar around the table, but the Texas people
of that time were too well bred to encroach upon men engaged in
business.

I was personally acquainted with only two members, Jesse Grimes
and John W. Moore, and did not see them in the building. The president, the Honorable Richard Ellis of Red River, was not presiding,
but a younger man occupied the chair. I took my stand on the right
of the chairman, a few feet from him. A gentleman stood, reading
part of the proposed Constitution of the Republic, section by section,
as a committee had prepared it. After a few minutes, another delegate addressed him as "Mr. Childress," and thus I learned that he
was George C. Childress, author of the Texas Declaration of Independence. The chairman called for the voice vote, by ayes and noes,
upon each section as Mr. Childress read it. All the sections passed by
what seemed to be a two-thirds vote.

During a short time after I began to observe them, all the delegates
seemed to take due interest in the reading but, after a few minutes,
some two or three turned their attention to a document which lay
on the table and called the attention of others to it. These delegates
arose and stood in a group about the document and quit attending
to the reading. The chairman frequently rapped for order, but with
little effect. As their number increased about the document, the votes
on sections grew weaker, till on one section there were only three
votes, two ayes and one no. Then a delegate called the attention of
Mr. Childress to the document under consideration.

Mr. Childress went to the delegate and seemed to be making some explanation. I judged that some section had been passed hurriedly and contained a provision that the majority did not approve. One delegate spoke for five or ten minutes, and then one of them used a pen for several minutes, probably correcting a mistake. A vote was taken, probably on the document as amended. Then Mr. Childress renewed his reading and again had the undivided attention of the Convention. After that, having observed all I could of a deliberative body in session, I left them sitting and returned to the street.

At Washington, our company was joined by eleven men from the United States who had been waiting several days at that town for an opportunity to join some company en route for the army. Among these were Alphonso Steele, from Kentucky, and James Gillaspie, of Tennessee, who later became our captain. Besides the eleven, we were joined by Zoroaster Robinson, a temporary resident of Washington, and James W. Robinson, ex-lieutenant governor of Texas during the provisional government, 1835 to 1836. These men were not related. The ex-lieutenant governor was unpopular in our company as most of us sympathized with Governor Henry Smith, whom the lieutenant governor and the Council had tried to depose. The two Robinsons swelled the number of our recruits to thirteen, and our company counted twenty-seven men. This was considered a respectable number of men in a company in those crude days.[5]

In the afternoon of the tenth of March our company retired from Lott's Hotel and encamped on a creek, probably a mile and a half north of the town. In Washington, my mess had purchased a bolt of Lowell (strong domestic), of which to make a tent. Therefore, we sat down, cut it into pieces of proper length, engaged ourselves in sewing, and soon had a good tent cloth.

I had also purchased a small supply of stationery and now improvised an unbound manuscript book in which to keep a diary of our marches and other doings. I commenced the diary by narrating all that had occurred from the sixth of March till the present time. I then made an entry in it nearly every day till about the time of the

[5] Zoroaster Robinson, son of Henry and Susan Robinson, was one of the veterans listed in "Survivors of the Texas Revolution," in *Texas Almanac for 1872,* pp. 103–104.

Battle of San Jacinto, when I accidentally spilled all my ink, and, from necessity, suspended my diary. But I preserved what I had written of it. Moths destroyed that manuscript many years ago, but I had read it so often that the facts became fixed in my memory. I also kept a diary during every subsequent campaign on which I served.

The man who had tried to sell a worthless gun to my father camped with us and had the gun with him. He had learned somehow that one of our young men had promised my mother to buy the gun for me if Captain Bennett should approve it, and he had come only to sell it. He urged the young man to buy it whether the Captain should approve it or not. As he was untiringly persistent in his wicked purpose, I here denominate him "my evil genius."

When my friend asked me if I wanted the gun, I said I did if Captain Bennett should approve it, but otherwise I would not accept it. I then went to the Captain and requested him to examine the gun. He said that he had already examined it, and that it was utterly worthless, that the lock was worn out and would snap four or five times for each time it would fire, that it would sometimes fire spontaneously on being slightly jarred, and that it would be not only unsafe in battle but dangerous on a march, as it would be liable to fire if I should stumble over a root and kill some of my comrades. He also advised me that if I should receive it, it would be difficult for him to draw a musket for me, because the public supply of arms was limited.

I then returned to my friend to tell him that I would not receive the gun, but "my evil genius" had him closely engaged in conversation and he acted as if he did not hear me. But I was sure that he did and thought that the matter was settled.

The next day "my evil genius" and my friend rode back to Washington. In two or three hours my friend returned alone, bringing the gun with him. He thrust the gun at me and said, "Here, Zuber. Here is your gun."

I impulsively took hold of it and said, "Where did you get it?"

"I bought it from ———," he replied.

"I told you yesterday that I would not receive it, so keep it."

"You *have* received it," he said.

"No, I have not."

"You *have*," he said, "and you now have it in your hand." And he turned away and left me.

I leaned the gun against a tree and immediately went to Captain Bennett and told him what had just occurred.

"Now you have placed it out of my power to draw a musket for you. If you had not received that old polk stalk, I could easily draw one for you when we reach the army, but now you have a gun and I cannot do so. You cannot have two guns," he said.

I replied, "*I have not received it.*"

"Yes, *you have*," he rejoined. "You have just said that you had it in your hand."

"I will not touch it again, but will leave it in this camp."

"That will avail nothing. I cannot draw a gun for a man who has thrown away his gun. Keep it and do the best you can with it."

"That is," I said, "break it or throw it away."

"Then you cannot go into battle," he said, "for I cannot draw a gun for you."

Thus I was compelled to proceed with "that old polk stalk" instead of a gun, which, as the Captain had plainly said, was worse than no gun. I found it to be as worthless and dangerous as he said it was, but, as I used it with great care, it subjected me to no accident. However, Captain Bennett's sudden change of demeanor assured me that he had become my enemy.

News from the Alamo

On the afternoon of the eleventh of March, our company marched from our camp near Washington to a few miles east and again encamped. Here Captain Bennett appointed his noncommissioned officers, with Samuel Millett, my schoolteacher in 1835, as orderly sergeant. Our march was very deliberate, and about noon on the thirteenth we arrived at Col. John H. Moore's ferry on the Colorado, where the town of La Grange stands.

At Colonel Moore's place I saw specimens of the old "blockhouses," built for fortification against assaults by Indians. It was a log cabin with the ground for the first floor, and built as other log cabins to a height of about eight feet. A round of strong logs jutted out on each side and end, and probably twenty inches beyond the wall below. On these were placed two rounds of logs, one immediately above the wall below, the other six or eight inches farther out, making an opening through which a man could shoot down upon an enemy approaching the wall. The inner-side logs served as sills, or plates, upon which to place joists, and a puncheon floor extended about three feet inward from the side, all around the house. This served as a platform upon which a defender could stand or walk from point to point, as occasion might demand. Then a second story was built upon the outer round of logs and finished as other log cabins. At the proper height in the upper story, portholes were made in the walls, through which a defender could shoot at an enemy before he could advance to the wall. I have never heard that Indians attacked a blockhouse, but, besides being a good defense, it was an excellent scarecrow to frighten them away.

We found that all the families residing on the Colorado had retreated east because of the belief that our garrisons at the Alamo and Goliad and our few companies at Gonzales all would soon fall and the whole country would be overrun by Mexican soldiers. So far as we could learn, not one family remained on the Colorado. This was the beginning of the Runaway Scrape, which soon extended to every American settlement in Texas. Colonel Moore's family also had gone, but we found six men occupying one of his houses, faring well on the provisions the family had left upon their exit. These men informed us that, on that morning, a lone man who had come down the river from toward Bastrop had hurriedly told them of a report that the Alamo had fallen on the sixth. It was now the thirteenth. We proceeded to the bottom and encamped.

Sometime after nightfall on the thirteenth Col. J. C. Neill rode into our camp but did not dismount. Sitting in the saddle on his horse, he, in my presence, confirmed the report we had heard on that day of the fall of the Alamo. He had been commander of our garrison in the Alamo, but had retired before the last siege on account of bad health. But on the eighth of March he was returning to the Alamo, probably to resume command of the garrison. The distance from Gonzales to the Alamo he estimated at seventy miles, and halfway between, at the Cibolo, Colonel Neill met Mrs. Dickenson, her babe, and Colonel Travis' colored servant Joe. Mrs. Dickenson told him of the catastrophe, in which every one of our men had died. Colonel Neill turned back with them, and, alternating with Mrs. Dickenson in carrying her babe, they returned to Gonzales or vicinity.

About the same time that Colonel Neill rode into our encampment, four young men, who professed to have come down the river from toward Bastrop, arrived and camped at the fire of my mess, but on the opposite side. According to their statement, they had assisted some families to start on the retreat and were now passing down the river in search of some friends who resided farther south. I learned the name of only the youngest, Mr. Scott, about eighteen years old, but I speak of another as Loquacity, because he talked so much.

Immediately after Colonel Neill's departure, Loquacity began to tell of some events which he said occurred during the storming of the Alamo, inferring that he had seen Mrs. Dickenson and learned of them from her. Green as I was, I drank in all his statements as facts. On the next morning, when the four men were about to depart, I asked one of Loquacity's companions, "Where did you see Mrs. Dickenson?"

"Pshaw!" said he, "you must not believe anything that he says. He talks to amuse himself. He made up all those stories as he told them."

During several succeeding days, some men of our company frequently repeated some of Loquacity's stories, without, I thought, believing them. And, for a time, I ceased to think of them. After the Battle of San Jacinto, however, I heard some of that man's stories repeated, with variations, and some of them were even received and believed by families after their return from the Runaway Scrape. One variation reached the ears of Gen. Martín Perfecto de Cós, who, doubtless hoping to relieve himself of his supposed perilous condition, made his own variation of the part relating to the fate of the supposed last victim in the Alamo.

Another variation found its way into published Mexican writings and, later, into Bancroft's *History of Texas*.[6] It is easy to understand how some false reports, originating with some of our own imaginative men, were credited and circulated as having been received directly from Mexican prisoners, many of whom professed to have witnessed everything.[7]

Flight from Gonzales

Having learned that the Alamo had fallen, we proceeded no farther toward it. On the morning of the fourteenth, we elected lieutenants for our company. James Gillaspie became first lieutenant and Matthew Finch, second lieutenant. Both were volunteers from Tennessee who had joined us at Washington and both were elected without opposition.

Then we commenced to dig an entrenchment on the east bank of the river, intended for use in repelling any attempt by the enemy to cross it. We felled a large cottonwood tree, a few feet south of the landing at the ferry, so that it lay on the brink of the bank and parallel to it. We stuffed under the tree some brush from its branches. Then we dug a ditch about five feet east of the fallen tree, parallel to it, about two and a half feet deep and three feet wide. We piled the excavated dirt by the tree, saving a space about two feet wide between the embankment and the ditch on which to stand or walk. Now our entrenchment was complete. If a body of the enemy should attempt to cross the river, we could stand on the space, use the embankment for a breastwork, and fire upon them. Then we could step down into the ditch and reload in perfect safety from the effect of their small arms. I think we could have repelled or destroyed a whole regiment if they had attempted to cross at that point, but we had no occasion for using our entrenchment.

On the fifteenth of March a number of families in flight from Gonzales encamped near us. I saw old Mr. Martin, the father of Capt. Albert Martin who fell at the Alamo. He was sitting on the

---

[6] H. H. Bancroft, *History of the North Mexican States and Texas*, II, 211–212.

[7] Much of the material on "Inventing Stories about the Alamo" is included in a letter from Zuber to C. C. Jeffries, written in 1904 and printed in *In the Shadow of History*, pp. 42–47.

bank of the river, gazing into the flowing stream. He shed not a tear, but his whole body was convulsed in grief. His son had been in command of the thirty-four citizens of Gonzales who had entered the fort on the night of March 1.

General Sam Houston had been in Gonzales and had assumed command. On the twelfth, the little force there consisted of about three hundred men. Then, on the night of the thirteenth, Mrs. Dickenson arrived in the camp and informed General Houston of the fall of the Alamo. The General ordered an immediate retreat.

This intelligence was not unexpected, but Mrs. Dickenson, suffering great fear, said that she believed the Mexican army would arrive before day. Her anxiety so excited our soldiers that they departed in confusion, some of them leaving their baggage and horses. The confusion and hurry was so great that they forgot to relieve their pickets west of the river. During the night, they retreated, very disorderly, over a dim and muddy road, to Peach Creek, ten miles east of Gonzales, where they arrived about daybreak on the morning of the fourteenth.

Arriving at Peach Creek, the front of the army, in obedience to the General's order, rested till the rear came up, and here the whole army rested for a short time. This rest allayed the undue excitement, and from Peach Creek the army continued the retreat in excellent order.

Mr. Connell O'Donnell Kelly was a member of the picket guard left behind when the army retreated.[8] He later told me that on the morning of the fourteenth, after the hour had passed when they should have been relieved, our pickets, judging that something extraordinary had occurred, recrossed the river to report and hear the news. They found the encampment vacant, except for some men who had returned to recover their horses and baggage left behind in the hurry of departure. They also found that all the families in the town had gone, leaving nearly all their effects, and that a company of men were burning the houses, on order of General Houston, to pre-

[8] Connell O'Donnell Kelly of the "Mobile Grays" was listed when "Brief Sketches of Survivors of the Texas Revolution" appeared in the *Texas Almanac for 1872*, p. 110.

vent the enemy from occupying them. But no enemy had yet arrived.

Another soldier, encamped at Peach Creek while en route for the army with a small company commanded by Capt. John Bird, told about seeing two women who were next door neighbors, whose husbands had fallen in the Alamo. They were at supper, with their children, when news came that the Alamo had fallen and that the army was hastily preparing to retreat. Having no means of conveyance, each woman immediately arose from the table and snatched and tied up a little bundle of drygoods. Then, each with two children holding to her skirts and one carrying an infant in her arms, they departed. They were a short distance ahead of the army and thus they traveled, over a wet and slippery road, ten miles to Peach Creek. They arrived at Captain Bird's encampment a short time before day and told the Captain of their sad condition. He mounted his baggage wagon, threw out two large boxes to make room for them, helped the women and children to mount, and seated them in the wagon. They rode on the wagon during the retreat to the Colorado, where they joined some other friendly retreating families.

On the Colorado

While General Houston and the army were retreating toward the Colorado, I was with Captain Bennett's company, encamped on the east bank of the Colorado at Moore's ferry. On the night of the fifteenth of March, our first guard was detailed. It was composed of three sergeants and six privates and divided into three reliefs, one sergeant and two privates to each relief. The reliefs were to stand on post alternately, each two hours at a time. Their duty was to watch the river, and, if they should see any man or body of men trying to cross from the west side, to hail them. Should they prove to be enemies, they should give an alarm by firing upon them, then run into the encampment and join their comrades in defense or in a retreat if such should be necessary. But no cause for alarm occurred. William Kennard and I were on this first guard. Neither of us having served previously, we were broken in by being placed on the first relief. We stood during the first tour and were also on post at midnight and at daybreak. Some fugitive families from Gonzales were yet encamped adjacent to us and near our post.

On the nineteenth of March, Captain Bennett received a dispatch from General Houston, ordering us to proceed down the river. We marched down to Ross's farm. Here, of course, the place was desolate. The barn and its contents were in ashes, said to have been burned by General Houston's men to prevent the enemy from using them. Thence we went a short distance to the encampment of Capt. Spencer Townsend and his company, of only twelve men, on the east bank of the river, immediately opposite Jesse Burnam's residence, which was on the west bank. Here we encamped, expecting to stay all night and perhaps longer.

That night, I was placed on guard to watch the river, as I had done at Moore's ferry. Only one sentinel was to stand at a time, and I was to be relieved at the end of two hours. After I took my post, Captain Bennett came to me and informed me that another dispatch had arrived, ordering him and Captain Townsend to march with their companies farther down the river. But he said that I must stay at my post till relieved, which should be in time for me to fall into rank and march with the company.

I stood till my two hours had expired, and then Captain Bennett visited me again. He said that my two hours had expired, but, as we would march within ten or fifteen minutes, it was not needful to relieve me till the moment of departure. He assured me that I should surely be relieved in good time.

Further, he admonished me that we were now under command of General Houston and governed by military law. He strictly charged me not to leave my post till relieved as death is the legal penalty for such an offense. Then he returned to his place.

I stood at my post at least two hours more, during which time I was not again visited. Most of the company was asleep. Finally I heard the Captain give the order "March," and, as the company passed near my post, I saw them start.

I spoke out rather roughly, "Captain Bennett, are you going to leave me here on post?"

"No!" he answered. "Why are you not in the rank?"

"Because I was not relieved. I am doing as you directed me."

"You should not have waited to be relieved," he said, "but should have fallen into rank when the company paraded."

Not another word was said, and I fell into rank. We marched during all the night of the nineteenth, and just at daybreak on the morning of the twentieth we arrived at the encampment of a detachment of the army under Captains Patton and Ware, in the bottom, near the north bank of the Colorado as it flows east at that point, opposite DeWees's Bluff, which is on the south side.

March 20, 1836. We were now part of the army, a detachment of four companies: those of Captains William H. Patton, William Ware, Joseph L. Bennett, and Spencer Townsend, embracing about seventy-five men, with Patton, as senior captain, commanding.

General Houston, with the main army, was encamped on the same side, at Beeson's ferry, about nine miles below by the road around the bend (but only three miles by the short road, crossing the river twice and going down on the west side). The Mexican general Sesma, with about eight hundred men, was encamped on the west side, midway between our two encampments, about one-and-a-half miles from each. Each army seemed to be awaiting an attack by the other. But we were all raw militia, destitute of ordnance, while Sesma's men were mainly drilled regulars and armed with an excellent twelve-pounder cannon.

Patton's and Ware's companies had made an entrenchment on the sand beach in the river's channel, near the water's edge. This was designed as a defense in case of an attack by the enemy from De-Wees's Bluff on the opposite side. On the twentieth, Bennett's and Townsend's companies built, for their own use, an extension of the entrenchment.

On the same day a company arrived from Nacogdoches, commanded by a lieutenant who was known by the appellation of "Black Hawk." They also went to work and built an extension to the entrenchment.

Our detachment now contained five companies, known as Patton's, Ware's, Bennett's, Townsend's, and Black Hawk's, and included about one hundred men, all commanded by William H. Patton, senior captain. Now our force at the two encampments was about equal in number to that of the Mexican Sesma. Yet we believed that we could easily defeat any force of the enemy, if they did not outnumber us more than two to one. Therefore, we solicited General Houston, through subordinate officers, to lead or send us across the river to capture or repel Sesma's command. But he declined, arguing that it was impossible for raw militia, destitute of ordnance, to contend successfully against an equal number of disciplined regulars, armed with a cannon.

On the morning of the twentieth, our orderly sergeant, Samuel Millett, had informed me that General Houston had ordered all boys under the age of seventeen years to be exempt from guard and fatigue duty, and that I had nothing to do but rest, to march, and to fight when occasion should require. But I had come to perform a man's duties, and I demanded to be excused from exemptions.

On the following morning, I was detailed on the camp guard to serve twenty-four hours, the first regular camp guard on which I ever served. Part of the guard line was in a dense canebrake. A narrow path had been cut through the cane, by which a sentinel could stand or walk, and relief or grand rounds could pass. Here I could see nothing but the wild cane, and in the night I could not see my hand. My parents had predicted that if I should be placed on guard at such a point, I would disgrace myself by becoming frightened and running away from my post. Now I gloried in the opportunity to demonstrate that they were mistaken.

On the twenty-second our scouts brought in two Mexican prisoners, the first that I saw. They had ventured a quarter of a mile from their encampment southwest of the river, and our scouts had slipped upon them while they were in a deserted house, searching for plunder.

On the morning of the twenty-fourth, our cavalry, commanded by Capt. Henry W. Karnes, crossed the river from our lower encampment at Beeson's and, under cover of timberland, marched by a circuitous route to a point a few hundred yards from the enemy's encampment. Here they surprised and routed the enemy's picket guard,

from whom they captured a horse. Now they were in plain view of
the Mexican army in their encampment. The Mexicans fired three
rounds of their cannon at them and sent their cavalry to engage them.
But our cavalry, with the captured horse, retreated across the river
to their own encampment. In this adventure, we suffered no casualty.

General Houston, judging that this encounter might provoke an
attack by the enemy which our force at the upper encampment was
too weak to withstand, dispatched Lt. Col. Sidney Sherman, assisted
by Adjutant Stauffer, with two hundred men to assume command.
As I afterward learned, Colonel Sherman proposed to General
Houston that he and his command would attack the enemy from the
north and withdraw them from their encampment, immediately
after which the General should assault them from the south. And
thus, holding them between two fires, our two columns would com-
pel them to surrender. But the General preferred to await an attack
by the enemy.

In the morning, at our upper encampment, we heard three reports
of the enemy's cannon and were alert for the reception of an attack.
Early in the afternoon, two other men and I were detailed to hunt
and butcher a beef. We found a cow in the bottom and wounded her.
Then we chased her, for perhaps two hours, by a circuitous and zigzag route, and finally killed her. While skinning the beef, we heard a
firing of small arms. Our detachment in the entrenchment and the
enemy's cavalry on the bluff on the south bank were firing across the
river at each other. Had we known this, we would have left the beef
and gone to them. But, bewildered by our tortuous chase, we thought
that our pickets beyond the river had encountered a body of the
enemy. Being footmen, we could not cross to them, so we continued
our work.

Just before finishing our butchering, we saw Colonel Sherman's
detachment advancing toward our encampment. When we finished
our work we returned to the camp and were mortified to learn that
during our absence our detachment had been engaged in a skirmish
with a party of the enemy.

In retaliation for our cavalry's demonstration, Sesma sent his
cavalry, about eighty strong, to annoy our detachment. They ad-

vanced to the brink of the bluff, opposite our camp. Our pickets saw them advancing, ran in, and gave the alarm. Our detachment hastened to the entrenchment to receive them. The enemy sat on their horses on the bluff and fired their *escopetas* at our men, but overshot them and did no damage. Our men returned the fire, but as the river was broad and the bluff high, they were not sure that any of them hit their marks. However, they believed that they wounded the Mexican commander, for he flinched as if hurt badly and ordered his men to fall back. They returned to their encampment.

Lieutenant Colonel Sherman was now commander of our detachment, and our troops here, as reinforced by those who had come with him, numbered three hundred.

Our army, from its arrival at Beeson's on the nineteenth of March, had received accessions almost daily, so that on the twenty-sixth, our number, including those at the two encampments and those known to be within a day's march of us, amounted to nearly seventeen hundred men. All these could have been massed together on the twenty-seventh, and on the twenty-eighth we could have captured or dispersed Sesma's command. But the delay and embarrassment occasioned by amassing our men, fighting a battle, caring for the wounded, burying the dead, and guarding and caring for prisoners would have given Santa Anna time to bring an overwhelming force against us, and our victory might have been followed by disaster.

On the night of the twenty-fifth Peter Kerr arrived from Goliad at our lower encampment. He reported that on the twentieth, Colonel Fannin's command, retreating from Goliad, had been overtaken and captured by the enemy and conducted back, prisoners, to Goliad. Then it was certain that Houston's personal command was the last and only hope for Texas. Had we then fallen into the enemy's power, our cause would have been lost.

General Houston judged that, as a matter of course, his men were intimidated by Kerr's report, and, to preserve their courage, he affected to disbelieve it. He emphasized his disbelief by causing Kerr to be arrested as a spy, and then sent him under guard to President Burnet at Harrisburgh. Kerr's report was later confirmed by intelligence, and the President set him freee. But the General misjudged the courage of his men. Kerr's report, far from intimidating them, aggravated their thirst for revenge and intensified their wish to storm Sesma's camp.

Now General Houston fully realized the seriousness of our condition. Deeming it suicidal to fight under the circumstances, he would not hazard an engagement, but, if he should remain here and refuse to fight, a general mutiny would occur and the army would dissolve. Thus he resolved to resume his retreat, believing that his retreating army would continue to grow.

Retreat from the Colorado

At the upper encampment, on the morning of the twenty-sixth, Colonel Sherman ordered an extra supply of beef to be slaughtered, but did not order it to be barbecued as if for a march. Early that afternoon, we were ordered to "pack up." We put our raw fresh beef into sacks and onto our pack animals. We fell into line and marched down the river, in the bottom, not knowing why we were marching, or whither we were going, but judging that, of course, we were going to join the main army, at the lower encampment. We felt confirmed in this belief, because a small picket guard at a ford above our encampment had not been called in. (These were afterward surprised by a body of Mexicans, but escaped and followed our trail to our encampment in the Brazos bottom.)

While marching in the Colorado bottom, we crossed a creek about twenty or thirty feet broad, but only about six or eight inches deep. A row of stepping-stones had been laid in it, on which we could, by long strides, step from stone to stone and cross dry-shod. In so doing, we had to cross slowly, in single file; hence, while some were crossing, those who waited their turn stood in a huddle.

While thus huddled, we naturally inquired of each other why and where we were marching. One young man answered that both we and the men at the lower encampment were moving out to the edge of the bottom, where we could have grass for our animals. He was asked how he knew this, and he replied, "Because, on this morning, I saw an express bearer hand a paper to Colonel Sherman, who handed it to Adjutant Stauffer to read for him. And I heard Stauffer read it to him. It was a dispatch from General Houston, ordering Colonel Sherman to march out to the edge of the bottom to a point at which there is plenty of fresh grass for the animals. It also informed Colonel Sherman that at the fork of the road he would meet a guide who would conduct him to where he would join the main army."

I did not observe the fork of the road when we passed it, as the road was dim, and, if Colonel Sherman met a guide, I did not see him. When we emerged from the bottom, we continued eastward marching till about midnight.

Our midnight halt was in a thicket of dead saplings, some of which we hacked down with our hatchets and used as fuel in building fires. Here we prepared and ate our supper, which was only green beef without bread. In order to cook the beef, each of us prepared a wooden rod, about one inch in diameter and three and a half feet long, sharpened at one end. On this we stuck a piece of fresh beef, which we held in the blaze till it became scorched black. Then we trimmed off the black enamel and ate the meat. Again we held the remnant in the blaze till it also became black, and disposed of it likewise. Fatigue had given us relish for our scorched raw beef; our repast was delightful and refreshing, and we ate of it bountifully. It was well that we did, for this meal served us not only for supper, but also for breakfast and dinner on the next day. Supper dispatched, we resumed our march and halted not again till daylight.

Between daybreak and sunrise on the morning of the twenty-seventh we came to the junction of the two roads by which our two bodies were retreating. This was in a long narrow prairie, extending lengthwise from west to east, and bordered on each side by open post-oak timberland. The other road led lengthwise through the prairie, and our road came to it obliquely from the northwest. Since the main army had not yet reached this point, our detachment halted, stood, and waited for it. Soon we saw their front guard, a small body of horsemen, emerging from the timber at the west end of the prairie. Then came the wagon train, consisting of six wagons drawn by oxen, then the unmounted infantry, and, lastly, the mounted infantry. The cavalry, being divided into two parts, formed the flank guards on the right and left of the central column. Looking down the line, not

much more than half a mile long, I was stricken with admiration for
what I thought was a great assemblage, since I had previously never
seen more than three hundred persons at one time.

I strained my eyes to see General Houston, but saw no man that
I would recognize as he. The most conspicuous person that I saw was
a large, plainly dressed man riding a large, stout, clumsy-looking
gray horse. He occupied a place beside the foremost wagon. He wore
plain coarse jeans, a white wool hat, and mud boots. I wondered who
that man was, and, notwithstanding his coarse attire, I thought that
he was the noblest-looking man that I had ever seen.

While I was trying to satisfy my curiosity, the foremost wagon
came opposite my place in the rank, not more than a hundred feet
distant, and the main army halted. Our position was oblique to theirs.
Then the part of the cavalry that formed the left flank passed through
the ranks and became part of the right flank. I then asked the men of
Black Hawk's company if they could show me General Houston. One
of the men answered: "Yes, don't you see that man on the big gray
horse? That is he."

"What," I exclaimed, "that plain-looking man by the wagon?"

"Yes. That is nobody else than the General."

At that moment, "the man on the big gray horse" rode across the
open space, bowed to Colonel Sherman, and said, "Good morning,
Colonel. I wish you would move your battalion so as to form the left
flank of the army."

His politeness was as striking as his plainness. The march was resumed, and Sherman moved his "battalion" as directed, forming the
left flank till we entered thick timber, when we necessarily fell to the
rear of the central column. After that, we were no longer a detachment, and the army was a consolidated body.

About nine o'clock on the night of the twenty-seventh, we arrived
at the Agua Dulce, where we encamped for the night. Since noon
of the preceding day, we had marched sixty miles from our abandoned encampment on the Colorado. During the march we had not
closed our eyes for sleep and had eaten only one meal, that of the
preceding midnight. Worn by our hard march, my mess did not even

erect our tent, but after taking supper, again of scorched raw beef, we lay down for the much-needed rest.

Here, at the Agua Dulce, several companies became detached from the army, to prevent the advancing enemy from crossing the Brazos. Captains Moseley Baker and John Bird, with their companies, both raised in and near San Felipe, guarded the ferry at that town. With Baker commanding, they encamped in the thick bottom near the east bank of the river. Another company, Capt. Wylie Martin's, guarded another crossing near Fort Bend, probably fifteen or twenty miles below San Felipe, where they encamped on a road some distance west of the river.

On the morning of the twenty-eighth, after breakfasting again on scorched beef, we departed from the Agua Dulce before day, marching up the Brazos on the west side. Recent heavy rain had left our road in wretched plight and had deposited beds of quicksand in the fords of the creeks that crossed our way, rendering our route almost impassable. Consequently, at the end of three days, we had marched only fifteen miles, and on the afternoon of the thirtieth, we arrived at Foster's plantation, which bordered on the Brazos bottom west of the river.

It was a short but troublesome march, and on this third day our first death occurred in my company. On the morning of the twenty-eighth, Felix Wright was detailed to fatigue duty. He had no breakfast and he worked all that day with no food, helping to pry and lift wagons out of the quicksand in the creeks. That night, intensely hungry, weary, and wet, he went to the camp of his mess, where he ate bountifully of charred raw beef. Then he lay down and tried to sleep. During the night, a severe case of cholera morbus ensued, which could not be allayed, and on the morning of the twenty-ninth he could not walk. He was hauled on a wagon to our next encampment, and died sometime during the following night.

On the morning of the thirtieth, when I awoke and left my tent, I found an open fresh grave about ten feet from my door. Two sections of bark, about four feet long, lay beside the grave. They had been peeled from green hickory trees to be used as a substitute for a coffin. I had been too weary and sound asleep to know that there was a death and a gravedigging, or even a sick man so near me.

Soon, Lieutenant Colonel Sherman came and had the dead man brought out of his tent, wearing his clothes just as he had put them on three days before. They wrapped him in his blanket and stitched it to prevent it from unwrapping. The blanket covered the dead man's face, but not his feet, and I saw that he was still wearing his shoes. Next they laid him in the grave, the floor of which was covered with water which seeped from its walls, and then a platoon of riflemen fired a salute. After that, one section of the bark was laid upon him, covering his feet and extending to near his waist, while the other section was lapped over the first, covering his head and face. Lastly, the grave was filled. We packed up and marched early, leaving the mortal remains of our comrade Felix Wright, uncoffined, buried in a lonely unmarked grave, in the midst of the forest.

Late that same afternoon of March 30 at Foster's plantation I visited headquarters, where I saw a woman with a girl about twelve years old. Both were beautiful and refined, and their clothing was neat and clean. The girl was holding the bridle of a horse which was hitched to a small sled containing bedclothing.

Later I learned that the woman lived nearby, and that her husband, because of some affliction, had gone to New Orleans to have his arm amputated, but was not expected to live to return. She had no children, and the girl was an orphan who lived with her. When she learned that the army was retreating and all families were flying before the enemy, she and the girl had hitched their only horse to the sled. Walking and leading the horse and sled by turns, they soon fell into our trail and followed it till they came to our encampment at Foster's plantation. They remained with the army until the twelfth of April. Friends supplied them with some needed articles and a tent, which was erected near the headquarters. During this time they made fine linen shirts to support themselves. Very few of our men knew their names, and they were generally known as "the widow woman and her girl." I saw them frequently, but never conversed with them.

On the morning of the thirty-first, still in our encampment at Foster's plantation, I strolled some distance from my tent to where a log heap was burning. Four young men were encamped there, apparently not attached to any company. I asked them what they thought of the stampede that seemed to be under way.

"Why, General Houston is giving up the country to the Mexicans," one replied.

"I cannot believe that," I answered. "If he were doing so, he would resign and give us a chance to defend our country without him."

"No, he is betraying his trust. We are going to leave him and take care of our families. But yonder he comes," he said, pointing to the General, who was passing by.

"See here, Boss," the man said, "what are you going to do with us? Are you going to march us across the Sabine and disband? We thought that we had come to fight."

The General made an emphatic gesture and replied, "You men are too impatient to fight. I have brought you here to an advantageous point. I am going to encamp you here in the bottom *and give you as much fighting as you can eat over.*" Then he passed on, and I returned to my tent.

We all were more or less dispirited. Some men professed unlimited confidence in the General, but the majority were almost hopeless. There had been some desertions, and we were holding ourselves together as the only hope for the country, just as a drowning man catches at a straw.

Early in the forenoon of the thirty-first, I was detailed on fatigue duty. Our fatigue detachment consisted of about thirty men, commanded by Lt. Nicholas Lynch. We were to cut a road a mile and a half long, going east through a dense bottom to a lake near the west bank of the Brazos, and to clear a camping ground for the army near the bank of the lake. If it had not been for an abandoned narrow road that lay through a continuous thicket of saplings, our detachment might have been occupied at least three days in cutting the road. But we worked to the lake in about four hours. Clearing the proposed camping ground was a laborious job, and we had to cut away and burn a great many wild grapevines, but we finished our work and arrived back in camp before night.

On our return to the encampment, we learned that during our

absence six men of Colonel Fannin's command had arrived. They had brought word that on the twenty-seventh, by order of Santa Anna, more than four hundred of those patriots at Goliad had been murdered. So far as they knew, none but themselves had escaped.

One of the men was known as "Kentuck," an appellation generally applied by Texas soldiers in 1836 to any man whose name they did not know. He was small, with handsome features, probably between twenty-two and twenty-five years old. But he was addicted to gambling. According to Kentuck, Colonel Fannin's army had been retreating from Goliad when overtaken by the enemy, on the twentieth of March, near Coleto. After a hard-fought battle of several hours the Texians surrendered, with the stipulation that they would be treated as prisoners of war and shipped to New Orleans. The condition was that they should not again bear arms against Mexico. They were conducted back to Goliad, thrust into a close prison, and fed for a week on a scanty supply of spoiled beef.

From his guards, Kentuck learned the Mexican game "monte," in which he excelled his teachers by winning about three hundred silver dollars. He was wearing thick, heavy clothing, consisting of jeans, pants, vest, a blanket overcoat, and mud boots. The total weight of the silver he had won was about eighteen pounds, and, from want of a sack in which to carry his money, he distributed it into several pockets of his garments.

On the night of the twenty-sixth, the prisoners were told that the next day they were to be shipped from Copano Bay to New Orleans, and they were made to believe that they were soon to be at home with their families.

On the morning of the twenty-seventh the men were marched out, single file, between two files of guards, each guard file as numerous as themselves. They were then separated into three divisions, two of which were marched to the river's bank, the other a few hundred yards west.

Kentuck was in one of the divisions that were marched to the river's bank. They were again made to form a line, single file, a few feet from the brink, and the Mexican file next to the river passed through them to the other side. Now the guard, outnumbering them two to one, were all on one side, and the prisoners naturally turned and faced them.

Instantly the prisoners realized that they were to be shot. At that moment they heard the firing by which the two other divisions were murdered and heard the screams of the wounded, who were shot again and killed. Kentuck and his comrades were then ordered to "face about," but many of them refused. They looked into the eyes of their murderers. The order was given to "Fire!"

But the man who faced Kentuck could not fire. Kentuck fell back into the river as if killed, and then began to swim across the stream. Weakened by confinement and saturation and encumbered by his heavy garments and his pockets loaded with silver, he made poor headway.

The current bore him down the river, but he finally reached the opposite bank, climbed up, and ran. His garments now were thoroughly wet and many times heavier than when dry, the heavy silver in his pockets beat painfully upon him, and the sloshing of water in his boots caused his feet to slide within them. Thus impeded he seemed to be scarcely moving. He looked back over his shoulder and saw that some of the Mexicans had followed him. They had left their muskets as they plunged into the river, but some of them had sabres. Looking again, he saw that they were gaining upon him.

When they were almost near enough to lay their hands upon him, some money jounced out of one of his pockets. His pursuers halted and scuffled for it, each trying to grab more than the others. As they again drew near, he threw down a handful of money, and again they halted and scuffled. Handful after handful went, till all his pockets were emptied. He then threw off his overcoat, which was a burden to him, and then his vest, and they halted and scuffled for each of these. His hard running had caused the friction of his feet against his water-filled boots to stretch them till he could kick them off easily. Again he delayed his pursuers for another scuffle.

The grass had recently been burned on the ground over which he ran and the sharp stubbles penetrated his socks and pierced his feet. The pain was great, but he was running for his life and did not relax his speed. His pants also were burdensome and he dropped them. But, being thoroughly wet, they did not slip easily from his extremities, and his effort to push them off compelled him to make a brief halt, during which his pursuers almost caught him. But the resultant scuffle enabled him again to lengthen the space between himself and them.

Now his underwear was the only garment that he yet retained, and it was so wet that he could not shed it without halting long enough to be caught. With no more "graft" with which to bribe them, Kentuck thought that he was "gone up." But his pursuers seemed to be satisfied with their sport and abandoned the chase, and Kentuck soon reached a chaparral in which he hid himself.

He pushed his way through the brush, while thorns tore his flesh and reduced his undergarments to shreds. He headed eastward, and fell in with a comrade who had also escaped from the wholesale murder. Shortly they were joined by four more, and these six men continued to travel east, avoiding roads so far as practicable. All families on their route had fled ahead of them, and they subsisted on food which they found in abandoned houses. They crossed the deep streams by swimming and finally struck our trail at the crossing of the San Bernard, arriving at our encampment at Foster's plantation on the thirty-first.

Kentuck was in a pitiable condition from his escape, but the other five were in better plight. Some of our men shared extra garments with Kentuck, and he drew a hat and shoes from the quartermaster's department. He and one of his comrades joined our army, but the other four continued their journey to the United States.

Also after our return from fatigue duty, I learned that our orderly sergeant, Samuel Millett, had been promoted to the office of assistant commissary. As Mr. Millett's successor had not yet been appointed, Lieutenant Gillaspie sent me to the commissary's department to draw meal for our company. While I was there, Mr. Millett told me that on that day he was issuing rations for eleven hundred men. I was surprised, considering our depletions from leaves of absence, desertions, and men on detached service at San Felipe under Capt. Moseley Baker. But these depletions had been partly remedied by reinforcements that had met us during our retreat from the Colorado.

A respectable number of our men reposed unlimited confidence in General Houston and were willing to follow him blindly and to do whatsoever he commanded. Some wondered how he held his army together. *They* held themselves together, as a last resort. But the General helped them to do so by his inflexibility, confidence of success, and courtesy to his soldiers. Also he kept no bodyguard. When we were encamped, the door of his tent generally stood open, and any soldier who wished could enter at liberty. General Houston never exchanged compliments with a man, however, or conversed with him unless on business, at which time he courteously answered necessary inquiries and gave needed advice and encouragement. He was skilled in inspiring men with hope, and his sympathy with his men was remarkable. When marching, he rode beside one of his teamsters, as is the custom of wagonmasters in regular armies, so that he might be near during their troubles.

To the believing Christian, the good hand of our Heavenly Father was visible in directing us to success. Very few of us were religious, but most of us had, somewhere, praying mothers, wives, or sisters, and, our cause being just, God granted their prayers for us. Surely He led us by a way which we knew not.

In the Brazos Bottom

On the first day of April, 1836, we marched from Foster's plantation over our newly cut road to our encampment in the bottom near the west bank of the Brazos. During the twelve days we encamped there, Captain Bennett and I were messmates. The General's tent and ours were erected side by side at this place, but I had no occasion to speak with him.

When Mr. Millett was promoted, Captain Bennett filled his vacant place of orderly sergeant with an unprincipled man whom I designate as "Bully." A man of gigantic stature and strength, he was proud of his ability to fight with his fist and his foot. Overbearing and insolent to men of inferior strength and pugilistic skill, he was submissive to those whose strength and skill were nearly equal to his own. He professed great admiration for brave men and contempt for cowards and deserters. His letters to his family were written in red ink, indicating that he was ready, if need be, to shed his blood for his country, and he bombastically displayed them to his comrades. He even said that he was willing to sacrifice his family for his country's rights and that, however great their distress, he would never go to their relief, with or without leave, till the invading Mexican army should be expelled from the country.

In case of Captain Bennett's promotion, Bully wished to become his successor and expected that the vacancy would be filled by popular election in the company. To secure his success, he sought to win the support of men whom he thought to be influential. The men detailed for duty on each day were taken from the companies pro rata, according to the numbers of names on the respective muster rolls. But Bully practically exempted his favorites from detail duty and took the daily number of details from those of us who remained, making our daily guard duty very heavy.

Captain Bennett was aware of this abuse of authority by Bully, but did nothing to correct it. Our men bore it patiently for a time, but one day two of them administered hearty cursings to the braggart. Bully endured the cursings meekly and afterwards ceased his abuses of all except William Kennard and me. From that day on, he detailed each of us to guard duty for twenty-four hours, alternating once every two days. Though not cowards, we were timid boys and endured the wrong without complaint, while Captain Bennett seemed to wink at the abuse. Friends advised me to relieve myself by claiming the exemption offered by the General to boys under the age of seventeen years. But I refused.

Early on the thirteenth of April our army crossed the Brazos on the steamboat *Yellow Stone*, which happened to be present. The day before, I had been detailed on horse guard at Foster's plantation, where the horses were pastured. When I returned to our encampment on the morning of the thirteenth, I found that the army had departed, with the exception of a few sick men and nurses. With some others, I proceeded to the river, crossed it, and rejoined our company, now encamped at Groce's plantation, on the east bank of the Brazos. There I met George W. Hockley, who had arrived in camp with two iron six-pounders, well mounted and equipped, a present from citizens of Cincinnati, Ohio. They had been named "The Twin Sisters." Prior to this time, we had no artillery or artillerymen.

On the fourteenth, the Honorable Thomas J. Rusk, Secretary of War, arrived, sent from Harrisburgh to our encampment by President Burnet. The same day, our army was reorganized, doubtless by order of the Secretary of War. First the companies were equalized. Captain Bennett's company, which contained only about thirty men, was raised to fifty-eight men, rank and file, two more than the law required.

The second step was to rearrange the volunteer infantry companies into two regiments. This done, the regimental officers were to be promoted, elected, or appointed. Lt. Col. Sidney Sherman became colonel of the Second Regiment, and Captain Bennett was elected its lieutenant colonel. James Gillaspie, who had been first lieutenant in Bennett's company, now became captain. Captain Bennett's old company, now Gillaspie's, had fallen into the First Regiment, but Bennett having become an officer of the Second Regiment, regained the company in exchange for another. Also, the army now consisted of five classes: artillerymen, cavalry, regulars, first regiment of volunteer infantry, and second regiment of volunteer infantry.

On the morning of the twenty-eighth of March, when we had departed from the Agua Dulce on the Brazos, a detachment had remained to guard the ferry at San Felipe under the command of Capt. Moseley Baker, with Capt. John Bird second in command.

Unfortunately, unkind feelings existed between General Houston and Captain Baker, and, later, their respective statements of what occurred there were in some particulars contradictory. General Houston said that two captains, alluding to Baker and Bird, refused to march with the army. Doubtless their purpose was to care for the town, which was the home of many of their men. They encamped in the thick bottom, near the east bank of the Brazos, but kept pickets at the west edge of the town, which was west of the river. In the meantime, though most of the families had retreated, some of them remained, including most of the merchants with their goods.

About the first of April, Captain Baker announced that he had received a dispatch, written in pencil, from General Houston, ordering him to burn the town. Most of his men advised him to disobey the order, but he replied that General Houston was inimical to him and he would obey him literally. He ordered his third sergeant, Moses Austin Bryan, to superintend the burning. Being a nephew of Stephen F. Austin, that gentleman requested the Captain to excuse him, saying that he was opposed to burning the town which his uncle, as Empresario, had "laid off," that is, caused to be surveyed.

The Captain accordingly excused Mr. Bryan and appointed another man to superintend the burning. The families and merchants were given three hours in which to move their effects across the river and hide them in the bottom, which they did. The furniture and goods being removed, the detachment burned all the houses in the town. It has been said that General Houston denied ordering Captain Baker to burn the town, but Baker's orderly, Joseph Baker, said that he saw General Houston's dispatch written in pencil, ordering Captain Baker to burn the town.

Some men of the detachment said that later General Houston sent an officer to supersede Captain Baker as their commander, but that the men unanimously refused to accept him. Based on the following occurrence, I believe that the officer alluded to was Lt. Col. Joseph L. Bennett.

One night Colonel Bennett came to me and requested me to lend him my shot bag and powder horn, saying that he was going that night to San Felipe and would need them. I complied with his request and inquired when he would return. He replied that he did not know that he would ever return. I then regretted that I had lent the articles to him, but let him keep them. That night he went to San Felipe, as he said that he would, but returned on the next afternoon.

"Colonel," I asked, "on what sort of an errand have you been to San Felipe?"

"It was on confidential business," he replied.

Captain Baker still kept a guard of pickets at the west edge of the ground on which the town had stood. About the eighth of April the men of this guard, Isaac L. Hill, James Bell, and Willie Simpson, were surprised by the sudden vanguard of a Mexican army. Our pickets fled, Simpson toward the nearest part of the river bottom, and Hill and Bell toward their boat at the ferry.

The Mexicans gave their first attention to Simpson, who was soon overtaken and captured. This gave Hill and Bell an opportunity to run a considerable distance before being pursued. But immediately after capturing Simpson, the Mexicans turned their chase toward them. As Hill and Bell reached the ferry, jumped into their boat, and pushed off, rowing manfully for the east shore, about three hundred Mexicans appeared on the summit of the bluff behind them.

One of them demanded in plain English that they "bring back that boat!" But the demand gave more energy to the rowers. The Mexicans then opened fire upon them, and our two men lay down in the boat for protection. They heard the bullets whiz over them and patter into the water like falling hailstones. The momentum they had given the boat drove it to the east bank, and Hill and Bell sprang out and safely hid themselves in the bottom.

Santa Anna Crosses the Brazos

The Mexican force that appeared at San Felipe was the same that Sesma had commanded on the Colorado, perhaps with some additions. But it was now commanded personally by Santa Anna. His purpose, evidently, was to cross the Brazos at San Felipe, but the stream, swollen by recent heavy rains, could not be forded. The only chance to cross there was to use the ferry, which he found impossible in the face of Baker's detachment. After waiting and reconnoitering for several days, Santa Anna marched his troops down the river on the west side, evidently to seek a crossing at some other point.

On the twelfth of April, judging that Santa Anna would advance on Harrisburgh, Captain Baker marched his company fifteen miles up the Brazos, on the east side, to Groce's plantation on the river bank, opposite our encampment on the west side, and sent over his report to General Houston. The next day the army crossed the Brazos at Groce's plantation, and Captain Baker's company rejoined it.

Captain Wylie Martin's company, all mounted, had been guarding the ferries at a place called Old Fort, or Fort Bend, on the Brazos. They were encamped on a road leading west from one of those ferries, perhaps a mile from the river. Mr. Joseph Kuykendall resided near the east bank of the river, on another road, and from this dwelling he could see the other ferry, which was kept by a colored servant man.

On the morning of the thirteenth, the vanguard of the division of the Mexican army, which Santa Anna commanded in person, arrived from San Felipe at the west bank of the river, at the ferry near Mr. Kuykendall's. In good English, one of the Mexicans hailed: "Bring over the boat!"

Mistaking them for Captain Martin's company, the colored ferryman took the boat to them. It was a flatboat, and as many of them as could stand in it crossed to the east side. Mr. Kuykendall was a cripple and not able to perform military service. He was at home with his family and some women and children of other families, preparing to flee if they should learn the enemy was approaching. When he saw the Mexicans crossing the river, they too, mistook them for Captain Martin's company and went to meet them. Drawing near the enemy, they realized their mistake, and the women and children, except one boy, fled up the road in terror. Mr. Kuykendall, who could not run, and John Fenn, a brave twelve-year-old boy, stayed behind. The Mexicans surrounded and captured them. The Mexican officers questioned the prisoners closely while Santa Anna's entire division crossed the river. Then, leaving Mr. Kuykendall and John behind, the Mexicans marched east across the great prairie for Harrisburgh.

The women and children who had fled were pursued, slowly and at a distance, by some of the Mexicans. They came to a pasture in which was a thicket, and halted to climb a fence. Those who had entered the pasture went to the thicket for concealment, and the others continued to run up the road. One woman carried a nursing babe in her arms, and she handed it to a young woman to hold while she climbed the fence. But just as she got through the fence, they all took fright and ran, the young woman carrying her neighbor's babe with her. Six weeks elapsed before the mother and the babe again came together.

Capt. Wylie Martin's company, having learned that the Mexicans had passed them on another road, marched in haste to the lower ferry, about two miles below that on which the enemy crossed. Here they crossed, and marched up the river on the east side, safely passing the enemy while they were crossing, and narrowly escaping them. They arrived at our encampment at Donoho's on the fourteenth of April and encamped with us that night.

March from Groce's Plantation to Donoho's

Having met our cannon and formed and drilled a company of artillerymen, our General put us on the march which led to victory.

Late in the afternoon of the fourteenth we marched from Groce's plantation three miles east to Donoho's, where we encamped for the night. Half of the infantry now had horses and rode as cavalry, and on this afternoon march the mounted men of our guard formed the vanguard of our army and the footmen, I being one of them, formed the rear guard.

We were in doubt as to our destination. There was a crossroad at Donoho's, the left end pointing north away from the enemy, the righthand side south, toward them, and a middle road pointing a little south of east. On the morrow if we should march on the left hand road, we were yet retreating; if on the righthand road, we were advancing toward the enemy. But if we should take the middle road, we would be in doubt till arriving at McCarley's, twenty miles distant, where there was another crossroad.

On the night of the fourteenth, I was posted as sentinel on the camp guard, to stand two hours of each six during the night. The countersign on that night was "Watch." The moon, which was at its full, rendered the night as light as day. During one of my tours, General Houston and George W. Hockley, who had brought the cannons to us, walked twice around the encampment as "grand rounds." As I had seen the General every day of the last twelve, though I had never had occasion to speak with him, his form and features were familiar to me, and I knew him well by sight. On their first round, when they came within about twenty feet of me, I hailed, "Who comes there?"

"Grand Rounds," one of them said.

"Advance and give the countersign," I called.

They both advanced, and the General inquired, "What is the countersign?"

"Any word by which I may know a friend on business," I replied.

"But," said he, "you are not to know any man when on guard."

"Not unless he has the countersign," I said.

"What special word is the countersign tonight?" the General queried.

"I'm not permitted to tell you," I answered.

Then Hockley became spokesman. "Is it 'Guard'?"

"I must not tell you."

"Do you not know us?" he asked.

"I know General Houston, but not the other gentleman."

"But," said he, "you are not to know *any man* when on guard at night."

"When I see a man every day and know who he is," I replied, "I'm *bound* to know him."

Then the General resumed. "I see that you are not fully instructed as to the duty of a sentinel. Give me hold of your musket and let me show you how to do."

The "musket" was my worthless rifle. I knew that it was unlawful to let any man touch my gun and that to do so would render me liable to court-martial. But I handed it to him for the sake of instruction by the General.

I expected him to reprove me, but he did not. He took my gun. "Now I am going to talk to this man as if there were one or more others with him," he said. "And he will act accordingly."

Then Hockley retired to a point about twenty feet distant. The General leveled the gun upon him, but held his thumb on the hammer of the lock and hailed, "Who comes there?"

Hockley advanced, leaned over the muzzle of the gun, and said in a whisper, "Watch!"

The General then said, "Advance, Grand Rounds!" as if there were others. Then handing the gun back to me, he said: "That is the way. Never let more than one man advance till after the first has given the countersign, for if they should be spies, they would overpower you. Let only one advance, and make him give the countersign in a whisper, over the muzzle of your musket. Yet hold the hammer of the lock, lest it should fire accidentally. Watch them closely, and if they prove to be spies, fire and call the officer of the guard. I have instructed you minutely, because you may wish to join someone's army sometime, and then you will want to know your whole duty." As if he were not "someone," and I had not already joined his army!

When they came the second time, I leveled my gun at them, holding the hammer with my thumb, and hailed, "Who comes there?"

One of them answered, "Grand Rounds!"

I said, "Stand, Grand Rounds! Advance one and give the countersign." Hockley advanced and gave the word in a whisper over the muzzle of the gun. Then I added, "Advance, Grand Rounds!" and the General advanced and said, "We congratulate you on learning promptly."

After giving me another brief lecture, the General concluded: "We are performing double duty tonight because we expect to fight a great battle very soon. We may be watched by spies, some of whom may be our own countrymen. Therefore, it is necessary to be actively alert."

Doubtless they thus visited every sentinel twice on that night.

From Donoho's to Harrisburgh

Just at daybreak on the morning of the fifteenth day of April, Col. Sidney Sherman called his regiment into line and marched on the middle road. Behind him was the rest of the army, in the following succession: First Regiment Volunteer Infantry, Col. Edward Burleson; Regulars, Lt. Col. Henry Millard; Artillery, Lt. Col. J. C. Neill. As on the previous day, the mounted men formed the front guard, and the foot soldiers the rear guard. The cavalry formed the flank guards, half on the right hand and half on the left hand, and in this order we marched over twenty miles of road to McCarley's, passing no habitation on the way.

We of the rear guard, being isolated, could not know the effect that our movement produced upon the army at large. Notwithstand-

ing the General's assurance that he expected soon to fight in a great
battle, we were yet in doubt as to which road we would take on the
morrow. I was a little homesick and melancholy, but Mr. William F.
Williams, known as "Buck" Williams, of Arnold's company, rallied
me to laughter by calling me "the pretty little man with a mouthful
of bones," alluding to my teeth, which were very large.

We arrived at McCarley's sometime after nightfall and were relieved of our guard duty. I was weary, but sought rest in sleep, though
my blanket had been stolen.

On the morning of the sixteenth, after preparing and eating our
breakfast, we marched on the righthand road, south, toward the
enemy. Then some of our men were heard to say, "The General is
right, after all." We marched in the same order as on the day before,
except that the artillery and the wagons were in front, because of the
bad condition of the road from the heavy rains.

About two miles south of McCarley's our road led through a dense
thicket that jutted into the prairie. Here our flank guards, from
necessity, fell into line. About fifty of our men, taking advantage of
the situation, left the ranks and concealed themselves in the thicket.
When we had all passed, they went to their homes or sought their
families who were retreating. Among these was the orderly sergeant,
Bully, of Captain Gillaspie's company, who took with him the muster
roll of his company. Moreover, when preparing to desert, he had
stolen my blanket, which was my bedding and my protection against
the drenching rains to which we were sometimes exposed when
marching. My friend and messmate William Kennard saw him as he
was leaving with my blanket wrapped around him and knew it by the
letters *WPZ* with which my mother had marked it.

On the night of the sixteenth, we encamped at Matthew Burnett's
on Little Cypress Creek, about eight miles north of Harrisburgh.
There Captain Gillaspie appointed my messmate Richard Chadduck
orderly sergeant of our company to replace Bully. A new roll had to
be made, which caused some temporary irregularities in detailing
men for special duty. But after going through the new roll once, the
detailments were regular and fair. Thenceforth, William Kennard
and I were no longer subjected to detail duty one day and night of

each two, but were permitted to serve equally with our comrades.

On the seventeenth, our scouts went to a point so near Harrisburgh that they saw the smoke ascending from the town, which the Mexicans were burning. When they reported this to General Houston that evening, he feigned to disbelieve them.

Santa Anna's Movements

The following is mainly extracted from a report to the Mexican general [Vicente] Filisola by Col. [Pedro] Delgado, a subordinate officer in Santa Anna's personal command, but it is somewhat modified by my personal knowledge of the route on which Santa Anna marched and by other facts which were then well known in Texas.[9]

When Santa Anna found it impossible to cross the Brazos at San Felipe in the face of Baker's detachment, he marched his army down the river to a crossing near Fort Bend, and on about the thirteenth of April they began crossing at the same time our army was crossing at Groce's plantation.

On the fourteenth, about four o'clock in the afternoon, Santa Anna, with his personal command of eight hundred or more men, marched for Harrisburgh. Upon reaching Oyster Creek, they found that the water was deep and the east bank steep, slippery, and boggy. Here the difficulty delayed them till after sunset.

The road led through the Stafford plantation, which had been turned out and, the night being dark, the Mexicans mistook for a prairie. The road was very muddy and Delgado says: "The night was dark; a great many men straggled off and our piece of artillery bogged at every turn of the wheel. Such was our condition when,

---

[9] Two English translations of the Delgado report were available to Zuber in 1910. One account was entitled "Mexican Account of the Battle of San Jacinto," *Texas Almanac for 1870*, pp. 41–53. The other is catalogued as:

Texas (Republic) Army. The Battle of San Jacinto: Viewed from Both an American and Mexican Standpoint. Its Details and Incidents as Officially Reported by Major-General Sam Houston of the Texan Army. Also, an Account of the Action Written by Col. Pedro Delgado of Gen. Santa Anna's Staff. Austin, Texas: Institution for the Deaf and Dumb, 1878.

The information in brackets within the quoted material from Delgado is provided by Zuber as footnotes in his manuscript.

about nine o'clock, His Excellency ordered a halt in a small grove, where we spent the night without water. [There was an excellent well, but it seems that the Mexicans did not find it in the darkness of that night.] On the fifteenth, at eight o'clock A.M., most of the stragglers, having joined, we started again."

About three-fourths of a mile from the Stafford residence the Mexican army halted to eat. Here Santa Anna committed his usual arson, burning the dwellings and gin houses. At three o'clock P.M. they resumed their march, Santa Anna, with his staff and escort going ahead, leaving General Castrillón in command of the infantry. They marched at quick time across the great prairie, twenty miles wide, to the residence of Mr. David Harris, one mile west of Harrisburgh, arriving there about eleven P.M. They did not burn this house. Delgado says:

"His Excellency, with his adjutant and fifteen dragoons, went on foot to that town, . . . where they succeeded in capturing two Americans, who stated that Zavala and other members of the so-called Government of Texas had left the morning before for Galveston. [Galveston Island was then totally uninhabited. President Burnet, Vice-President Zavala, the heads of departments, and other refugees fled there and lived in tents till after the Battle of San Jacinto.] A part of the infantry joined us on the following morning at daylight on the sixteenth. We remained at Harrisburgh, to await our broken-down stragglers, who kept dropping in until two or three P.M.

"On the opposite side of the bayou [Buffalo Bayou], we found two or three houses well supplied with wearing apparel, mainly for women's use, an excellent piano, jars of preserves, chocolate, fruit, etc., all of which was appropriated for the use of His Excellency and his attendants. I and others obtained only what they could not use. [Delgado fails to mention the wine which they plundered. They also appropriated some fine fabrics for ladies' dresses, which were recaptured at San Jacinto.]

"On the same day, Colonel Almonte started from Harrisburgh for New Washington, with the cavalry.

"On the seventeenth, at three o'clock P.M., His Excellency, after instructing me to burn the town, started for New Washington, with the troops."

Delgado seems to have made quick work of burning the town, and to have gone with the troops, for he proceeds by saying:

"It was nearly night when we finished crossing the bayou. . . . At seven o'clock we resumed our march. Our piece of artillery bogged at every moment in some hole or ravine. As it was found impossible for the draught mules to cross a narrow bridge [Vince's bridge on Vince's Bayou], rendered still more dangerous by darkness and rain, His Excellency ordered General Castrillón to ford the bayou with the cannon three leagues above [not more than three miles], with an escort of only one company of infantry."

They were bewildered in the night, and had to halt till day, standing in ranks and exposed to heavy rains. Delgado continues:

"On the morning of the eighteenth, we moved on, our cannon being still far away. At noon, we reached New Washington, in which we found flour, soap, tobacco, and other articles which we issued to the men. His Excellency instructed me to mount one of his horses, and, with a small body of dragoons, to gather beeves for the troops. In a short time, I drove in more than a hundred head of cattle, so abundant are they in that country. General Castrillón came in at five o'clock, with the cannon. On the nineteenth, His Excellency ordered Captain Barragan to start with a detachment of dragoons to reconnoitre Houston's movements. We halted at that place, all being quiet."

Camp Opposite Harrisburgh, on Buffalo Bayou

When we arrived at our camp opposite Harrisburgh, in the afternoon of April 18, we found that the enemy had burned the town. General Houston dispatched Erastus Smith, known as Deaf Smith, in search of their trail. Smith found the trail easily and proceeded on it for some distance. While doing so, he met and captured two white Mexican couriers and conducted them, bound, into our encampment.

I had strolled to our guard line, near the point at which they entered. When I first saw them, they were yet outside the line and had dismounted. They crossed the line near where I stood and proceeded to General Houston's tent. I saw the men hurrying from all parts of the encampment to see the prisoners and to learn the news.

Before reaching the tent, I met a young man who told me the contents of a dispatch that one of the couriers carried, from Santa Anna to General Cós. It instructed Cós, on his arrival at Harrisburgh on the night of the twentieth, not to halt and await further orders as formerly instructed, but to proceed by force march to New Washington and join him there. This dispatch revealed two important items: Santa Anna's locality, and the anticipation of Cós's arrival at Harrisburgh. Unless Cós should receive a duplicate of the captured dispatch, he would probably remain and give battle to such of our men as he should find in the vicinity. The couriers were bearers also of extensive mail from some of Santa Anna's officers to their friends at home.

On reaching the tent, I saw the two prisoners with their elbows drawn slightly back and tied with cords. The sight shocked me, for I had never before seen white men thus bound. One of them was a fine-looking man, of genteel appearance, said to be an officer of high rank.

I entered the General's tent in search of further information. No furniture had yet been deposited, but the tent contained a pair of small saddlebags and a wastebasket. The skirts of the saddlebags were made of what seemed to be hogskin leather, tanned with the hair on it. I have been told that the smooth underside of one of the skirts had plainly written on it the name W. Barret Travis, showing that they had been the property of Colonel Travis and had been captured at the Alamo.

I found only one man in the tent. He was a Spanish scholar, and he was very busy taking the little scraps of mail, one by one, from the saddlebags, examining them, and dropping them into the basket. The air in the tent was very hot, and perspiration was dripping from his clothes. I also was unpleasantly warm and and soon emerged into open air.

Soon after the arrival of the captured couriers, we had the only authorized "false alarm" of which I was cognizant during that campaign. It was given to test the men's courage. We were ordered to parade, and word was passed from man to man that the enemy was within half a mile of our encampment and advancing. Nearly all our men promptly fell into line and waited in silence two or three minutes. Then we were order to "break." We knew that we had been fooled, but we had renewed confidence in each other.

On the morning of the nineteenth, General Houston ordered that about a hundred men be detailed pro rata from the several companies, to remain at our present encampment and care for the sick and guard the baggage while the main army marched to New Washington in pursuit of Santa Anna. This order was a severe tax upon the men, since nearly everyone wished to fight. If Cós, with 600 or more men, should arrive at Harrisburgh the next night as we expected him to do, he would probably cross the bayou and treat our little detachment left behind to the enjoyment of as much fighting as they desired. But the prospect for the main army to engage Santa Anna was regarded as certain, and none doubted victory.

Two small companies were added to the detachment, and the detailed men, together with a few teamsters, amounted to about 150 men capable of fighting. Their condition was critical if General Cós and his men should arrive. But we had about 50 men prostrate with measles, and they could not be left behind; nor could a larger force be spared from the proposed attack upon Santa Anna.

When I learned that ten of the men to be left would come from Captain Gillaspie's company, I approached the Captain and assured him that I was unalterably averse to being left there. He assured me that I was in no danger of being left contrary to my wish, for he had determined to detail only those who volunteered to stay. He thought that many men would be glad of the opportunity to avoid battle, but he was mistaken. All the other captains had likewise determined, but in no instance did the desired number volunteer.

At this juncture, Col. Bennett interposed for my discomfiture. Privately he told several men that it would be extremely dangerous to the company for me to go into battle with my tricky gun and incited some of the men to clamor for my detailment. In respect to the clamor that Bennett raised, Captain Gillaspie yielded and detailed me.

I remonstrated with Captain Gillaspie, and he promised that if I would get a well-armed man to exchange places and guns with me, I should yet go into battle. Though thankful for his promise, which was undoubtedly made in good faith, I did not make the effort, knowing all my comrades were as eager to fight as I. My mortification was so great that I involuntarily wept, and, since I regarded weeping as unmanly, my tears, far from relieving me, only aggravated my chagrin. After that I was generally known as "the boy who cried to go into battle."

While I was thus weeping, my friend Alphonso Steele approached and said, "Zuber, what are you taking on so about?"

"I have enough to make me take on," I replied. "I came to the army to fight for the rights of my people, but now I am deprived of this last opportunity to do so."

"What will you give me to exchange places with you?" he asked.

I drew out my purse. "Here are ten dollars and a half, all the money I have in the world. If you will exchange places and guns with me, it is yours, and if I had a thousand dollars you should have it all."

"I wouldn't exchange with you for *two* thousand dollars," he said.

A bystander then remarked, "Steele, if you get wounded in the battle, you will wish that you had taken Zuber's offer."

"I would," said Steele, "but I feel that I shall not receive a scratch."

Next I was approached by Ben Johnson, who was said to have fought courageously in the Battle of Concepción in 1835. He said to me, "Zuber, I want to exchange guns and places with you and let you go into battle."

I again drew out my purse, but he refused the money. "Then why do you want to exchange?" I asked.

"Because I'm afraid to go into battle."

"But you fought bravely at Concepción," said a bystander. "Why are you now afraid?"

"Because," said Johnson, "I heard some Mexican bullets whiz by my ears, didn't like the noise, and I don't want to hear any more of them." Thus we agreed and fairly understood that Johnson was to occupy my place in the detachment and I was to go into the battle.

On learning of my bargaining with Johnson, Colonel Bennett went to him. "Johnson," he said, "you are a fool. If you want to be in the less dangerous place, go into battle. When Cós arrives at Harrisburgh tomorrow night he will come over and storm this camp. He, with no incumbrances, will outnumber you four to one. The danger here will be more than twice as great as in the general battle."

Johnson then came to me. "Zuber," he said, "I'm sorry to break my promise to you, but I must back out." He went into the battle, was said to have acted bravely, and came out unhurt. Steele was severely wounded in the battle but recovered.

My mortification at being prevented from being under fire in the approaching battle was truly great. My involuntary weeping at my disappointment humiliated me. But later, I was surprised to learn that I had thereby won applause. Even Colonel Bennett became, ostensibly, one of my best friends.

Further Movements of Santa Anna's Troops

While at New Washington, the Mexican army, after several days of marching and starvation, was treated to an abundant supply of the green beef which they had appropriated. Then on the twentieth, they again made ready to march. Delgado continues in his report:

"On the twentieth, about eight o'clock A.M., everything was ready for the march. We had burned a fine warehouse on the wharf, and all the houses in the town, when Captain Barragan rushed in at full speed, reporting that Houston was close on our rear, and his troops had captured some of our stragglers and had disarmed and dispatched them. . . .

"There is in front of New Washington a dense wood, through which runs a narrow lane, about half a league in length, allowing passage for pack mules in single file only, and to mounted men in double file. This lane was filled with pickets, the drove of mules, and the remainder of the detachment.

"His excellency and staff were still in the town. Upon hearing Barragan's report, he leaped upon his horse and galloped off at full speed for the lane, which, being crowded with men and mules, did not afford him as prompt an exit as he wished. However, knocking down one and riding over another, he overcame obstacles, shouting at the top of his voice, 'The enemy are coming! the enemy are coming!'

"The excitement of the General-in-Chief had such a terrifying effect upon the troops that every face turned pale, order was no longer preserved, and every man thought of flight, or finding a hiding place, and gave up all idea of fighting.

"Upon reaching the prairie, a column of attack was formed, with trepidation and confusion, amidst incoherent movements and contradictory orders.

". . . Meanwhile, the officers having dismounted and taken their stations in front of their command, we marched on in search of the enemy, with flankers on both sides to explore the woods . . . At two o'clock P.M., when we descried Houston's pickets at the edge of a large wood in which he concealed his main force, our skirmishes commenced firing. They were answered by the enemy, who fell back in the woods. His Excellency reached the ground with our main body, with the intention, as I understood, to attack at once. But they kept hidden, which prevented him from ascertaining their position . . . Our cannon, established on a small elevation, opened its fire. The enemy responded with grape, which wounded severely Captain Urriza, and killed his horse."

Delgado then says that "His Excellency" withdrew all his force except Delgado, doubtless with a small guard, leaving him in charge of the ordnance stores, with only two mules with which to move them, and established a camping ground which Delgado says was "in all respects against military rules" and "at least one mile from where I had been left." Then Delgado tells what befell him:

"At length, at five o'clock P.M., my duty was performed; and as I entered the camp with the last load, I was closely followed by the enemy's cavalry. His Excellency noticing it, instructed me to order

Captain Aguirre, who commanded our cavalry, to face the enemy, without gaining ground. This movement checked the enemy for a few moments, but soon after, they dashed upon our dragoons, and were close enough to engage them with the sword, without, however, any material result. Then, His Excellency, deploying several companies as skirmishes, forced the enemy back to his camp, on which he entered sluggishly and in disorder."

The "enemy's cavalry" here alluded to was a select body of mounted men, including the cavalry, commanded by Col. Sidney Sherman, whose purpose was to bring on a general engagement. Sherman expected the entire Texas army to follow him, and when he saw that they did not, he returned to camp.

The Battle of San Jacinto

April 21, 1836, was the day of Santa Anna's great defeat.

Delgado describes what is known as "the Mexican breastwork": "At daybreak on the twenty-first, His Excellency ordered a breastwork to be erected for the cannon. It was constructed with packsaddles, sacks of hard bread, baggage, etc. A trifling barrier of branches ran along the front part and right."

The Mexicans had nothing that we call packsaddles. What Delgado or the translator of his statement calls packsaddles were cushions, made of pliant leather and filled with hay. The Mexicans called them *terrejos*, and they were used as we use packsaddles. Most of them were so large as to cover a mule's back from withers to cropper; they were so soft as to enable the animal to carry a great weight of baggage without being bruised by it. Of about two hundred captured packmules, I did not observe one with a sore back.

After the battle I saw what was left of the "breastwork." The "packsaddles, sacks of hard bread, baggage, etc.," had been removed. Two parallel rows of brush heap, about thirty feet apart, extended about seventy feet up a rising ground and were about six or eight feet high. I saw no opening through which to discharge either cannons or small arms. The brush would of course have deflected the course of rifle balls and weakened their force, but could be no defense against cannon shot. Its only practical use for defense would be to arrest a charge, as an enemy could not have leaped or climbed over it. The removed articles might have arrested rifle balls, but not cannon shot.

A long table, improvised of undressed scantlings and planks, extended nearly the full length of the brush heaps and midway between them. When I saw this table, it was perfectly nude, but men who saw it immediately after the battle said that it was covered with tablespreads and bore many cakes, bottles of wine, and goblets. As a defense, this structure was also worthless.

Delgado continues:

"We had the enemy on our right, within a wood, at long musket range. Our front, though level, was exposed to the fire of the enemy, who could keep it up with impunity from his sheltered position. Retreat was easy for him on his rear and right, while our troops had no room for maneuvering. We had, in our rear, a small grove extending to the bay shore, and to New Washington. . . .

"A few hours before the engagement, I submitted to General Castrillón a few remarks on the situation, suggested by my limited knowledge. But he answered, 'What can I do, my friend? I know it well, but cannot help it. You know that nothing avails here against the caprice, arbitrary will, and ignorance of that man.' This was said in an impassioned voice, in close proximity to His Excellency's tent.

"At nine o'clock A.M., General Cós came in with a reinforcement of about five hundred men. His arrival was greeted with a roll of drums and with joyful shouts. As it was reported to His Excellency that these men had not slept the night before, he instructed them to stack their arms, to remove their accoutrements, and go to sleep in the adjoining grove.

"No important incident took place until 4:30 P.M. At this fatal moment, the bugler on our right sounded the advance of the enemy upon that wing. His Excellency and staff were asleep; the greater part of the men were also sleeping; of the rest, some were eating, others were scattered in the woods in search of boughs to prepare shelter. Our line was composed of musket stacks. Our cavalry were riding bareback, to and from water.

"I stepped upon an ammunition box, the better to observe the movements of the enemy. I saw that their formation was a mere line in one rank and very extended. In the center was the Texas flag; on both wings they had two cannons, well manned. Their cavalry was opposite to our front, overlapping our left.

"In this disposition, yelling furiously, with brisk fire of grape, musketry, and rifles, they advanced resolutely upon our camp. There the utmost confusion prevailed. General Castrillón shouted on one side. On the other, Colonel Almonte was giving orders. Some cried out to commence firing. Others, to lie down to avoid grapeshot. Among the latter was His Excellency.

"Then, already some of our men were flying in groups, terrified, sheltering themselves behind large trees. I endeavored to force some of them to fight; but all efforts were vain—the evil was beyond remedy. They were a bewildered and panic-stricken herd.

"The enemy kept up a brisk crossfire upon the woods. Presently, we heard, in close proximity, the unpleasant noise of their clamor. Meeting no resistance, they dashed upon our deserted camp.

"Then I saw His Excellency running about in the utmost excitement, wringing his hands, and unable to give an order. General Castrillón was stretched on the ground, wounded in the leg. Colonel Treviño was killed, and Col. Marcial Aguirre was seriously injured. . . .

"Everything being lost, I went, leading my horse, which I could not mount because the firing had rendered him restless and fractious, to join our men, still hoping that we might be able to defend ourselves, or to retire under shadow of the night. This, however, could not be done. It is a known fact that Mexican soldiers, once demoralized, cannot be controlled unless they are thoroughly trained to war.

"On our left, and about a musket shot from our camp, was a small grove on the bay shore. Our disbanded herd rushed for it, to obtain shelter from the horrid slaughter carried on all over the prairie by those bloodthirsty usurpers. Unfortunately, we met on our way an obstacle difficult to overcome. It was a bayou, not very wide, but rather deep. The men, on reaching it, would helplessly crowd together, and were shot down by the enemy, who was close enough not to miss his aim. It was here that the greatest carnage took place.

"Upon reaching that spot, I saw Colonel Almonte swimming across the bayou with his left hand, and holding up the right, in which he grasped his sword.

"I stated before that I was leading my horse; but, in that critical situation, I vaulted upon him, and, with two leaps, he landed me on the opposite side of the bayou. To my sorrow, I had to leave that noble animal mired in that place, . . . As I dismounted, I sank in the mud waist deep, and had great trouble to get out by taking hold of the grass. Both my shoes remained in the bayou. I made an effort to recover them, but soon came to the conclusion that, did I tarry there, a rifle ball would certainly make an outlet for my soul, as had happened to many a poor fellow around me. Thus I made for the grove, barefooted.

"There I met a number of other officers, with whom I wandered at random, buried in gloomy thoughts upon our tragic disaster. We still had a hope of rallying some of our men, but it was impossible. The enemy's cavalry surrounded the grove, while his infantry penetrated it, pursuing us with fierce and bloodthirsty feelings.

"There they killed Colonel Batres, and it would have been all over with us had not providence placed us in the hands of that noble and generous captain of cavalry Allen, who, by great exertion, saved us repeatedly from being slaughtered by the drunken and infuriated volunteers.

"Then they marched us to their camp. I was barefooted. The prairie had been burned up, and the blades of grass, hardened by fire, penetrated like needles the soles of my feet, so that I could scarcely walk. That did not prevent them from striking me with the butt ends of their guns because I did not walk as fast as they wanted. . . .

"At last, we reached the camp. We were seated on the ground by twos, as we had marched. On the bay shore, our thirst had been quenched with an abundance of water which Allen and others had allowed to pass from hand until all were satisfied. . . .

"After having kept us sitting about an hour and a half, they marched us to the woods, where we saw an immense fire, made up of a huge pile of wood, even whole trees being used. I and some of my comrades were silly enough to believe that we were to be burned alive, in retaliation for those who had been burned in the Alamo. . . . We were considerably relieved when they placed us around the fire to warm ourselves, and dry our clothes."

The bayou, rather slough, flowed through an extensive marsh in the prairie which extended to the grove. The marsh was covered with water, generally about four inches deep, and rushes grew all over it as thick as they could stand, about five feet high. The Mexicans, in their flight, were much obstructed by those bulrushes and they trampled down thousands of them.

Though narrow, the bayou was deep and boggy. The Mexican horsemen, as well as their footmen, crossed it where they came to it. Their horses mired down and could not get out; those of the riders who were not killed had to leave them. The mired horses were so numerous and crowded that they could not struggle, and the Texas infantry crossed on them as if they were a bridge, stepping from saddle to saddle. The Texas cavalry and other horsemen found a better crossing, and most of them reached the grove in time to witness the surrender of the residue of the enemy.

Some Mexicans escaped from the battle, but were overtaken and killed. Their nearest and only safe route to Filisola's encampment on the Brazos, twenty-five miles distant, was due west across the prairie, but only one took that route. The rest took the road to Harrisburgh, and were overtaken by our cavalry and killed. Captain Barragan, the only Mexican known to have escaped death or capture, took the prairie route, and arrived safely at Filisola's encampment.

When the army had advanced, General Houston mounted his horse, galloped through the line, and took position between the two armies, exposing himself to two fires, that of the enemy and that of his friends. While advancing, he received a wound in his ankle, which for a time disabled him from walking. When about thirty yards from the enemy's line, his horse was killed. Then his aide-de-camp, Alexander Horton, who rode by his side, dismounted. He lifted the General onto his own horse, setting himself on foot.

On the morning of the twenty-second, Sgt. James A. Sylvester and five comrades rode out on a scout, seeking fugitive Mexicans. In the heat of the day they halted and sat down to rest in the shade of a branching tree. While thus resting, they saw a man squat in the tall prairie grass, which was about as high as a man's waist, perhaps a hundred yards distant. One of the scouts rode to him and brought him to the others.

His comparatively fair features and linen dress appeared so American-like that they would readily have received him as one of their countrymen. But he spoke only Spanish, and they knew he was a Mexican. The jewelry in his shirt bosom and his broad silver spurs caused them to judge that he was an officer of considerable rank. Only one of the scouts, Joel W. Robinson, could speak Spanish, and he interpreted for his comrades and the prisoner.

In answer to questioning, the prisoner said that he was a private soldier in the cavalry, that he had been forced into the army against his will, and that he had done nothing but what he had been compelled to do. Also, should he regain his liberty, he would never fight the Americans again. The prisoner was not able to walk. Therefore, Robinson took him up behind him on his horse and they rode double into our encampment.

Arrived in camp, the scouts took their prisoner to the prison guard, where other prisoners were crowded so close they had scarcely room to sit. These prisoners recognized the newcomer, and exclaimed impulsively, "El Presidente! El Presidente!"

The scouts now knew that their prisoner was Santa Anna. They dismounted, and, while Robinson was fastening his horse to a tree with a tie rope, Sergeant Sylvester, leaving his horse loose, took the prisoner's arm, conducted him to where General Houston, being wounded, lay on a pallet in the shade of a tree, and introduced General Santa Anna to General Houston.

At the Upper Encampment

On the nineteenth of April, the main army had departed from our upper encampment on Buffalo Bayou, opposite Harrisburgh, leaving our detachment to guard the sick, the baggage, and the horses. When the army halted about four hundred yards distant, we heard the voices of General Houston and Colonel Rush, as they delivered patriotic addresses, and the cheers of their audience, but could not understand a word that was said.

On the forenoon of the twentieth, we held our second funeral. The deceased was a young man named Hunter, who had been sick with measles for four weeks. Like Felix Wright, he was buried with military honor but without a coffin. That afternoon we heard the cannonading between our army and the enemy.

That night General Cós arrived and encamped across the bayou as we had expected, but so quietly that we did not know it until there was a long, loud blast of his trumpet at about nine o'clock. We judged that he was preparing to come over and give us battle, and all fires were extinguished and all noise hushed. But he did not come.

After the bugle sound, quiet reigned. We later discovered that Cós had received a dispatch from Santa Anna, ordering him to proceed by forced march to New Washington and join him there. His bugle sound was to call his men into ranks for the march. He left twenty footsore men in a thicket near the town, but we did not know of them.

On the morning of the twenty-first, four of our boys rambled down the bayou about half a mile and found, near the bank, a pile of planks and some tools and nails. Knowing that when we should move we would need a raft to cross the bayou, they commenced to make one of this lumber. On the other side, the footsore Mexicans heard their hammering. They came down to the bayou opposite the boys and fired across at them, severely wounding one of them in the left leg. His comrades moved him behind a cluster of bushes and bound up his wound with their pocket handkerchiefs. The Mexicans returned to their camp. Our guard mustered and marched to the scene of action, and on the way we met the wounded boy on a horse. So far as we could see, every thread of his bandage was deep red with his blood, but the bleeding had stopped. We proceeded to the bayou, but saw no enemies. Then we returned to our encampment.

On our arrival, our wagonmaster, Rohrer, hastily mustered a few men and went in search for enemies. They went some distance down the bayou, found a skiff in which they crossed to the southwest side, and went up to where the town had been. Smoke led them to the enemy's camp, where the men were broiling and eating their fresh beef. Rohrer's party crawled through the thicket and fired, killing eight and capturing the rest. The party then returned to our encampment and deposited their prisoners at the headquarters of our camp guard, with the two whom Deaf Smith had captured.

On the afternoon of the twenty-first we heard the roar of firearms from the battle of San Jacinto, and on the morning of the twenty-second, Maj. Robert McNutt received a dispatch from our Secretary of War, Col. Thomas J. Rusk, informing us of the victory. Our acting sergeant major, Jesse Benton, read it many times to us all, coming a few at a time. It elicited no great demonstration, for nearly all of us were confidently expecting such joyful news. That afternoon we decamped and marched for the main army.

We marched some miles down the bayou to a crossing. We took most of the camp equipment across on a raft, floated the wagons across, and swam the horses and oxen, while most of the men crossed in a skiff.

The tide of the bayou had drifted up from the battlefield, and a dead Mexican floated in an eddy. One of our young men swam to the body and brought it to the southwest side to be inspected. It was that of a white Mexican, dressed in a respectable traveling suit, and we judged that he had been an officer of rank. One of our boys cut open his clothes in search of treasure and found much blood, showing that the man had not died by drowning. Doubtless he was one of those who was shot in the bay. The boy unbuckled and drew out a money-belt in which there were twenty-six Mexican silver dollars. Someone else found a pocket compass in the dead man's watch fob.

We finished crossing a few minutes before sunset and resumed our march. The moon was full and gave a bright light. We saw, scattered along the road, the bodies of more than a dozen Mexicans who had been overtaken and killed in their flight.

Just at daybreak on the morning of the twenty-third we arrived at the encampment near the battlefield and resumed our places in our respective companies and messes.

Exploration of the Battlefield

After breakfast on the morning of the twenty-third, I walked alone to the battlefield. The slain Mexicans were a ghastly sight. Exposed first to a drenching rain and then to a burning sun, they were decaying rapidly and could not be moved without breaking to pieces. They sent forth a sickening stench. As their number equaled that of our army, our men could not bury them, and they rotted on the field. When all their flesh had disappeared, the cattle of that locality chewed their bones, which imparted such a sickening odor and taste to the beef and milk that neither could be used. The citizens finally buried the bones, except some of the skulls which the cattle could not chew, to stop the ruin of the beef and the milk. Some of the skulls were found on the ground years later.

The bodies which I saw lay thickest at the upper end of the "breastworks," but they were thick elsewhere as well. I did not go to the bay shore, where, it was said, they lay thickest.

As I was returning to the encampment, I saw our whole army returning from a point in the prairie. I asked one of the men what had happened. "Our scouts have brought in General Cós," he replied, "and we went out to see him. Don't you see those men guarding him?" And he pointed to about a dozen armed men who stood in a circle.

While attempting to escape, Cós had contracted a hard-shaking ague. When he and his guard arrived at this point, a paroxysm overcame him and he could go no farther. He halted and lay down, and a large blanket was spread upon him. Then he covered himself, head and feet, and shook as if being pulled to pieces. When I arrived at the place, I asked to see General Cós.

"Lift the blanket and look at him," one of the guards replied.

I did so. Cós raised himself on his elbow and stared at me, his eyes black and piercing. He was a white Mexican of manly appearance. He wore a heavy black beard, and his mustache drooped below his mouth. After a moment, I let go of the blanket and he lay down again, covered his head, and continued to shake.

I proceeded to the encampment. Santa Anna's tent, now occupied by General Houston, was embellished with brown and white stripes, each four inches broad, and the door opened on the east end. Cós's tent, now occupied by Santa Anna and his suite, was solid black. His door opened on the west end and faced the door of General Houston's tent, about eight feet away, and the doors of both tents were generally kept closed. We had a "Santa Anna guard," on which I was never detailed. It was composed of twenty-four men who were detailed daily and divided into three reliefs, with eight men on each relief. Six of these guards surrounded the two tents, and two "inside sentinels" occupied the eight-foot space between them. When the door of the black tent was opened, the inside sentinels could look in and see the Mexican general.

March to the West

About the time of the Battle of San Jacinto, I accidentally spilled all my ink, after which I could not make entries in my diary. Therefore I cannot give precise dates for what happened later, though I state the facts correctly.

Five or six days after the battle, the stench from the battlefield became intolerable and we decamped and marched up to Harrisburgh. We encamped many days near that town, which was in ashes. Then we marched slowly but continuously to Victoria on the Guadalupe. After encamping there, we marched to Goliad and buried the bones of Colonel Fannin's command.

General Houston had gone to New Orleans for medical treatment of his wound, and our Secretary of War, Col. Thomas J. Rusk, was appointed brigadier general to command the army, with Mirabeau B. Lamar filling his place as Secretary of War. By agreement of Santa Anna and Rusk, the Mexican general Filisola was ordered to march the remaining of the Mexican army out of Texas. Filisola was then encamped at San Antonio. He sent a flag of truce to General Rusk, asking permission to march to Goliad before proceeding farther west, because of the bad condition of the road between San

Antonio and the Rio Grande. But Rusk replied that our men's passions were so excited while burying our butchered brethren that if Filisola should come that way our men could not be restrained from taking vengeance. Therefore he declined to grant his request. So Filisola proceeded to the Rio Grande on the miry route. He was allowed reasonable time to evacuate, and it was stipulated that the Texas army, in its advance west, should not approach nearer the retreating army than twelve miles. Hence, the march of our army was slow and partly by short stages.

During our march up the bayou, I was on the rear guard, the camp guard for the next day, and we encamped on the north bank of a lagoon, a branch of Buffalo Bayou heading west. The army had preceded us and had gone about two hundred yards farther and encamped. Sometime afterward an escort brought Santa Anna and suite up the lagoon in a boat and landed a few steps from our camp. They then proceeded up the hill to our general encampment, where they deposited the prisoners in a house. This was the only time that I ever saw the Mexican general.[10]

At Victoria, on the first day of June, I was honorably discharged from a service of three months, from the first day of March to the first day of June, 1836. On the third day of June, with five comrades, I left the army for home. We were all on foot, and some of my comrades were so weakened by hard service that they could not travel

[10] On March 1, 1882, the *Houston Post* printed Zuber's "The Burning of the Bodies of the Heroes of the Alamo . . . First Full Account of the Massacre of the Alamo . . . Most Horrible Recital on Record . . . ," which Zuber said was based on a report of Alamo events given him by the captured Mexican soldier, Apolinoño Saldigua, whom Zuber first saw on this march westward. It is interesting to note that a manuscript account of "the receipted prisoner" (a victim of Santa Anna's Tyranny [1881], Zuber Collection, Texas State Archives, Austin) omits the details given in the newspaper article: of Santa Anna's thrusting his sword through the dead body of Travis and of Bowie's tongue being torn out. These prisoners must have constituted a rather small group, as most of the Mexican army reached the Rio Grande by May, 1836. Some of the officers were detained. Delgado related that the officers were taken on the *Yellow Stone* to Galveston, then moved to Anahuac and finally to Liberty, where they were detained at Judge Hardin's until April 25, 1837. See "Mexican Account of the Battle of San Jacinto," *Texas Almanac for 1870*, pp. 41–53.

fast. The rest of us had to delay with them, and so it took me about two weeks to make the trip.

I arrived home about the middle of June, and was not sixteen years old till the sixth of July. Though my parents had been bitterly opposed to my going into the service, now that it was done, they were very proud. Then my mother told me of the troubles of our family on the Runaway Scrape.[11]

The Runaway Scrape

After the fall of the Alamo, when the army began marching east from the Brazos, most of the people believed that General Houston was giving up the country to the enemy, and they began retreating eastward in what has since been called the "Runaway Scrape." They did not take time for needed preparation for their journey, but hastily loaded wagons or carts with needed articles, hitched their teams, and departed. Others took what they could pack on horses, and some drove cattle before them. What they could not carry in these ways, they abandoned.

Our family at home consisted of my father, my mother, my ten-year-old sister, Mary Ann, and two Negro girls who were large enough to travel on foot. They had a cart and only one yoke of oxen. They had several head of horses, but only one gentle enough to be ridden, an old mare and the mother of the other horses. When they left our home in Grimes County, they were accompanied by a couple named Goodbread, their son John, one grown daughter, another half grown, Eliza, who was about eight years old, and a baby boy four years old. The Goodbreads had no wagon or cart, but each member of the family, except John, Eliza, and the baby, had a horse to ride. They carried what dry goods they could under them in the saddles on their horses, and Eliza rode behind one of her sisters.

---

[11] In his Eighty Years in Texas manuscript, Zuber makes no mention of the story of Moses Rose's escape from the Alamo that his parents related to him upon his return from the army. See the appendixes to this volume for his account of the Moses Rose story, "An Escape from the Alamo," and for the historiography of the Rose escape.

My father, being consumptive and not able to travel on foot, rode our mare, while the other horses followed their dam. They had hastily packed a scanty supply of the more valuable household goods into the cart, and made room for my sister and the Goodbread baby. Then they hitched their yoke of oxen to the cart, which John Goodbread drove, and departed, with my mother walking behind the cart, holding to a strap which hung to the hind gate. They left behind about sixty bushels of corn, three hundred chickens, all nearly grown, and a valuable stock of hogs.

About two miles north, they fell into the Coushatta Trace, the road leading northeast from Washington-on-the-Brazos to Duncan's Ferry on the Trinity. This road, like all others, was a bog of mud and water, and continuously crowded with retreating families.

Soon they met Mrs. Zoroaster Robinson, from Washington-on-the-Brazos, whose husband had ridden his family's only horse into the army. She had fled across the Brazos when the people of Washington stampeded, and was now wading in the mud with her three children, one a babe in her arms, born after its father had gone into the army, and the other two wading and holding to her skirt.

My mother got John Goodbread to halt the cart while they rearranged its freight and deposited Mrs. Robinson's two elder children with my sister and the Goodbread baby. Then they proceeded, my mother and Mrs. Robinson wading behind the cart with Mrs. Robinson carrying her babe.

Sometime later, they were overtaken by Mr. Robinson, who had heard of the stampede in Washington and of his family's distressful flight, and had taken absence without leave to search for them. During two or more nights he had slept on the wet ground without a tent and without food or fire. Hence he had contracted a severe cold and was so hoarse that his most intimate associates could not recognize his voice. Falling in with the throng, he inquired of his family, describing them. Someone told him that they were some distance ahead and that he would find his wife and another woman wading in mud behind a cart and that his wife was carrying an infant in her arms.

He found them. The women wore sunbonnets and looked straight ahead at the cart, holding to and steadying themselves by some straps that were hung to the hind gate. They did not turn their heads and did not know when he approached.

At first, he could not speak, but soon recovered and addressed his wife: "Madam, you have a hard lot to wade in the mud and carry that babe."

Not recognizing his voice or looking back, she replied, "Yes, sir, my husband is in the army and my lot is hard."

Then he inquired, "Can I do anything for you?"

She answered, "No, sir, I am with kind friends, and they are doing all that can be done for me."

My mother thought him too officious and turned and faced him, saying, rather sharply, "Mrs. Robinson has friends who will care for her."

Then he said, "Why, Martha, don't you know me?"

Mrs. Robinson turned, faced him, and exclaimed, "Why, it is Mr. Robinson!"

He dismounted, took the babe from its mother, probably caressed it for a moment, for this was the first time he saw it, passed it to my mother, and lifted his wife into the saddle on his horse. It was a Mexican saddle, not suitable for a woman's use, but much better than no saddle. Then he took the baby from my mother and they proceeded, Mr. Robinson wading in the mud and carrying the baby, and Mrs. Robinson riding.

Sometime before the twenty-first of April, they arrived at a creek three miles southwest of Duncan's Ferry on the Trinity. The stream was much swollen and could not be forded and was not subsiding. Someone had built a raft on which persons and goods could be ferried across the stream, but this was not without trouble. The wagons or carts must be unloaded and then floated and drawn across by hand. The women and children and the freight must be ferried across on the raft, and the teams and loose stock must be made to swim across. Then the teams must be rehitched to the wagons and carts before the families might proceed on their retreat. Since only one family could cross at once, they awaited their turns in the order of their arrival, and only a few families could cross in a day. As the number of arrivals exceeded that of the departures, the encampment grew large.

On the afternoon of April twenty-first, my parents and their friends were awaiting their turn to cross the creek when they heard the sound of artillery far southward and they knew that a battle was being fought. My father and Mr. Robinson, hopeful of a victory, determined to wait at this camp till they could learn the results of the battle. But the Goodbreads, being fearful, crossed the creek and continued to retreat.

The next day a man rode into the camp at full speed and shouted, "Hello! Halt! Do not cross that creek! All danger is passed! Turn and go home in peace! On yesterday Houston met Santa Anna's personal command of the Mexican army, and they fought a battle in which every Mexican was killed or captured."

This man had participated in the battle and had come to publish the victory. He seemed an honest truthful man, and the people believed him. The campers crowded around to hear particulars of the battle. When a company was named to him, he could tell the number of killed and wounded, if any, but could not remember their names. My mother asked him if there were any casualties in Gillaspie's company.

"Yes," he said. "A youth about seventeen years old is dangerously wounded, but he may live."

"Is his name Zuber?" my mother asked.

"Yes, I believe that is the name," the man answered.

Then my mother cried, "O, Lord! My only son is killed, and I shall never see him again!"

The man then said, "No, Madam, I was mistaken. The youth who was wounded is a volunteer from the United States, and recently from Kentucky." But my mother believed that the man was telling a fib and would not be comforted. My father would have departed immediately for home, but my mother's grief was so great that she was not able to travel.

On the twenty-third another man arrived from the army bearing a dispatch from the Secretary of War, Thomas Rusk, and a list of the killed and wounded. From him my mother learned that the name of the wounded man in Gillaspie's company was Alphonso Steele, and she recovered from her paroxysm of grief.

That day my parents departed for home, with Mr. Robinson driving the cart. On the way they met two men with four bushels of meal. They asked them where they had gotten it, and the men said that they had found some corn in a crib. They had shelled it, leaving only a few ears, and had brought it by a mill and had it ground. Now they were taking it to their families on the road. When they described the place where they had found the corn, my mother recognized that it was our home. She told them that they had deprived her family and they cheerfully surrendered the meal.

Arriving at home, my parents found our corncrib empty and their lot of three hundred chickens reduced to four or five. But their fine herd of hogs was undisturbed. When I arrived at home in June we finished cultivating a crop of corn they had planted and partly cultivated before the Runaway Scrape, and we gathered a plenteous harvest.

4

Defending the Republic

Frontier Defense

During the next two years, 1837 and 1838, I was in actual service, protecting the frontier against the incursions of hostile Indians and at the same time cultivating the soil. The people of Robertson County gave us partial protection, being between us and the country occupied by these Indians. But occasionally the Indians came down undetected into our section, between the settlements of Robertson County, stealing many horses and committing some murders. With every family likely at some time to be attacked by Indians or to lose property by these thefts, every man or boy able to bear arms was a guard for his family.

But the crops still had to be cultivated to sustain life. The field in which I plowed was bounded at the ends of the rows by a dense thicket. Therefore I plowed with my gun lying in the middle of the row next to that in which I was plowing, so that, if attacked, I could run to my gun and defend myself and my family.

On June 3, 1837, nineteen men, including myself, took the trail of a body of Indians who had, on the preceding night, stormed a house and committed murder. We trailed them for two days, advancing between forty and fifty miles, but they discovered our pursuit and scattered, so that we could trail them no farther. Thus they escaped, and we had to abandon the chase and go home.

Our militia company, which occupied a large territory, was divided into six platoons, each having a commanding officer appointed. Each platoon served a week at a time by turns. Our service was to scour the woods for a week, hunting for Indian trails. But the Indians learned what we were doing and quit raiding. So even though we made no discoveries, we kept them back in their northern haunts, the range of the Comanches, between the counties of Robertson and Fannin, and thus protected ourselves and the settlements south of us.

I cannot clearly justify our taking the Indians' country from them by force or fraud. But our ancestors adopted this policy toward them through the pretended "right of discovery," we inherited it, and we could not well avoid it. In their wars against us, as well as in their intertribal wars, the Indian policy was to kill all the old people and all men able to bear arms, and to subject all the women and children to a captivity worse than death. And we, being born and brought up in their country, must fight and exterminate them to secure our own existence. If our case against the Indians was just, this necessity is what justified it. If our cause was just, I have never participated in an unjust war.

Thus, during the two years, I and all able-bodied men who resided in what are now the counties of Grimes, Walker, Madison, and Brazos were in actual though not regular military service, protecting our country from the depredations of savages.

In 1839 the Cherokees had immigrated from the United States to Texas without permission and were regarded as intruders. The combined forces of Burleson and Rusk, under the command of W. Henry Daingerfield, stormed the Cherokees, defeated them, and drove them across the Red River into Indian Territory. Such a force of white men, though not operating directly against the Comanches, intimidated them, and they remained north of Robertson County and did not raid the settlements during that year. So we of our section rested one year from fighting Indians.

The Tidwell Campaign, 1840

In 1840, in the Indian Territory on the north bank of the Red River, opposite Fannin County, a man named Holland Coffee owned and operated an establishment called "Coffee's Trading House." It was licensed by the United States government and the license gave Coffee permission to trade indefinitely with the Indians. Being in territory belonging to the United States, this establishment was not controlled by Texas. Coffee, or men connected with him, bought horses from the Indians which they had stolen in Texas, drove them to more distant localities, and sold them for a profit. This trade encouraged the Indians to increase their thefts in Texas and, incidentally, to increase their murders. Some Comanches and other Texas Indians engaged in these transactions, but they were mostly operated by Cherokees and Kickapoos who had been expelled from Texas.

In May of that year, with both President Lamar and Vice-President Burnet absent, our Secretary of War, Branch T. Archer, assumed the responsibility to issue a proclamation ordering all the militia of Texas to enter service for the purpose of exterminating all Indians from Texas. This proclamation was generally believed to be illegal, and was surely impractical, since, if all able-bodied men were called into service, they could not raise corn for their families.

In his proclamation, the Secretary divided the Republic into five districts. The first embraced all territory west of the Colorado River; the second, that between the Colorado and the Brazos; the third, that between the Brazos and the Trinity; the fourth, that between the Trinity and the Sabine; and the fifth embraced the counties bordering on the Red River. Secretary Archer designated a place of rendezvous for each district and ordered the militia of each district to meet at the appointed place on the first day of June and encamp there until further orders. Believing the proclamation illegal, and knowing it to be only injurious if practicable, most of the districts paid no attention to it. In the second district a few men of Washington

County assembled on the east bank of the Colorado between La Grange and Bastrop and discussed the situation for a day or two. Then they unanimously voted to go home.

In the third district, however, the proclamation was partly obeyed in Montgomery and Navasota counties. Montgomery, the "Mammoth County," embraced the territory of the present counties of Montgomery, Grimes, Walker, and Madison. It contained five organized companies, constituting one regiment, with a colonel-elect named Wheeler.

At the time appointed, men of every company in Montgomery County rendezvoused on the west bank of the Brazos near Nashville, a town now defunct, in Milam County. I was one of those men, and we were about 300 in number. A few men from Navasota County rendezvoused with us, but they soon returned home. The rest of us waited for further orders. Some of our men returned home nearly every day, so that by the first of July, we were reduced to about 150 men.

At that time Senator Beden Stroud, a wealthy bachelor who represented the counties of Robertson and Milam, owned and resided on a plantation covering the site of the present city of Calvert, eighteen miles northeast of our encampment. Stroud had two neighbors in limited circumstances, Mr. Tidwell and David Hollis, who lived on farms adjacent to each other and northwest of Stroud's plantation. Settlements extended farther up the Brazos and Trinity rivers, in and near their respective bottoms, but on the dividing ridge between those rivers there was not a habitation between Stroud's plantation and the settlements on the Red River. This route was a continuous, almost unbroken prairie, except for the first eighteen miles from Stroud's to the Little Brazos and a strip of timbered land, averaging three miles in width and extending northeast from the Waco village on the Brazos to the Red River.

Late in June a band of forty Cherokee and Kickapoo Indians came down from the Indian Territory on this route to the residence of the Tidwell family. At his residence nearby Senator Stroud heard the Indians yelling and judged that they had killed the entire Tidwell family and would commit other murders. After arming and instructing his Negroes how to defend themselves in case of attack, he rode to our encampment eighteen miles away and reported what he thought had occurred.

He arrived in the night, and as soon as it was light enough to find our horses, we saddled up and marched for the scene of the tragedy. Arriving there about noon, we found that the Indians had killed Tidwell and captured his wife and three children. We found their trail, which was the same one they had made while coming down, and followed it. Nine men of Robertson County, including Senator Stroud and his nephew, Logan A. Stroud, went with us. We followed the trail for eight or ten days, subsisting on the flesh of buffaloes that our best hunters killed.

At the head of the Navasota River our commanding officer, Colonel Wheeler, and about half our regiment turned back. The remainder of us chose to proceed, and we elected J. G. W. Pearson our captain.

Some days later Captain Chandler, commanding the squad from Robertson County, and W. R. Saunders, a lieutenant of Pearson's company, awakened those of us with reliable horses who were most eager to chastise the Indians and rescue the captives, intending that we should ride fast and try to overtake the enemy in one day. We left the rest of our squad asleep.

We had gone about two miles when the others awoke and saw us leaving them. Five or six of them rode and overtook us, but the rest followed slowly. With about thirty men in the lead, including the nine from Robertson County, we rode fast through the Cross Timbers. But the Indians discovered us and eluded us by riding up the bed of a running creek where the water spoiled the tracks of their horses, while we continued on the trail they had made when coming down. And so we unconsciously got ahead of the enemy.

In the evening we arrived at a point where three streams came together to form Nolan's River, a branch of the Brazos, and we encamped without food or fire. Here we found that all our horses, including mine, were so broken down that we could go no farther in pursuit and we reluctantly decided to turn toward home. So the next morning we commenced marching, going very slow on account of our horses. About noon we joined up with the others and continued toward home.

Further on the way we met Felix Huston, major general of all Texas militia, with his colored servant and four or five citizens of Robertson County, the latter bringing biscuit and coal flour for our relief from hunger.[1]

Arriving at the Stroud's, we found Colonel Wheeler and those who turned back with him from the head of the Navasota encamped and awaiting our return. That night we encamped there, with General Huston commanding, and set our camp guards. The following morning General Huston issued an honorable discharge to each of us for a service of eighteen days, after which we departed for our respective homes. We never learned why our Secretary of War, Branch T. Archer, issued his eccentric proclamation, or why he did not issue to us further orders, as he intimated that he would do.

The Indians took Mrs. Tidwell and the children to Coffee's Trading House in the Indian Territory and proposed to let Coffee ransom them at a certain price, but Coffee refused. As they were about to leave, a citizen of Arkansas arrived who lived fifty miles from the Trading House. Coffee told him about the Indians encamped near him and the prisoners they were holding for ransom. The man went to the Indian camp and was granted permission by the chiefs to talk with the prisoners. He discovered that Mrs. Tidwell was a sister of one of his near neighbors. He then told the chiefs that if they would wait three days longer he would send a man who would pay the ransom. They promised to wait.

The man hurried home and told his neighbor where his sister and her children were, and of the ransom that the Indians proposed to take for them. The man had part of the required money on hand, and he hurriedly borrowed the rest from some neighbors. Then he went to the Indian camp, paid the ransom, and took the captives to his home in Arkansas. Mrs. Tidwell later wrote to Senator Stroud, telling of her captivity, her ransom, and her situation at her brother's residence in Arkansas.

[1] The term "coal flour" is as Mr. Zuber stated, although I do not know what it is. JBM.

She said that excepting the murder of her six-week-old baby, which they had killed on the first day of their return, and her fatiguing rides, the Indians had treated her kindly, but had told her they would kill her rather than permit her to be rescued. They were northern Indians and not quite so brutish as the Comanches. She also said she would never again return to Texas. This is the last that I ever heard of Mrs. Tidwell.

The Vasquez Raid, 1842

In March 1842 the Mexican border general, Rafael Vasquez, with a force of rancheros, entered San Antonio. Most of the inhabitants fled, those loyal to the cause of the Republic going east, those in sympathy with the invaders going west. But some remained, including some Americans with Mexican wives. One of these was Hendrick Arnold, a loyal citizen; in his charge many who went east left their property. The motive of Vasquez and his raiders is not known, but I think it was a test of the public sentiment, in the vain hope that they might sometime reconquer Texas. After taking the town, they abandoned it and returned to Mexico.

As soon as this raid became known to our people at large, there was a general rush for San Antonio, to drive the raiders back to Mexico. Our men did not take time to organize, but went in haphazard squads, expecting to join an organized force on arriving at San Antonio. Among those who went as private patriotic citizen-soldiers were Generals Sidney Sherman and Moseley Baker. On arriving at San Antonio, the foremost squad found that the raiders had gone back to Mexico and left the town deserted. Furthermore, there was no organized force for them to join. They waited a few days, but, when reinforcements did not arrive, they returned home. On their way home, they met other squads who had started out later. They finally all went home without an encounter with the enemy or even an organization. I think the number of men who went to San Antonio on account of the Vasquez raid was at least a thousand, but they did no fighting.

I was one of thirteen men who on that occasion went to San Antonio from Alto Miro, Montgomery County—now Anderson, Grimes

County. On the way we met some squads going home. Before entering the town, we rode through the Alamo grounds, then about four hundred yards east of the town, with a mesquite thicket intervening.

Arriving at San Antonio, we at first encamped on the river a little below the town, but because of rain and mud which soon hampered us, Hendrick Arnold invited us to occupy one of the houses left in his care. We stayed there about four days, during which time other squads arrived and yet others departed. Then we returned home. On our exit from the town we again rode through the Alamo grounds. On our way home we met still other squads going to San Antonio.

This was a campaign without an organization or any active service. However, in 1862 our state legislature recognized it by paying a small sum to each man who had engaged therein.

The Somervell Campaign, 1842

About September 14, 1842, a Mexican general, Adrian Woll, with a force of about 950 soldiers suddenly entered San Antonio. The district court was then sitting in the city, and Woll captured the judge, the jury, the lawyers, the plaintiffs, the defendants, the witnesses, and several citizens. He deposed all the officers of Bexar County and the city of San Antonio and appointed an *ayuntamiento* of *alcaldes, regadores,* and *síndicos.* He also deposed the Roman Catholic priest, a man of good reputation whom Bishop Odin had appointed pastor of the parish, and reinstated his predecessor whom the Bishop had dismissed for gross immoral conduct.[2] By these acts Woll seemed to think that he had taken permanent possession of San Antonio and its environs.

Having thus arranged affairs in the city, Woll marched east, apparently expecting to reconquer the whole Republic. He was said to have been reinforced by 150 Mexicans of San Antonio, increasing his force to 1,100 men and two cannons.

---

[2] Woll deposed the Reverend Michel Calvo and restored the Reverend Refugio de la Garza to the San Fernando pastorate (Ralph Bayard, *Lone-Star Vanguard: The Catholic Re-Occupation of Texas, 1838–1848,* p. 302).

Upon reaching Salado Creek, five miles east of San Antonio, Woll was ambushed by 201 Texians under Col. Matthew Caldwell, and 300 of Woll's men were killed. On retreating, however, his forces engaged a company of Texians under Capt. Nicholas Dawson, who was trying to join Caldwell, killed 45 of Dawson's men and captured six. Only two others escaped. Then Woll returned to San Antonio, but, upon learning that another considerable force of Texians was advancing, he took his men and their captives and retreated to Mexico.

In order to avenge Woll's invasion and rescue the prisoners, President Houston ordered a draft of one-third of all the militia, except that of Montgomery County, whose militia had been more liberal than those of any other county in service against both Mexicans and Indians. The President appointed Alexander Somervell to command the expedition. The other counties did not submit to a draft, but a sufficient number of their men volunteered. After a lapse of several days, however, the men of Montgomery County were surprised by an order to draft two-thirds of its militia. This was a hardship, for all our clothing and blankets were worn out by service on previous campaigns, and we had no time to send to Houston for others.

The militia of the county was already organized as a regiment, commanded by Col. Joseph L. Bennett, Lt. Col. James Gillaspie, and Maj. Robert Smither. The captain of the company at Alto Miro was William Bowen. I belonged to his company and, after being drafted, I went into service like many others, not equipped for a campaign. No place was appointed for a rendezvous, but Colonel Bennett, who resided at the town of Montgomery, started with two companies that resided there, and the other companies fell into line as he marched.

We commenced our march about the last of September. Crossing the Brazos at Washington, which was then the temporary seat of government, we encamped one mile west of the town. On the next morning the President and his staff visited us. Houston delivered an eloquent and patriotic address in which he predicted that we would invade Mexico, release all Texas prisoners, and administer to the

enemy a strong rebuke for their raids upon our border.³ Then we
marched to Gonzales, where we halted some time before continuing
up the Guadalupe to Seguin. Here we were detained several days by
a rise in the river, finally crossing on a raft and swimming our horses.
We then marched to San Antonio and encamped several days on
the river below the city. From there we proceeded to the Leon, a
creek ten miles west of the city, where our regiment encamped on a
high hill, a peninsula nearly surrounded by the creek, whose west
bank was a high bluff. Our camp was all open prairie, a very bad
location in case of a storm.

We had been drafted for a term of ninety days, and the fiftieth
day elapsed while we were there. Over a hundred of our regiment,
weary of inactive service, signed an address to General Somervell. It
respectfully requested him to inform us whether he was going to
march us to Mexico or keep us in camp till the expiration of our term
of service. I did not sign this address, because I feared it might have
been written by some men who wished to break up the expedition.
The address was not presented through the commander of our regiment, however, but by a selected man. The General received it po-
litely, promising to give a written satisfactory answer soon.

But General Somervell was an arbitrary man, consulting with his
soldiers only through their officers, and, though the address was
reasonable and respectful, he treated it as a mutinous document. He
sent a copy of it to Colonel Bennett, and it was read to the regiment
on dress parade. The reply, addressed to Colonel Bennett, not to the
men, read, "What the President will order me to do I cannot say."
At the same time, he ordered Colonel Bennett to punish all mutinous
combinations in his regiment. This answer, tendered indirectly and
disrespectfully, only aggravated the anxiety of those poorly equipped
and suffering men. On the next morning, more than forty of them
elected a captain and departed for home. This was a wholesale de-

³ Houston wrote that he got to Washington on October 2. He commented:
"But what will be done in war matters I cannot pretend to say! Since I got here
Colonel Bennett passed . . . with part of his command, and as they wished me, I
gave them a speech" (Houston to Thomas M. Bagby, *Writings of Sam Houston,
1813–1863,* III, 171).

sertion. A freezing norther was blowing and a mixture of snow and sleet so dampened the patriotism of those remaining that for the next three mornings other wholesale desertions occurred, reducing our regiment to a company.

I did not desert, but my want of equipment and the inclement weather so impaired my health that I obtained a furlough for forty days, which was to the end of my term, and I returned home.

General Somervell marched his army down the Rio Grande, to a point opposite Mier, and there encamped. Later the General and his staff left the army in the command of Maj. Peter Hansborough Bell and returned home. Major Bell was ordered to march the army back to San Antonio and disband. Three hundred men, unwilling that their expedition be in vain, determined to cross the river. Their disobedience eventually led to the disastrous Mier Expedition. Thus ended one of the most laborious and soul-trying campaigns to which the Texians ever submitted. It was seemingly without purpose and badly managed from the beginning.

5

Politics, Religion, and Learning

A Voter

I was a qualified voter in army elections from the beginning of my service, but I could not vote in civil elections till after my twenty-first birthday on July 6, 1841. The following September I cast my first civil vote for Sam Houston to be President, not because he bore the reputation of "the hero of San Jacinto," but because I approved his financial policy during his first administration. I voted for Memucan Hunt as Vice-President and Andrew J. Harper as representative of Montgomery County because I thought them good men. Houston was elected, but Hunt and Harper were defeated.

In 1857 I voted for Sam Houston for governor simply because it was my habit to vote for him, but Hardin R. Runnels was elected. In 1859 my judgment was that I ought to vote against Houston because he had supported the admission of California as a free state, but, influenced by friends, I voted for him because he had opposed the repeal of the Missouri Compromise Act, by which measure the floodgates of abolition immigration to the Southwestern territories, soon to become states, were opened and the future abolition of African slavery in the South was secured.

After our annexation to the United States I became a Democrat, because the Democratic party opposed one central national bank and a protective tariff. Since that time I have voted the Democratic ticket, reserving the right not to vote for a nominee whom I knew to be unworthy.

Annexation

From the beginning of the Texas Revolution a majority of our people wanted to be annexed to the United States. Therefore, in 1837, Dr. Anson Jones, our minister to that country, in obedience to instructions, made a formal application for the admission of Texas as a state of the Union. But the United States refused to admit us, and our application was withdrawn. Northern states had opposed the application mainly because Texas was a slaveholding country, but in 1845 some of the Southern members of the United States Congress introduced a bill for the acceptance of Texas. The bill provided that four new states be formed out of the state of Texas, with the consent of said state, and that such of those states as should be south of parallel thirty-six degrees thirty minutes north latitude (the Missouri Compromise line) should permit Negro slavery and such states lying north of said parallel should exclude it. The bill passed and the Texas Congress called a convention to consider the subject. It met at Austin, and formed a constitution for the state, which was later approved by the United States Congress. The Texas Congress, which was then sitting, called for an election to determine whether we, the citizens of the Republic, should be annexed to the United States and whether the proposed constitution should be adopted.

At that time many people of Texas were opposed to annexation. Our population was divided into two parties, the annexationists and the anti-annexationists. The annexationists tried by intimidation to convert the anti's or, failing this, to prevent them from voting. Mass meetings were held in some localities in which it was resolved that those who were present would never support for any office or patron-

ize in business any man who would vote against annexation. Doubtless for the same purpose the convention provided that the vote
should be given viva voce and each voter's name and vote be recorded
in a poll book, either "for annexation" or "against annexation," and
"for the constitution" or "against the constitution." Thus anyone
might know how a man voted by examining the record.

I opposed annexation for several reasons. First, I was proud of the
honor we had won by founding one of the nations of the world, and
wished to hold it. Second, I was indignant that the United States had
rejected us in 1837, and I wished to remain independent of them.
And third, I was opposed to dividing Texas into five states and especially to restraining Negro servitude in part of our present territory.
Had I been aware that our financial embarrassments were so great
I think I would have been an annexationist. But I did not fully realize
the situation and acted accordingly.

At the time of the election a Methodist camp meeting was in progress in Montgomery County, with about three hundred voters attending, or about one-third of the voters of the county. Our county
chief justice, Judge Guinn Morrison, was present, and, to enable the
men to vote without leaving the meeting, he made the campground
an election precinct. I was present and determined to vote on my own
judgment, but to avoid excitement I tried to say nothing about it.
However, I was teased to tell how I would vote and reluctantly did
so. Then, as I feared, I met vigorous opposition and I was reminded
of the consequences should I do so. Some said that the first Texas
gun fired in the Battle of Concepción was an annexation gun, and
others said that the voters at that point were determined that the
vote of that precinct should be unanimous for annexation. They said
that I should vote for it or not vote at all.

I waited until the managers of the election gave notice that they
would close the polls in ten minutes. Then I registered my vote
"against annexation" and "for the constitution," which at this point
was the first opposing vote cast.[1] I walked away, but in five minutes
returned and found that one more vote had been polled, exactly as

---

[1] Zuber undoubtedly voted *for* the constitution in the belief that annexation
would probably pass and the constitution would be necessary.

I had voted. These were the only votes cast against annexation of the more than three hundred that were cast. I expected a serious time after voting, but the ultra-annexationists never executed their threats against me or against any of those who voted against annexation, so far as I know.

The Republic continued till [February 19,] 1846, when J. P. Henderson, our first governor, was inaugurated. That day the Texas flag was lowered and our last President, Anson Jones, said, "The Republic of Texas is no more." Then the United States flag was raised and Mr. Henderson took his oath of office. We were now one of the United States.

I took no part in the Mexican War of 1845 and 1846, which resulted from annexation, because, since we had given ourselves to the United States, I believed that government ought to take war off our hands.

My Conviction of Sin

In Louisiana, in 1829, when I was nine years old, I had thought that I was very religious, because I prayed three times each day and imitated the acts of those adults I thought to be most religious. In my ignorance, I chose to follow the example of those who were most noisy and attracted the most attention. However, after we moved to Texas, in 1830, we heard preaching not more than three times a year, and some years not at all, and, with no religious associates, I dropped my religion and became very profane.

When we moved to the edge of Lake Creek bottom, there was a thicket of red haw trees near our house that made a beautiful shade, and when I had leisure I often went there to study. In 1836, while I was in the army, I often became weary of the noise of my comrades and retired to my tent and lay down to meditate on what I should do in the future. I was disgusted at my own profanity, and I would remember the beautiful shade of the haw thicket near home and think what a good place it might be for secret prayer. And so I resolved that when I returned home I would go to the thicket to pray and there reform and become a Christian. After my return home when I went to the thicket I sought the best place to stop and pray and passed through the thicket without praying and returned to the house. Then, strangely, I thought that my tent in the army was the best and only place in which to pray. As I expected never again to go into the army, I decided that my damnation was sealed and abandoned my intention to try to be religious.

Then one day in 1838, while in the forest driving the milch cows home, I was again impressed with a sense of shame for my profanity. Believing that I was ungrateful and dishonest toward God, I resolved that if I must go to Hell, I would go praying. I purported to use no more profane language and to pray three times each day. If business should prevent me on any day from praying my allotted three times, I would, on the first opportunity, pray as many extra times as I had missed. During a long time I faithfully complied with this resolve and easily dropped my profanity, except when angry. But I was very passionate, and found it impossible to restrain myself from anger or to avoid swearing when angry.

In 1839, our first Methodist missionary preacher, the Reverend I. L. G. Strickland, came to our section and formed a circuit, including our home, extending from the Trinity River nearly to the Colorado and embracing all of Montgomery and parts of Liberty, Washington, and Lee counties. It was called the "Washington Circuit," and the Reverend Mr. Strickland arrived on his round once every four weeks.

I acknowledged to him my desperate condition and told him of my inability to abstain from swearing when angry. He answered, "Just resolve never to swear another oath and adhere to your resolve, and you will succeed." But I knew that he was mistaken, for I had already done that and had failed.

After Mr. Strickland had preached two or three times over his circuit, the Reverend Littleton Fowler, superintendent of the Texas Mission and acting presiding elder for all Texas, exchanged the circuits of Mr. Strickland and the Reverend Joseph P. Sneed of the Columbia Circuit. I explained my condition to Mr. Sneed.

Mr. Sneed interrogated me thus: "Have you ever prayed to God to help you to quit swearing?"

"No," I replied. "I never thought of that."

Then he advised me: "Well, just ask the Lord, for Christ's sake, to enable you to quit swearing and He will do so."

I made no promise, but secretly resolved to do as Mr. Sneed advised. To my joyful surprise I soon quit both swearing and becoming angry at trifles. But, from want of proper instruction, I still clung to my erroneous belief that I must win salvation mainly by my own works and failed to obtain the blessing that I sought. I yet thought that abstaining from outward sin and praying often were my entire duty, not knowing that my whole spiritual nature must be so changed that I would hate everything sinful and love God and all His creatures, especially my fellow man. And so I was unhappy and did not feel at peace with God.

In June, 1839, I attended a Methodist Quarterly Meeting at a private residence near the present town of Anderson, ten miles from our home. Like all Methodist meetings of that period, it was intended to be both a business and a revival meeting, and the Reverend Mr. Fowler presided. Early in the meeting it was announced that there would be a camp meeting in the Robinson settlement, eight miles southeast of the present town of Huntsville and twenty miles east of Lake Creek bottom. It was to commence Thursday afternoon, September 26, and continue till the morning of Monday, September 30. At the Quarterly Meeting I knelt at the "mourner's bench" and the Reverend Mr. Fowler prayed for me. While thus kneeling, I resolved to attend the camp meeting, where I felt I would experience conversion from sin to righteousness.

Therefore I planned a program by which I expected to obtain this blessing. On Thursday I would go to the meeting, attend the preaching, and have my mind stirred up for the desired change. On Friday I would kneel at the mourner's bench and be prayed for. On Saturday I would join the church as a seeker of religion. On Sunday I would be converted. And on Monday I would come home a true Christian. How presumptuous I was in planning to do what God alone can do!

A day or two before the camp meeting, a neighbor boy about my age asked my father to send me to swap work with him in gathering and housing corn. He said it would take me three days—Thursday,

Friday, and Saturday—the first three days of the camp meeting, and he promised to help me do similar work during three days of the next week. Though my father was aware of my calculation to attend the camp meeting, he promised the boy that I would do as he requested. I was not present when this arrangement was made, and my wish to make peace with my Heavenly Father outweighed my wishes to obey my father and accommodate the boy. But I reluctantly promised to help him during the first two days, even though this interfered with my program. However, I declared that I would go to the meeting on Saturday, hoping that the Lord would provide for my success somehow.

I worked during the first two days with my neighbor, but suffered much anxiety. Then, just at sunset on Friday evening, as I was departing for home, the boy said, "Be here by sunrise in the morning, and we will finish our work."

"No," I said. "I only promised to help you two days."

"But you must come tomorrow to finish the job."

"But that would prevent me from going to the camp meeting, and you know I am determined to go."

On Saturday morning my father said, "William, I think you ought to help that boy finish gathering his corn."

"No, Father," I said. "You know my anxiety to go to the camp meeting, and I must go."

I reached the campground at noon and found more than a hundred persons present, many of whom were young, new converts. Some were old professors of religion, however, and some were neither. We had expected the Reverend Mr. Fowler to be present, but he did not come. Therefore, the circuit preacher, the Reverend Mr. Sneed, presided at the meeting. Besides Mr. Sneed, the following were present: the Reverend Jesse Hoard, pastor of another circuit; the Reverend Robert Hill, a local Methodist preacher; the Reverend Mr. Fullenwider, an old-school Presbyterian preacher; and Mr. Richard Davidson, a Methodist exhorter. The preachers all preached with power from on high, and Mr. Davidson exhorted eloquently, but I was most edified by Mr. Hoard's preaching. The Reverend A. J. McGowan, a Cumberland Presbyterian preacher, was also present, but he did not preach. He and I arrived together, as we had fallen in with each other on our way to the meeting.

Being late, I needed to work fast to fit my four-day program into two days. So, to relieve myself as much as possible from worldly chores, I hired a trustworthy colored man to care for my horse.

I heard the afternoon sermon by Mr. Hoard and was much encouraged by it. Mourners were called, and I knelt to be prayed for, while the prayers and shouts of new converts rang out about me. The invitation was given to unite with the church, and I joined as a probationer. I had now completed my program to date, and confidently expected to be converted on the next day, Sunday, as I had planned.

On Sunday, however, I was discouraged. I had lost confidence in my plan and threw myself solely upon the mercy of God and hoped He might yet bless me. As if in answer, it was announced that the meeting would be continued till the morning of Tuesday, October 1. Thus far the noise of the young converts had annoyed me, so I determined to seek some seclusion where I could pray alone, and where, if I should shout like the others, none but God could hear me.

Accordingly, early Monday afternoon I retired about a mile from the campground and, in a thicket at the foot of an ancient pine tree, I knelt down and said to myself, "Here will I remain on my knees till I either get religion or die."

My Conversion, September 31, 1839[2]

With my eyes closed, I remained on my knees at the foot of that pine several hours, wrestling with God in prayer. I thought that I mentally saw an ecstatic vision. My soul was then filled with love for God, for the angels, for the departed saints, and for all living persons. I confidently believed that I was a converted man, a new creature. I then joyfully arose and started to return to the campground.

But after going a short distance, the thought came that I might be mistaken and still in sin. I returned to the foot of the pine and renewed my supplication. Soon I again believed that I was converted

---

[2] In his *Ancestry and Kindred of W. P. Zuber, Texas Veteran* (1905), Zuber gives September 28, 1839, as the date he joined the Methodist church. He has stated earlier in this chapter that on that date he joined "as a probationer."

and again started for the campground. But again I had misgivings. So once more I returned to my place of prayer. The third time I felt certain that I was converted. This time my confidence was steadfast and I never again doubted my conversion.

But another temptation soon attacked me. Before I reached the campground, the following thought was forced upon me, and I believe it was suggested by the enemy of the soul: Now, I have got religion, but, hardened to sin, mentally weak, and subjected to many severe temptations, I cannot continue faithful, but will surely fall from grace. Then my condition will be worse than if I had not become religious; so I would have done better had I remained as I was. Then involuntarily, for a brief moment, I regretted that I had sought and obtained the blessing.

But a better thought instantly came to my relief, and I believe that it was prompted by the Holy Spirit: The Lord has sustained me thus far and will not forsake me. He is all wise and almighty, and if I continue faithful at heart, which I am determined to do by His help, He will lead me to be a Christian as long as I live. This thought renewed my courage, and since then I have never felt a regret for my change.

A thicket of bushes extended to the open campground, which had been cleared of such obstructions. Just before reaching this open ground, I met Brother Job Collard, who had been a Christian and Methodist probably six months.

"Brother Zuber!" he said. "You have got religion."

"Yes, Brother Job," I replied. "But how do you know?"

"I see it in your face," he said.

As I entered the open ground, I wondered how he could see it on my face. The sun was setting and the congregation was going from the arbor to the tents. Then I realized that some of their faces glowed with a flush of peace and joy such as I had never seen before. Was this what Brother Collard saw on my face?

After prayer on Tuesday morning Brother Sneed dismissed the congregation and we departed for home. My traveling companions were four wicked young men, some of whom were scoffers. Their conversation was uncongenial to me, but I paid little attention to what they said to one another. I meditated on the camp meeting and its results to me and others. To me, the sighing of the wind through the treetops seemed to be songs of praise to God.

Arrived at home, I told my pious mother of my happy change, and she rejoiced. Doubtless it was in answer to her prayers that the Lord had borne with me in my apparently hopeless condition and had conducted me to my present hopeful one.

My Religious Experiences After Conversion

For a time I felt it my duty to apply to the church for license to preach and to take a circuit if permitted. I knew that I was ignorant, but, if I should be given a circuit, the church would supply me with lessons to study and thus prepare me for my work as I should practice it. But pride prevented me.

At that time our custom was to allow to each unmarried circuit preacher one hundred dollars and his traveling expenses, and no more. If by gift his financial receipts amounted to more than one hundred dollars, he was required to give the surplus into a common fund to be distributed to those who did not receive their full allowance. However, the lay members residing on his circuit were permitted to supply him with a horse and clothes. Also, he was expected to raise his allowance (the term "salary" was not then used) by explaining his services and the necessity for his support, and then sending a brother to pass a hat to each person present into which each contributor deposited a small piece of money. This money was given to the preacher for his allowance, and the manner in which it was collected was commonly called "begging."

Here was where my pride interposed. I thought begging disgraceful and would not condescend to it. This pride was sinful, but I soon repented of it. Then I thought that if the Lord required me to preach, He would inspire some devout members of our church to advise me to do so. For a time, no member spoke to me on the subject, though several nonmembers did. I thought, however, that God would not call a man to preach through nonprofessors of his own religion. Later, I concluded that preaching was not my duty, quit thinking about it, and commenced the study of medicine. Soon after this, one of our most faithful local preachers expressed to me his disappointment at my not studying divinity. But I was averse to changes, had begun another study, and would not abandon it.

That same year, 1839, my father sold his place near Lake Creek bottom and moved to another site on his headright league. Since the new place was unimproved, we lived for a time in a camp while we built our first log cabin. We cut down trees, trimmed the logs and cut them the proper length, and hauled them home. Then we called some neighbors to help us raise the house. With help, the walls of a house were generally raised in a day, and the work done on these occasions was called a house-raising.

Among the guests for our house-raising was a man who, though an acquaintance of several years, was a new settler in our vicinity. I thought well of this man, even though he was irreligious, but at our house-raising he said to my father, "Mr. Zuber, you ought to have had this raising on Sunday, which would have saved a day for you and your neighbors."

"You know that I am not able to work at house-raisings," said my father. "Instead, I send William. Since he has joined the church, however, I do not believe he will break the Sabbath."

"Church or no church," replied the man, "I intend to have all my house-raisings on Sunday, and if any man refuses to help me, I will have no more to do with him, and he and I will be strangers."

I was present and heard this conversation, but did not utter a word. A short time later the man came around to invite me to his first house-raising, which was to be on the next Sunday. I was not at home, and he delivered the message to my father. When I returned, my father relayed the message to me. I replied that I would not work on the Sabbath.

"You have heard what he has said on the subject," my father replied. "If you do not go, you will lose his friendship."

I rejoined, "I will not forfeit God's approval for man's friendship."

I did not go to that house-raising. I judge that the attendance was small, for though many of our neighbors were not religious, they yet respected Sunday as a holiday. This man remained in our settlement several years, but he had no more house-raisings on Sunday, and seemed to respect me more than before.

My Self-Education

In 1844, William L. Porter, who lived ten miles east of my parents in the western part of what is now Walker County, proposed to employ me to teach school for himself and his neighbors. He wanted to build a little schoolhouse and to board me for the tuition of his own three children. His neighbors were to pay me $1.50 per month for each pupil, to be paid at the end of the term. The neighbors were thinly settled on a territory about three miles in circumference, and he believed that they could supply about a dozen pupils.

I was then twenty-four years old, and my education was so limited that the proposal that I teach school was a surprise to me. At first I declined on the plea of incompetency, but Mr. Porter urged that all the children were young and not far advanced in study, that they were so few in number as to be easily managed and taught, and that I could find some moments of leisure in which to prosecute my own studies. Thus advised, and conscious of my need of the pittance I might earn, I determined to take the school if I could start with a dozen pupils. Mr. Porter went with me to see his neighbors, and we obtained the promise of twelve pupils.

On the day appointed, I commenced teaching my first school. All my pupils were of the elementary grade, were easily controlled, and learned well with one exception. I discovered in myself an aptness to teach. My business was pleasant, and I found some leisure in which to teach myself. But at the end of my term, when I attempted to collect my pay, I failed. Mr. Porter had paid me his part in board, but, the cotton crop having failed, the others could not pay any money. They all gave me orders on merchants in Huntsville for goods to the value of their dues, all which I took in fabrics for women, as a present to my sister. Thus, my first school was a financial failure, but it was a benefit to my pupils and afforded to me opportunity and pointers for self-improvement. It also inspired me with confidence in myself as a teacher.

In 1845 I took another school, in what later was called the Goshen settlement in Walker County. Here again my school was small, but not so small as the first. Most of my patrons, however, were of a different sort from the first. The parents did not control their children at home. The children were hard to control and to teach at school and did not learn well. They gave me much trouble and little or no opportunity for self-improvement. At the end of the term, half or more of the patrons did not pay me. My only profit therefrom was some unpleasant experience in teaching. But all gave me a certificate stating that I had taught to their entire satisfaction.

In 1846 I received an invitation to teach school at a place about three miles north of the site of the present city of Hempstead. Here I taught nearly two years. Most of my patrons were wealthy and well-educated, and all were courteous and hospitable. All my pupils were well-trained at home, easily controlled, and learned well. I had ample leisure to prosecute my own studies, and my patrons paid me every dollar that I earned in specie.

In 1848 I took a school in the Bedias settlement, eighteen miles north of our residence. Here I combined teaching and the study of medicine, teaching by day and reading a medical book by night. I prospered during about six months, but, on the twenty-fourth day of November, my father died, and I had to abandon both teaching and the study of medicine to administer upon his estate.

Further Religious Experience

In 1848 I desired a Sunday school in our vicinity near the site of the present hamlet of Prairie Plains, but our local Methodist society was weak and not able to support one. A majority of our settled population were immigrants from South Carolina who had been Lutherans in their native state, but had joined the Cumberland Presbyterians here. Having no denominational Sunday school system, they preferred union schools. This being the case, I tried to build a union school.

To begin this work, I prepared a subscription, a promise of the subscribers to pay the sums annexed to their respective names for the purchase of suitable books to be used in a union Sunday school at a certified place. I prevailed upon a prominent neighbor to call a meeting for the purpose of raising funds. The meeting was respectably large, but I found that the people had but small sympathy for the cause. However, most of them reluctantly subscribed to pay small sums amounting in all to ten dollars, of which my own subscription was two dollars. From appearances, I judged that most of the subscribers feared the money would not be collected, so I advanced the ten dollars from my own pocket and bought a small supply of books. We afterward bought more.

I then procured the calling of another meeting for the purpose of organizing a Sunday school. One man, not a member of any church, whose height of six feet four inches made him prominent, professed to know all about such matters. He took the lead and successively nominated all the officers but one. Instead of a superintendent and assistant, he nominated a president and vice-president, who were elected, while the tall man was elected secretary. Then followed the election of a librarian. All this when there was no prospect of starting with more than half-a-dozen pupils. But, as I afterward learned, the tall man was opposed to any public enterprise unless he was boss. The president then appointed me first teacher and, while other teachers were appointed, all the teaching devolved upon me.

After the election of officers, a class of eight pupils was enrolled, and I found no trouble in getting them interested in their studies. We met each Sunday morning in a little schoolhouse, the place of worship for both Methodists and Cumberland Presbyterians. The officers soon tired of their work and ceased to attend, but my little class and I continued to meet every Sabbath. We prospered and I hoped that interest would grow and our school would be enlarged.

But the tall man busied himself telling the people that Sunday schools were peculiar to cities and towns and could not be sustained in rural districts. Also, that they were wasting their children's time by sending them to a country Sunday school and ought to quit doing so. To my astonishment, his listeners agreed. They ceased allowing their children to attend the school, and thus, through the opposition of the two-faced man, we had no Sunday school for some years.

Soon after my failure to establish a Sunday school, the Cumberland

Presbyterians built a house of worship called Prairie Plains Church, which was comfortable for what was then a large congregation. They invited the Methodists to use it with them, which we did, each using the building alternately once every two weeks.

When a young man, I believed that the constant society of a pious woman would be helpful to me as a Christian, and so, on the seventeenth of July, 1851, when I was just thirty-one years old, I married Miss Louisa Liles, a pious young woman recently from Missouri. She was an efficient help in my Christian duties and was the mother of my children.

In about 1859 the Reverend Milton Estill, a citizen of Walker County, and pastor of Cumberland Presbyterian at Prairie Plains, at one of their regular meetings proposed organizing a union Sunday school. My baby had cried, and I had taken it from its mother and stepped out to quiet it when the preacher called for a nomination for superintendent. A Cumberland Presbyterian brother nominated me. The preacher then insisted that to make the election interesting it should be a race, and that another nomination should be made. But there was no other nomination. The vote was taken by ayes and noes, and I was unanimously elected. When I reentered the house, I was duly informed of my election and accepted the position.

I served that Sunday school as superintendent till my departure for the Confederate army in March, 1862. When I returned in 1865 I again served as at first, till the rulers of the Cumberland Presbyterian church, who controlled the house, tendered the use of it to the colored Baptist church, whose members were then free, except when the Cumberland Presbyterians and the Methodists were using it for preaching purposes. For a time, the Negroes used it every hour of every Sunday when neither of the two white churches were using it for preaching. Then, there being no time to operate our Sunday school, it was suspended. When the Negroes ceased to use the house so much, the Sunday school was revived, but I had already moved my church membership to another locality.

My Writings

While acquiring knowledge of useful subjects, I desired also to learn how to make that knowledge useful, and, for this purpose, I practiced writings of various kinds: letters to imaginary persons and compositions on literature, history, religion, and science, so far as I understood them. I did not indulge in fiction. Of course, as I practiced writing, I improved my style, but for a long time my diffidence was so great that I burned all my manuscripts and offered nothing to the press, lest, from want of appreciation of its merit, my work would be rejected.

My first writing for the press was in 1855, when I was thirty-five years old. It was a short note to the *Galveston News*, a correction of an error that another correspondent had made in stating an incident which occurred a few miles from our residence. To my delight it saw the light in due time. Thus encouraged, I wrote for the *Texas Almanac* an army sketch, "The Baggage-Guard." After this, I was no longer diffident about writing for the press, but wrote other articles for the *Texas Almanac* and some newspapers, nearly all of which were published. Some of them were extensively copied into other publications, and, to my regret, some copyists did not credit me or the paper or periodical in which they first appeared. During my later years, I have seldom used a *nom de plume*, because every writer ought to be responsible for what he writes.

6

Campaigning in Arkansas and Missouri

The Confederate War

I call said war the "Confederate War," not the "Rebellion" or the "Civil War."

A rebellion is an attempt to throw off the authority of a superior power, but the Northern states rightfully never were a superior power to the Southern states. The original states voluntarily adopted the Constitution, came into the Union, and assumed the right to participate in its counsels. Having that right, they had a right to abandon the right to participate in the counsels of the Union and to resume their original independence. The new states that were formed out of the United States territory, whether originally owned or acquired, were admitted on an equality with the older states and had the same moral rights with the original thirteen states.

The Constitution forbids the forming of a combination within the Union by any two or more states; hence, each of the seceding states seceded as an independent power before joining the Confederacy, and each state had the moral and constitutional right to secede and form a confederacy. The other states had no moral right to coerce them back into the old Union. Therefore, the Confederate States, in their war of defense, were not attempting to throw off a rightful superior power, but were simply defending their natural rights. Thus they were not rebels.

A civil war is a war in which the people of a government are divided against each other and fight either for different principles or for different leaders or chiefs. But we were fighting for a just government for our country, which was unjustly invaded by a foreign power, the United States. Therefore, the war in which we were engaged was not a civil war.

As our war was neither a rebellion nor a civil war, the proper name for it is the Confederate War. "The War between the States" is applicable, but I prefer to call it the Confederate War because the term is more brief and because it indicates that the Confederacy was really and justly an independent power.

I Join the Confederate Army, March, 1862

When it became known that Abraham Lincoln, that hardheaded abolitionist, was elected to the presidency, the South resorted to the necessity of secession and formed a confederacy, hoping that the North would recognize the new government by entering into an international treaty with it. I did not share in this misguided confidence, however, but resolved to join the Confederate army.

But I was embarrassed with debt and did not see how I could leave home without bringing my family to financial ruin. I now had a wife and four children, whom I loved ardently, and during 1861 and part of 1862 I tried to arrange my business so as to make the best possible preparation for their support during my absence in the army. I had enough milch cows to supply them with milk and butter, enough hogs for their meat, with some to sell, and a flock of several hundred sheep, the wool of which would bring some money. I let my sheep out on shares to a herder and employed a neighbor, Elisha Floyd, as my agent to see to the butchering of my meat. He was instructed to sell as much of the meat as my family could spare, and to sell the wool to the penitentiary at Huntsville, the proceeds of which he should use for the support of my family and the liquidation of my debts. With this provision, I requested my wife not to accept any gifts from the committee for the support of soldiers' families, and she did as I asked. Also, she earned some money by weaving cloth for soldiers' garments.

By March, 1862, I was prepared for service. The war had progressed, the first conscript law had been passed, and no men were being received in the army for a shorter term than "three years or during the war." Also, it was determined that no more cavalry should be received. Rev. George W. Carter, president of Soule University, had already obtained permission to raise a regiment of mounted lancers. He had gotten commissions for himself, Rev. Fountain C. Wilkes, and Rev. James C. Gillaspie, respectively, as colonel, lieutenant colonel, and major.

I preferred cavalry service, but determined to join Carter's Lancers rather than go into the infantry. The first conscript law, which required all men between the ages of eighteen and thirty-five years to enlist, did not include me, because I was in my forty-second year. Later, the second conscript law required all men to enlist who were not past fifty years old.

My family and most of my friends stoutly opposed my purpose to join the army, but on the twentieth of March I visited our post office in Prairie Plains. There I found a man recruiting for a company that was being raised by Capt. John R. Alston to join Colonel Carter's Lancers. Thereupon I was sworn into service for "three years or during the war" and was instructed to meet with the company at Hempstead for rendezvous on the first day of April, when we would organize.

When I returned home from Prairie Plains and told my wife what I had done, her grief was great. She had hoped that I would abandon my purpose. I now know that I did wrong in enlisting. The passing of the conscript law ought to have convinced me that our cause was hopeless. My duty to my family was greater than that to my country, and I ought to have stayed and suffered with them.

On the first day of April, 1862, I met with the company in Hempstead, and we elected John R. Alston captain; Augustus D. Edwards, first lieutenant; John Cross Jones, second lieutenant; and John B. Ashford, third lieutenant. We then went into camp on Clear Creek, three miles southeast of Hempstead.[1]

Camp on Clear Creek

Besides our company, twenty-seven other companies had assembled to join our regiment, and two more were on their way. Colonel Carter had gone to Richmond, Virginia, to report his command to the Confederate government and to have our service changed from mounted lancers to cavalry. Also, he planned to change the regiment into a brigade of three regiments and to bring colonels commissions to Lieutenant Colonel Wilkes and Major Gillaspie. Carter, being senior colonel, was to be the brigade commander. However, Lieutenant Colonel Wilkes and Major Gillaspie were at present commanding our regiment and drilling us as cavalry.

At Galveston Gen. Paul Octave Hébert, commander of all troops in Texas, claimed the right to include us in his command and cautiously delivered orders to Wilkes. But Carter had arranged to receive orders directly from the Secretary of War at Richmond and did not recognize Hébert as over him. Therefore, in order to avoid contest with Hébert, Wilkes obeyed some of his minor orders.

We were bountifully supplied with what tableware and kitchen furniture was transportable on baggage wagons, such as tin plates, tin pans, tin cups, spoons, knives and forks, iron ovens, kettles, and frying pans; each company had a baggage wagon and six mules to pull it. We had also drawn Lowell (cloth) of which our women had made tents, and we had manufactured portable wooden tent poles and posts. Every mess had a tent and each mess had from four to twelve men. Some of our men were wealthy and brought into camp

---

[1] Blessington, of Walker's Texas Division, located Camp Groce three or four miles from Hempstead. Opposite that camp and on the railroad was Camp Hébert and "here was encamped Colonel Carter's Brigade of Cavalry" (Joseph P. Blessington, *The Campaign of Walker's Texas Division*, p. 22).

black servants whom they sent out to purchase such dainties as the government did not supply.

We had some sham fights, one party mounted and representing cavalry, and the other on foot, representing infantry. In these, we shot paper wads at each other, recklessly wasting powder. Several men were accidentally hurt, and some of them were disabled for further service during the war.

I received a letter from my wife stating that our baby, James Andrew, was dangerously sick. I applied to Captain Alston for a furlough to go home to see him, perhaps to bury him, but the Captain said that Colonel Wilkes had received an order from General Hébert instructing him to grant no more furloughs. I replied that I did not believe Colonel Wilkes was subject to orders from General Hébert. The Captain then agreed to go with me to Colonel Wilkes and urge my case.

We went to Wilkes's tent and the Captain called him out and stated my case. "I don't know what I am to do," Wilkes replied. "I am ordered not to grant any more furloughs." He turned his back on us and re-entered his tent.

Captain Alston and I returned to our company, but he said that he had a right to detail a man to go out recruiting for his company during ten days and he would detail me. So he did, and I went home.

Arriving there, I found that baby Jimmie had recovered, so on the tenth day I departed again for the army. My three elder children, Ann, Daniel, and Rachel, all cried bitterly when I was leaving. Their mother said, "Don't cry, my darlings. It is your father's wish to go into the army, and we must submit to it."

I said to her, "Don't say it is my *wish*, but my *duty*." But she seemed not to understand what I meant by *duty*. She could not realize that our country was invaded by an overwhelming army determined to ruin us, and that it was every man's duty to try to repel it. I was sorely grieved, but felt that I was just performing my duty.

Arriving at our encampment on Clear Creek, I found that great changes had occurred. The encampment looked desolate, with all the tents standing and the men gone. While I had been away, Colonel Carter had returned from Richmond with orders to reorganize his regiment into a brigade of cavalry containing three regiments of ten companies each, to be styled the Twenty-first, Twenty-fourth, and Twenty-fifth regiments of Texas Cavalry, but also to be recognized as the First, Second, and Third regiments of Carter's Brigade, and to be commanded respectively by George W. Carter, Fountain C. Wilkes, and James C. Gillaspie, for each of whom he had brought a commission as colonel.

Colonel Carter divided his thirty companies by lot into three regiments of ten companies each and lettered each company by lot. But Captain Taylor's company contained about twenty more men than was allowed by law. Therefore, the surplus men were permanently detached from it and, commanded by Captain Rock, were added to the Twenty-first Regiment as Company L. Then Colonel Carter assumed commany of the Twenty-first, Wilkes of the Twenty-fourth, and Gillaspie of the Twenty-fifth.

Carter, being senior colonel, also commanded the entire brigade. He then had furloughed all the men for a few days, except one man in each company, who, assisted by several colored servants, stayed to care for the wagons, teams, and baggage, with the adjutant or sergeant major of each regiment to direct them. When I arrived Colonel Wilkes was in camp commanding the whole, but Colonel Carter was in Hempstead, posting up the books of the command, which the subordinate officers and clerks were not able to do. The officers and privates of each company had been ordered to come together on a certain day at Crockett, Houston County, while the teamsters were to come back to this encampment to convey the wagons, teams, and baggage to Crockett. Alston's company, Company H, Twenty-first Texas Cavalry, in which I served, had been left in care of our third lieutenant, John B. Ashford, and he occupied my tent. I stayed with him one night, but on the next day I again went home to enjoy the society of my family.

March to Cherokee and Smith Counties

At the end of my brief furlough I again bid farewell to my wife and children. Their grief and mine was great, but my sorrow was much aggravated because my dear wife still did not appreciate my motives. She yet spoke to our children of my *wish*, instead of my *duty*, to go to the army, even though she, like myself, was an ardent secessionist. But she believed that it was every man's duty except mine to go to war and fight for our rights. I tried to explain that if every Southern man with a family stayed at home, there would be no resistance to Northern oppression. And so I departed.

On the day appointed, our regiment came together at Crockett, but Colonel Carter was yet at Hempstead. From Crockett we marched to Alto, Cherokee County. With his regiment, Colonel Wilkes had preceded us and encamped half a mile east of the town. But Colonel Gillaspie had marched with his regiment to a point farther east. We encamped with Wilkes's regiment for several days, until Colonel Carter overtook us and resumed command. Then we were all disappointed because he had not brought our bounty and back pay, and we grew restless because of our inactivity. We had enlisted expecting to achieve one or more victories before this time, but we had done nothing of importance and there seemed to be no hope of doing anything soon.

From Alto we marched to Rusk, Cherokee County, and from Rusk to a spring in Smith County, near a hamlet called Mount Vernon, whose post office was called Seven Leagues. Here we completed the organization of our regiment by electing Capt. DeWitt Clinton Giddings lieutenant colonel, and Benjamin D. Chenoweth of Houston, major. Lieutenant Colonel Giddings, who proved himself to be a brave and able officer, was succeeded as captain by his first lieutenant, Mr. Lusk, of Brenham, Washington County.

While we were encamped near Mount Vernon, many of our men became sick from the measles and many died. When my messmate, John Edmunds, was seized by a fever, I was detailed to take him to the residence of a Mr. Burrell Thompson in the hamlet of Mount Vernon and care for him and his horse till he should recover or die. Mr. Thompson was a merchant and postmaster, and he and his family were very kind to us. Edmunds was carefully attended to by Dr. Huson, of our regiment, and after several days was able to be up and dispense with my services. But by then my fatigue and loss of sleep from caring for him and our horses had caused me to become very sick. And so Edmunds, in turn, became my nurse.

Every residence in the hamlet contained sick soldiers and their nurses. During our illness, Edmunds and I were visited by Walter A. Stewart of Captain Lusk's company from Brenham, who almost a year later saved my life by generously risking his own. When I was able to be up and move about a little, Dr. Huson gave Edmunds a furlough to go home to recuperate, and he departed.

Sometime before I was able to travel, our regiment marched for Shreveport, Louisiana, but Dr. Huson tarried a while to minister to me and others. A few days later he also followed the regiment, after giving me a sick man's furlough for thirty days. He advised me that I could go home as soon as I should feel able to travel, and if I had not quite recovered at the expiration of my furlough, I should report by letter to Colonel Giddings at Shreveport.

I gradually recovered strength and early in July I left Mount Vernon, though I was so weak that I could not mount my horse from the ground, but had to lead him to a block, from which I mounted. I traveled by short daily rides, and, though my riding fatigued me much, I grew a little stronger each day.

One night I tarried at the residence of a Mr. Wright. On the next morning, as I was waiting for Mrs. Wright to prepare my breakfast, her son, Hynch Wright, departing for the army, came in to tell her good-bye. He spoke in a subdued tone, and she asked in a similar tone, "When will you come back?"

He answered, yet subdued, "I do not know that I will come back at all."

Not another word was spoken. The mother and son grasped each other's hands, and Hynch departed. Not a tear was shed, for their sorrow was too deep for tears.

As I rode along, I realized that it was the sixth of July, and that I was forty-two years old that day. The next day my ride was long, as the road lay through an unsettled section and there was no habitation at which I could obtain entertainment. That evening I arrived at Crockett.

On the last day of my journey I rode till late in the night. It was midnight perhaps when I arrived home. The moon was shining bright as day. I dismounted, hitched my horse to a tree, crossed the yard fence, and was advancing toward the house. I could not walk straight, but naturally formed curves toward my left, which I laboriously corrected at every step, walking very slowly. My wife was sitting up and by some means knew that someone was approaching the house. She came out into the hall to see who it was.

She did not recognize my staggering walk, but inquired, "Who is that?"

I answered, "A soldier." I thought that she would recognize my voice, but sickness had so changed it that she did not.

She retorted, "Then soldier away from here, for you are not welcome."

But I continued to advance. She returned to her room, closed and locked the door, and seized an axe that she kept for defense.

Her mother, who occupied another room, bravely came out into the hall to see who the intruder was. I had now entered the hall and said to my mother-in-law, "You know me, don't you?"

"I don't know whether I do or not," she replied.

Then I said loudly, "Oh, my dear Louisa! Don't you know your husband?"

"Oh. It's Mr. Zuber," my mother-in-law cried. "Come out, Louisa, it's Mr. Zuber."

My wife came out cautiously, and then followed a scene of joy.

While sick at Mount Vernon I had written to her, stating my situation. She had hired a man to go with a buggy after me and bring me home, and he was to start the next day. But my arrival prevented his trip.

I had also written to my cousin whom I had never seen, William Moss Zuber, postmaster at Minden, Rusk County, telling him of my illness. Soon after I arrived home I received a letter from him, stating that he had gone with a buggy to Mount Vernon, to take me to his house, but had returned alone when he found that I had gone home.

Ride to Cotton Plant, Arkansas

I remained at home about two months until my health was restored. Then my friend Edmunds and I rode to Shreveport, where we expected to rejoin our regiment.

On the way we sojourned two days and nights at my cousin Moss Zuber's, at the Minden post office. He and his wife had one son, William, and two daughters, Martha and Amanda. Zuber and many other Georgians had settled in this vicinity some years previously, and it was called the Georgia Colony. William was eighteen years old in 1862. Shortly after our visit he enlisted in Col. A. W. Terrell's regiment of cavalry. After the Battle of Yellow Bayou in 1864 he was captured by the Yankees and conveyed to Elmira, New York, and there he was confined in prison, where he died of prison fever.

On arriving at Shreveport, we found that our regiment had marched to Pine Bluff, Arkansas, under the command of Colonel Giddings, while Carter had returned to Hempstead. I learned later that Colonel Carter had sent Colonel Wilkes to Richmond to draw the bounties and back pay for our brigade. After he had drawn the money, Wilkes told the authorities at Richmond that there was no such body as Carter's Brigade. Then he returned, bearing instructions to himself and Colonel Gillaspie which showed that they commanded unattached regiments. Colonel Wilkes then appropriated the brigade's money for the use of his own regiment. He and Gillaspie, who preferred infantry service to that of cavalry, arranged for the dismounting of their regiments and, with them, joined General Churchill's command at Arkansas Post. When the Yankee general Sherman captured that fortress, nearly all those men became prisoners and were conveyed to the North and confined in prison.

Edmunds and I left Shreveport and proceeded to Pine Bluff, where we found that Colonel Giddings had marched our regiment to Cotton Plant, beyond the White River, and attached it to Col. William H. Parsons' regiment, the Twelfth Texas Cavalry.[2]

[2] W. H. Parsons, *The Brief and Condensed History of Parson's Texas Cavalry*

We later learned that when Colonel Giddings had arrived at Pine Bluff with our regiment, General Theophilus Hunter Holmes had caused notices to be sent from Little Rock to Pine Bluff and posted at every street corner, ordering all officers of cavalry arriving at that city to dismount their men and turn their horses over to the local quartermaster. But Colonel Giddings had not read those notices. A few days later Colonel Giddings received a special order from General Holmes instructing him to dismount his men and turn over their horses. This was an unreasonable demand, for throughout the Trans-Mississippi Department every cavalryman's horse was his private property and many of the dismounted regiments were permitted to send their horses home by men detailed to conduct them. Colonel Giddings put the order into his pocket unread. Instead, he wrote Colonel Parsons saying that if he needed an additional regiment of cavalry, he should request General Holmes to order Giddings, with his regiment, to report to Parsons and make the two regiments a brigade, which Parsons did. Soon after this, Giddings received another special order from Holmes, this time instructing him that if he had not dismounted his men, to proceed immediately to Cotton Plant and report to Colonel Parsons for duty. This order he read and obeyed. Thus he saved our regiment from being dismounted.

From Pine Bluff I went to Des Arc, on the White River in Prairie County. There I heard that our regiment was somewhere nearby, east of the river. I crossed the river and proceeded through a bottom twelve miles wide, extending from the White to the Cache River.

As I rode through a very muddy lane, my horse, Pomp, stepped on a tire nail that had dropped from a wagon wheel. It stuck into the frog of one of his hind feet, penetrating very deep, and lamed him badly. I dismounted and drew the nail out of his foot, causing the foot to bleed profusely, and then I threw the nail into a gully. Lame though he was, I remounted and rode Pomp to the encampment of our regiment, about two miles east of Cache River, and doctored

---

Brigade, 1861–1865, gives a roster of the several units "as far as obtainable." Not a name is listed for Companies G, H, or K of the Twenty-first Regiment. Zuber belonged to Company H.

him as best I could.[3] But we moved camp, and the mud in this region was poison to his flesh. It required about six weeks to cure my horse, and his lameness prevented me from participating in some exciting scouts and one battle.

Religion and Masonry

Soon after my arrival at our regiment's encampment near Cotton Plant, Arkansas, my comrade E. Boder, of our company, asked me to take a walk and pray with him, which I did. Thereafter, we retired and prayed together nearly every night. Other comrades soon discovered our custom and followed us. Our number increased, and we soon had a nightly prayer meeting which was largely attended. I was recognized as the leader, and I think our prayer meetings would have effected much good in our Master's service had my deportment been consistent with my position. But I sometimes yielded to the numerous temptations incidental to army life, and uttered language that disgraced me as a leader of prayer and paralyzed the good influence I ought to have exercised.

Our company had very few religious men, but many gamblers and profane men, and I was not happy in my association with them. But three other companies of our regiment each contained a mess of pious men in whose conversation I delighted and whom I frequently visited. One night I went to Company I, to the mess of James and John Walker. All members were present, and after conversing a few minutes, one of them said, "Gentlemen, it is time to go to that meeting."

"So it is," said another, looking at his watch. Then all except John Walker arose and started away.

"Aren't you going, John?" one of the men asked.

"No," John answered. "I'm tired, so I'll stay and keep camp."

Then James said, "Brother Zuber, aren't you going?"

"Of course I am," I said, and I started to go with them.

[3] Carter's regiment arrived at the Cache Creek encampment about August 19, 1862 (Orr Brothers, *Campaigning with Parsons' Texas Cavalry Brigade, CSA*, p. 63).

"William," John asked, "do you know what meeting you are going to?"

"Yes, of course," I answered. "It is a prayer meeting."

"No," he said, "it is a Masonic meeting."

When I said that was something I knew nothing about, he said, "I thought so, and that's why I called you back."

So I stayed with John, and all the others left. We talked for a few minutes, till he fell into a profound sleep. Then I departed.

Next I went to another mess, in another company, where I found only one man, whom I did not know. He said that all his messmates had gone somewhere and had left him to keep camp. Then I visited my third neighbor mess and found the same situation—only one man keeping camp while his messmates had gone away together. I felt sure that all Masons of our regiment had a meeting somewhere, so I returned to my own mess.

Up to this time my opinion of Masonry had been unfavorable, as I had been told that long ago, in Georgia, some Masonic brethren had betrayed my father's confidence and subjected him to poverty. But now I discovered that nearly all the men whom I preferred as associates were Masons. I judged that their order was ennobling and resolved to join them when I should have opportunity of doing so.

As I afterward learned, the Masonic meeting that night was to prepare and forward to the Grand Lodge of Texas a petition for a dispensation for the establishment and operation of a lodge of Masons in the Twenty-first Regiment, Texas Cavalry, Confederate States Army. The dispensation was granted, and the lodge was duly organized. The dispensation provided that the regular meetings should be held twice in each calendar month, as the regiment moved so often that the lodge could not hold enough regular monthly meetings to preserve its dispensation from forfeiture.

When I learned that the Masons had a lodge in our regiment, I sent in my application to be admitted into their order, but the frequent moves of the regiment, combined with my affliction and long furlough, retarded my progress to the sublime degree for about a year.

I was initiated on Spring River, in the northern part of Arkansas, becoming an Entered Apprentice in April, 1863, while on our march to Missouri under General Marmaduke. Our lodge room was an unused log cabin, about twelve by fourteen feet, with one door but no window. A tent was erected in front of the door and joined to the cabin for an antechamber.

Just after our return from Missouri to Arkansas in May, 1863, I was passed to the degree of Fellow Craft in a local lodge room on the west bank of the Saint Francis River, in the presence of some members of the local lodge. Then in May, 1864, while on our silly march to Texas, to arrest conscripts, I was raised to the sublime degree of Master Mason, in the Masonic Temple in Shreveport, Louisiana, in the presence of some members of the Shreveport Lodge and some visitors. Owing to unavoidable circumstances, I have never taken the higher degrees of Masonry.[4]

At Cotton Plant

We encamped in and about Cotton Plant, frequently moving from place to place in the same vicinity. Months later Colonel Nathaniel M. Burford's regiment, Nineteenth Texas Cavalry, and Major Charles L. Morgan's squadron, Texas Cavalry, were attached to our brigade. The army contained no better squadron than Morgan's.

The Confederacy had no better regiment of subordinates and privates than Parsons', notwithstanding the timidity and want of resolution that the Colonel had displayed early in the war when attacked by the Yankees. Due to the eloquence of the speeches that he delivered from the saddle, he was extremely popular with his own and Burford's regiments. But he was not popular with ours.

We now had two commanders, although Colonel Carter was never with the brigade when Colonel Parsons was present. I did not know the cause of this till a short time before the breakup in 1865. Both Parsons and Carter claimed to be the senior colonel of the brigade and entitled to its command. But Parsons was already in com-

---

[4] According to Grand Lodge records, Zuber was affiliated with Orphan's Friend Lodge No. 17, Bremond Lodge No. 350, and Zion Lodge No. 313 (*Texas Grand Lodge Magazine* [May 1959], 180–181).

mand and retained the position, with but two short interruptions, till a decision was made at Richmond. Parsons' first commission as colonel of the "six-months" men antedated Carter's commission. But Carter's commission antedated Parsons' second commission as colonel of men enlisted for "three years or during the war," by virtue of which he now commanded his regiment. Carter applied to the Secretary of War at Richmond for recognition as Parsons' senior. The case was referred to a select committee, which did not report till a short time before General Lee's surrender, when the committee decided in favor of Carter. However, Carter knew that if he should assume command of the brigade both Parsons' and Burford's regiments would mutiny. Therefore, he withdrew from it and attached his regiment to Gen. Walter P. Lane's brigade. The authorities at Richmond were culpably slow in business, and I think this was one cause of our failure.

After my horse recovered from his lameness, I participated in several scouts toward Helena. Once, with Alston's company only, we were returning toward Cotton Plant. After galloping several miles we came to Big Creek, where the water is deep and very cold. My horse was hot from hard riding, and he became severely chilled by fording the stream. If we had resumed our gallop immediately after crossing, I think the exercise would have relieved him of the effect of his bath. But a few steps from the creek we found the tall stump of a fallen tree on fire. Captain Alston halted his company to warm by it, and we remained there about half an hour, during which Pomp suffered greatly. It was nearly night when we left this place, and unfortunately we rode slowly. The sky was obscured by clouds, and, when night overtook us, it was very dark.

We halted at the gate of Rev. John Groves's. Here, Captain Alston dismounted and left us sitting on our horses while he went into the house. He was gone for more than an hour, eating his supper, as I afterward learned, while his men sat outside, chilled and unfed. When he finally returned, remounted, and ordered us to march, my horse could not move. The Captain then told me to dismount and stay behind with the Reverend Mr. Groves till my horse should become able for service. Two other men of our regiment were halting to care for their sick horses, and they helped me to move Pomp into a comfortable stable.

The Yankees at Helena had threatened to arrest and imprison Parson Groves, and when our company arrived at his gate he hid, fearing the Yankees had returned. After the company departed, he came out. I told him who I was and why I had halted at his house, and he bade me welcome. He and his family were most hospitable during the two weeks I remained. He was very pious, holding family prayers night and morning, and, when he learned my church standing, he invited me to alternate with him in conducting family worship.

One of the guests of the Reverend Mr. and Mrs. Groves, a Mrs. McCulloch, was the wife of a citizen whom the Yankees had imprisoned and sent to St. Louis on a charge of "bushwhacking." This mode of warfare was believed to be honorable, since the business of soldiers is to kill their enemies. Bushwackers would waylay a body of the enemy in a thicket beside a road on which they were about to pass, and, on their arrival, would shoot some of them and then would escape through the thicket.

Sometime earlier that year several citizens, including Mrs. McCulloch's husband and an elderly man named Johnson, met at a house on a roadside to form a company of bushwhackers. The men were sitting on the front piazza, waiting for the arrival of others, when two strangers arrived. The strangers rode to the gate, dismounted, hitched their horses, walked up onto the piazza and took seats. They were dressed as citizens and their appearance was suspicious. All the men there except Johnson feared they might be enemies in disguise and so were uncommunicative. But Johnson, confident that they were friends, had no secrets.

After sitting in silence a few minutes, one of the newcomers said, "We're hunting for some bushwackers and wish a brief conference with them."

Johnson, quite unsuspecting, replied, "We have assembled and are waiting for some others to form a company of bushwhackers."

The spy ingeniously questioned Johnson, and he "let the cat out of the wallet" and even gave the names of the purposed company, including some who were absent.

Just as the spy had obtained the information he sought, a whole company of Yankee cavalry rode up to the house and captured the purposed bushwhackers. They were taken to Helena, where Johnson took the oath of allegiance to the United States government, was liberated, and went home. All of the others, including Mrs. McCulloch's husband, rejected the oath and were sent to prison in St. Louis.

While at the Reverend Mr. Groves's, the two other Texas soldiers and I took our disabled horses each day to a new ground field, half a mile away, and there we rubbed them down and fed them on the green fodder of standing cornstalks that had failed to bear ears. We generally stayed at that field most of the day, lest some of the Yankees find us at Groves's residence and kill or capture us. At the expiration of two weeks, my horse seemed well and I returned to our encampment near Cotton Plant.

This section where we encamped was a dense forest of tall trees, and in rainy weather, mostly at night, one of the trees would fall, crushing the branches of many others and making a roaring noise that could be heard several miles away. This occurred frequently and on such occasions, Colonel Parsons acted strangely. Either thinking or pretending to think that the sound was the enemy's artillery shelling the forest, he would order his brigade to saddle up and mount. Sometimes, after keeping us sitting on our horses for an hour or more, he would move us to another locality in the vicinity to encamp.

The people in and around Cotton Plant were mostly loyal secessionists, but some were secretly Union men and we could not always know who were friends or foes. At the residence of a Colonel Harrelson, we found some men who were badly crippled by wounds received in the battle of Cotton Plant. Most of their wounds were healed, but some of the men still had detailed nurses. My sympathy was especially drawn toward a young man named Wigginton, whose home was in Leon County, Texas. He had broken the bone of a thigh, and it was set so badly that he could not walk. Also, a ball had passed through his face, from side to side, breaking his lower jaw and cutting off his tongue so that he could not speak plainly. He lay in a swinging berth. His wounds had healed, but he was in bad condition. I afterward learned that his father came and took him home, where he had his thigh broken again and reset so that he could walk.

I once rode out to the Cotton Plant battleground. It was a dense forest and thicket, and I was unable to learn anything important by exploring the grounds. So I went to Mr. Hill's residence nearby, where I found his nephew, an intelligent youth apparently twelve or thirteen years old, who had been there when the battle was fought. Mr. Hill had not been at home.

Near the battleground were two knobs, or hills, each in the form of an old-fashioned loaf of sugar. On one of those knobs the Yankees had buried all their dead except one man. He had been mortally wounded and they took him into a room of Mr. Hill's home, where he died. Mr. Hill had a tool chest, seven feet long, and they took the tools out of it and used it for a coffin. They placed the dead man in it and took him to the top of the other knob, which was the private cemetery for Mr. Hill's family and friends. There they buried the Yankee, marking his grave with a headstone that they robbed from a woman's grave. Her name, the date of her death, and her age were engraved on one side of it, and on the other side they engraved the name "W. W. Sloan." After the battle Mr. Hill visited Helena on business and conversed with a Yankee general, who asked about Sloan's grave.

"I shall visit that section again and examine the grave," he told Hill. "If I find that it has been disturbed, I shall hold you personally responsible."

After learning what I could from Hill's nephew, I returned to the battleground, where I fell in with Lieutenants Wright and Cox of Captain Neal's company, Parsons' regiment, who had participated in the battle. Together we visited Parley Hill's private cemetery and saw Sloan's grave. I was indignant at the impudence of the thieves who put him here, and made the following entry in my diary:

Poor fellow, there he lies,
In a stolen coffin,
And a stolen grave
Marked with a stolen headstone.

After camping long at Cotton Plant, our brigade marched south
to De Valls Bluff, a hamlet on the east bank of the White River
twelve miles below Des Arc. Here we encamped till the end of that
year.

Battle of Shell Creek, 1862

While my horse was still lame, a detachment from our regiment,
commanded by Colonel Giddings, went on a scout toward Helena.[5]
In a long lane near a stream called Shell Creek, they met a large
foraging party of Yankees more numerous than themselves. Our
men fired on the Yankees, put them to flight, and pursued them, still
firing. They passed a house where a Mrs. Blount came out and
cheered our men.

As some Texians outran others, they became greatly scattered, and
near Helena they abandoned the chase and returned toward Cotton
Plant. In the meantime, a much larger Yankee foraging party had
gone out on another road, nearly parallel. Hearing the firing, they
had cut across a dense forest to the head of the lane, and, coming up
behind the Texians, had pursued them. Captain Alston and some
other men were now returning toward Cotton Plant, going west, and
the sun, nearly setting, shined in their faces. When they saw the second force of Yankees about to meet them, the sunlight so blinded
them that they mistook the Yankees for friends. The Yankees were
numerous enough to crush Alston and his companions, but at that
moment they again passed the Blount house. Mrs. Blount saw both
the Texians and the Yankees and understood the mistake of the Texians. She ran out into the lane in front of the Texians shouting, "Halt,
Captain, those men are Yankees!"

The Texians halted, and, shading their eyes with their hands,

[5] Henry Orr reports that this scout toward Helena, Arkansas, took place about
November 7, 1862 (*Campaigning with Parsons' Texas Cavalry Brigade*, p. 80).

they saw that she was right. Mrs. Blount ran to the fence near her house and opened the gate. "Ride in here where the standing corn will hide you," she said.

They rode in and she closed and fastened the gate and returned to the house. The Yankees usually burned a house near the scene of a battle. But not knowing the Texians had gone into the fields, they went down the lane at quick time, thinking they were still in pursuit. The Texians rode through the cornfield, leaped several broad ditches, and escaped.

Colonel Giddings, with seven private soldiers, also met a body of Yankees and retreated at right angles through a narrow strip of heavily timbered land between two thickety pastures. When beyond sight of the lane, they opened a gap into one of the pastures and proceeded to the farthest fence from the lane, where they halted to open another gap through which to go out. A man named John Ross dismounted and was throwing down two panels of the rail fence when about fourteen Yankees overtook them and ordered them to surrender. Ross seized his gun, but, seeing a number of Yankee guns presented at him, he surrendered, and so did all the others.

This was named the Battle of Shell Creek. In it, the Yankee loss was more than fifty men killed, with many wounded and about sixteen prisoners taken, one of whom was a major. The Confederates loss was none killed, four wounded, and fourteen prisoners taken, including Colonel Giddings.

Soon after, the Texians began to retire toward Cotton Plant. Some of them were guarding three prisoners who could not be made to "trot" (they were dismounted and were on foot), and were walking at a creeping gait, doubtless hoping that some of their friends might overtake and release them. The Texians kept telling them to trot, but they would not. Finally they were overtaken by two other Texians, who inquired, "Why don't you go faster?"

"Because these prisoners won't trot," the guards answered.

"Well," said one of the newcomers, "I can make them trot." And he drew his pistol and shot one of the prisoners dead. Then the two remaining prisoners trotted.

The Yankee prisoners were sent to Little Rock, where they were confined, while the Texas prisoners were conveyed into Helena and sent from there by steamboat to St. Louis to be confined. Colonel Giddings, being a field officer, fared moderately well, but the private soldiers were confined in the medical college building, where they suffered at night from want of bedding and ate their rations at the dissecting table, which was stained all over with grease of human subjects.[6]

Colonel Carter negotiated with the Yankee general at Helena for an exchange of the prisoners of both parties captured in the Battle of Shell Creek, the exchange to be effected in Helena. On the appointed day Colonel Carter took a detachment of men from our regiment to Helena as an escort for himself and his prisoners; he also took a wagon and team for the transportation of a load of goods, which he expected to purchase there. The driver of the wagon was Mr. Roman, of Captain Branch's Company A.

The Yankee major and two privates were liberated in exchange for our Lieutenant Colonel Giddings. Both Colonel Giddings and the Yankee major had requested that their horses and horse rigging, as well as their pistols, be kept separate and exchanged with them, and this was done.

After the prisoners were exchanged, Colonel Carter purchased some goods at the stores in Helena and had them placed on his wagon. Then he and his exchanged prisoners, their escort, and the teamster departed for our encampment near Cotton Plant.

Among the Yankee prisoners who were exchanged were the two who had been with their comrade when he was killed because they would not trot. Thinking they recognized one of Carter's men as the

---

[6] Ralph J. Smith, one of several Texans who experienced imprisonment at St. Louis, wrote of his capture at Shiloh: "My wound was bandaged and together with many officers of both blue and grey I was sent to St. Louis, Mo. where a hospital for prisoners was fitted up by some angels in female forms called Rebel Sympathizers. Human Sympathizers would have been a much more appropriate name, for those big-hearted ladies I am sure knew neither North nor South. . . . The hospital was located in McDowell's College on Gratiot street and many a wounded Confederate had cause to thank heaven and woman-kind for the delicate care he received therein" (*Reminiscences of the Civil War and Other Sketches*, p. 6).

man who had killed their comrade, they raised a body of men from their fellow soldiers and followed Carter's men beyond the limits of the town. There they halted the wagon, turned it upside down, and spilled the goods out of it. They then told the suspected man that they had come to kill him. His denial was of no avail. But several of the Texians present knew both this man and the man who had killed the prisoner and finally assured the Yankees that this one was not guilty. The Yankees were not thoroughly convinced, but they were made to doubt the suspected man; so they returned to their garrison in the town. Carter's men reset the wagon, reloaded it with the goods that had been spilled out and pursued their journey without further molestation.

Misfortune and Wandering

On January 1, 1863, we were still encamped at De Valls Bluff on the west bank of the White River in Arkansas. At about eight o'clock in the morning we were ordered to "pack up and load," then to "mount and fall into line." We were then marched one or two hundred yards, not knowing why. There we halted a few minutes, then countermarched each company and mess to the respective places that they had just abandoned, with orders to "break." Each mess then re-erected and re-occupied its tent on the spot it had left a few minutes before. We all wondered about this strange movement, but it was never explained to us.

At this encampment, Brig. Gen. J. M. Haus [Hawes][7] arrived and assumed command of our brigade, in obedience to an order by the Secretary of War. This was the first suspension of Colonel Parsons' command of our brigade. General Hawes was an approachable and

---

[7] Zuber gives "J. M. Haus" and uses this "Haus" spelling (or misspelling) throughout. Certainly Brig. Gen. James Morrison Hawes is the officer referred to and will be thus cited. Another member of the Parsons' brigade reported on the new command: "We have another brigade commander now. Gen. Hawes, a Kentuckian—took command a few days since. Don't know how we will like him yet. . . . So Col. Parsons comes to his retirement. I judge he *does not feel so elevated as he has been feeling*" (Orr, *Campaigning with Parsons' Texas Calvary Brigade*, p. 76).

courteous gentleman and an able commander, though his command of the brigade was brief.

Soon after, we marched up the White River to Des Arc, crossed the river, and scouted far toward Helena. But we had no adventure with the enemy. Then we marched back to Des Arc and encamped a mile west of that town on Bayou Des Arc.

On our second night there, we were aroused to hear a telegram read from General Holmes at Little Rock, informing us that the Arkansas Post was threatened by the enemy. He ordered us to proceed by forced march to that point via Pine Bluff. We were told that we would march at daybreak.

On that day I had taken my dirty clothes and some belonging to my messmates to a nearby house to have them washed, so I had to bring them back that night or lose them. When I got to the house, I found the clothes washed but still wet, so I packed them all into a small sack and sewed it shut. Then I took the sack back to camp and put it on a baggage wagon. I did not see the wagon again for a long time and judged that the clothes had rotted. But one of the teamsters, John Morris, found the sack when the train halted to camp. He ripped it open, took out the clothes, and dried them in the sunshine. Then he put them back into the sack and sewed them in again.

While we had been encamped on Bayou Des Arc, we could not obtain food for our horses, and my horse, Pomp, ate nothing for several days. Early on the morning after our receipt of General Holmes's telegram we departed for the Arkansas Post via Pine Bluff. On that day we marched to Hicks Station on the Memphis and Little Rock Railroad, De Valls Bluff on the west bank of the White River then being its eastern terminus. At Hicks Station we drew corn for our horses, and I shelled fifteen ears for Pomp that night, which he ate. In the morning I shelled twelve more ears, but he ate only part of the twelve.

We continued our march toward Pine Bluff, but my horse soon began to show signs of foundering, grew worse, and could not keep up with the command. So I was left behind.

Near the edge of the Arkansas River bottom Pomp became unable to travel, so I halted at the house of an ex-overseer named Autrey and obtained permission to stay till my horse should get well or die. Mr. Autrey seemed to be a liberal and kindhearted gentleman, and he and his family entertained me well. He had not stable or shelter for Pomp, so I had to cable the horse to a post in the yard. On that night fell the deepest snow that I have ever seen. In the morning, after measuring in several places on level ground where there was no drift, I found it was eleven inches deep. Pomp was down, lying on his side, and could not rise. I had no means of doing anything for his relief or comfort, but had to let him suffer.

On the second morning my suffering horse was still alive, but apparently no better or worse. Mr. Autrey said he thought he could save him, so I told him that if he could, the horse was his, not mine.

I had to leave my horse rigging, but Autrey promised to take care of it and deliver it to me on my order. I offered to pay him for my entertainment and for the trouble that I had been to him and his family, but he refused, saying that I did not owe him a cent. So I started on foot to find our brigade, carrying my saddlebags on my shoulder.

I crossed the Arkansas River into Pine Bluff, but found no soldiers there except a few in the courthouse guarding about a dozen Yankee prisoners who had been captured below the Post while robbing a hen roost. On inquiry, I learned that the Post had fallen. Some of the men blamed General Holmes because of the frequency with which he had changed his own orders. They called him the "accommodating old gentleman who is influenced by the wearers of brass buttons" and said that he always granted the requests of the latest callers— even if by so doing he revoked his last previous order. Some officials had thought that relief ought to go to the Post from Little Rock and Pine Bluff by the road leading down the Arkansas River on the east end, while others thought that it ought to go by the other road, on the west side. So, after taking the advice of first one and then the other, and then the first again, the General caused the soldiers at Little Rock and Pine Bluff to cross the river six times, thus wasting so much time that help did not arrive at the Post soon enough to assist in its defense.

Late in the evening I engaged entertainment for the night and morning at a private dwelling in Pine Bluff. That night a few refugees from the Post came in. They had been on detached service when the Post fell, guarding the wagons a mile distant. Upon learning of the disaster, they abandoned the wagons and fled up the river to Pine Bluff, where they had been quartered in the courthouse. In answer to my questions, they said they thought the soldiers who tried to go to the relief of the Post were returning up the river. But they could not give any particular account of any regiment.

On the next morning, as I roamed about the city seeking further information, I met General Hawes. He had resigned his command of our brigade, and Parsons was again in command, but he did not so inform me, doubtless thinking that I already knew. He said that all the soldiers who had tried to reach the Post were now returning up the river, excepting our brigade. It had taken quarters at a plantation near the Post, because the enemy had abandoned the fort. He advised me to go down on a steam boat as far as it could carry me. At that point, he said, I would be very near the brigade, which I could easily find. Then he gave me a steamboat pass.

Soon after seeing General Hawes I met John H. Bowen, my comrade of Captain Alston's Company H. His horse had also broken down and was not yet able to carry a rider. We agreed to go down the river together on the righthand side. Our progress was very slow on account of the horse, which Bowen was leading. On the second night from Pine Bluff we arrived at the residence of Mr. O'Neal, whose wife was a Creole French lady. Here we engaged entertainment for the night and the morning, occupying the only spare bed in the house.

After Bowen and I had retired to bed a body of infantry soldiers arrived and encamped a hundred yards or less north of Mr. O'Neal's residence, between it and the river. The night was very rainy and our room was soon filled by refugees from the afflicting rain. Many of them had spoken for lodging, but could not get it because Bowen and I had preempted the only spare bed. However, since our bed was broad, we lay close together and made room for Dr. Middleton, a gentleman whose home was in Bastrop County, Texas. The others sat up all night laughing and joking about the hard times.

The men were generally of the opinion that all the forces that had tried to reach the Post were now marching up the river, either to Pine Bluff or to Little Rock. So the next morning, despairing of finding our brigade, I resolved to return to Autrey's to get my horse rigging and try to dispose of it, as I could no longer use or care for it. But Bowen preferred to proceed down the river in search for our regiment, and so we parted.

During my first day's travel from O'Neal's up the river, I overtook a lad named Garrett, whose home was at San Felipe, Texas. He belonged in some infantry command in the army and had marched with it to relieve the Post. But on the return march he became so weary he could not keep up, and they left him. As I too was very weary, I proposed that we proceed together to Pine Bluff, where he expected to rejoin his command, and he accepted my companionship. That night we arrived at a ginhouse that was surrounded by a patch of large turnips. Here we halted to spend the night, expecting to lodge on the bare floor without covering and nothing to eat. But, on entering the ginhouse, we found it occupied by part of Captain Highsmith's company from Parsons' regiment.

They had made themselves comfortable in the cotton left in the ginhouse and were dining on turnips that they had gathered from the surrounding patch and had roasted in a fire under the ginhouse. They shared with us their warm roasted turnips, which fatigue and hunger made us relish. We lodged comfortably in the cotton and in the morning we breakfasted on more warm turnips. Then, taking leave of our comrades, Garrett and I resumed our journey toward Pine Bluff.

About a mile and a half below the city we found the lifeless body of a soldier who had frozen to death in a mud hole. Several comrades who had been searching for him were standing by him. On the preceding night, in a paroxysm of delirium from fever, he had escaped from the military hospital in Pine Bluff. He had found this road and traveled on it down the river till he came to the mud hole where he had fallen and frozen to death. The steam from his perspiration was yet ascending in a large volume from his lifeless form.

Between this fatal hole and the city we met a comrade who informed young Garrett that his father, who had been left as a guard at

Pine Bluff, was sick and in the hospital. Upon arriving at Pine Bluff, the lad and I separated. He went to the hospital to see his sick father, and I went to a private boardinghouse at which I had been entertained before going down the river.

My landlady was a widow whose patriotism had died while I was gone down the river. On my former visit she had professed delight in entertaining Confederate soldiers. But now she received me and others with reluctance, saying that she did not want to entertain us any more because we paid her in depreciated currency—Confederate bills. But, she continued, when the Federals capture the town, she would take pleasure in entertaining them, because they would pay her in specie.

On the morning after my arrival, I left Pine Bluff. I crossed the river to its northwest side and proceeded up it about twelve miles to the residence of Mr. Motière Davis, whose house was about two hundred yards from the river. Here, weary and hungry, I obtained entertainment for the night and the morning.

During the night I was seized by a scorching and numbing fever, which grew so intense that by morning I was quite delirious. I imagined I was at home with my wife and children and kept calling my children by their names. Mr. Davis had lived long in this malarious district and had become his own physician. His close attention to me soon had me convalescing. I remained there several days, in a little house in the front yard that he called his office.

One day during my early convalescence I was sleeping restfully, but was awakened by a man's voice. "What! Have you swapped away your clothes?"

Opening my eyes, I saw that the interrogator was a heavy, fine-looking man, about forty years old, dressed in the blue uniform of a Yankee private soldier, and that the persons addressed were six or eight young men dressed in the seedy apparel of citizens. The man in blue had arrived alone, while the others, who were traveling together, had called a few minutes later. They were all deserters from the Federal army and had voluntarily entered our camps and surrendered in exchange for paroles, by which they hoped to reach their homes.

The man in blue said that he was a native citizen of Ohio and was drafted into the army against his wish. The others had swapped away their uniforms for badly worn civilian clothes in which they hoped to travel in disguise to avoid arrest by Confederate soldiers. On being asked what command they belonged to, several answered, "The Thirteenth Kentucky."

They also said that they were volunteers. When I heard Kentuckians say that they had voluntarily fought against Southern rights, my indignation became so great that I let it boil over. "This gentleman is a Northern man and was fighting for his country. But you are Southern men willingly fighting against your country's rights. Every one of you ought to be shot." They made no reply or demonstration, but soon departed.

When I became able to converse on business, I told Mr. Davis why I was traveling alone on foot, including my misfortune of leaving my foundered horse to die at Autrey's. Since Autrey's residence was only a few miles away, Mr. Davis sent a servant to him, bearing my written order for my horse rigging. But, to my astonishment, the servant returned without the rigging, saying that Autrey would hold the rigging till I paid him for my board. So the next day Mr. Davis again sent the servant with my written order and the required money. This time the rigging came.

As I could not take care of the rigging, I sold it to a man who lived with Mr. Davis. He bought it for the circuit preacher for that vicinity. The preacher had asked the man to purchase a first-rate Texas-made saddle and rigging, and I judge that he got the best that he ever saw. I had bought it from a young man for only twenty dollars, but it had cost him more, since he had it made to order.

When I became able to travel, Mr. Davis sent me on horseback to the ferry at Pine Bluff. He also sent a little servant boy to bring back the horse. He would not take pay for his kindness.

In Pine Bluff I learned that our regiment wagon train was encamped about three-fourths of a mile southeast of the city. One of our wagon guards, Hampton Carter, had charge of a mare that was the property of the Confederacy. The mare had been worked with mules in a wagon train and by hard pulling had strained her loins and become useless. She never could recover enough to be useful in cavalry service, but, by judicious treatment, Carter had so revived her that he felt she could be used for ordinary saddle purposes. Since I was on foot, he transferred her to my care. By good luck I was able to buy a good Texas-made Mexican horse outfit, a saddle, *correas*, blanket, and bridle, but not so good as that which I had sold. So I was again mounted, after a fashion.

At the encampment of our wagon train I learned that our regiment was stationed at "the Jordan Place," a plantation on the southeast side of the Arkansas River about ten miles above the Arkansas Post and four miles above De Valls Bluff. Our regiment was now our nearest important force to the Mississippi River.

From the camp of our wagon train I proceeded to the Jordan Place, riding the disabled government mare, and rejoiced to be again with my regiment after an enforced absence of perhaps a month.

First Encampment at the Jordan Place

The Jordan Place took its name from Dr. Jordan, its builder and owner, who had come to this vicinity and bought five thousand acres of redeemed government land. With a small Negro force, he began to prepare some of it for cultivation, and in due time had a fine plantation. He was an excellent physician and soon established a lucrative practice, which enabled him to prosper faster than his neighbors. His plantation, though a continuous open farm, was divided by his buildings into two parts. The first part fronted on a bayou emerging from the Arkansas River, which here flows east. The bayou runs parallel with the river, which turns south after more than a mile, and then flows into it. The second part of the plantation fronted on the west bank of the river below the bayou.

In 1861, the first, or upper, part of Jordan's plantation embraced an overseer's house, a fine lot of livestock with stables and provender, probably more than one hundred Negroes, a long row of Negro cabins, and a house containing a cotton gin and a gristmill. And the second, or lower, part of his plantation contained a fine two-story frame mansion with some lesser houses.

Dr. Jordan's gin was operated by steam, and he put one thousand pounds of cotton lint into each bale, but it was so compressed as to be only half as large by bulk as one of our five-hundred-pound bales, while the great number of steel hoops and ties needed to compress it and hold it together rendered bagging unnecessary. His last crop was five hundred bales, each weighing a thousand pounds. He said that his ambition was to raise a thousand bales annually.

At the beginning of the Confederate War, in 1861, Dr. Jordan was very liberal in expending thousands of dollars for provisions and clothing for Confederate soldiers, and he acted as agent for other capitalists in Arkansas who were liberal in the same cause. As such, he engaged the service of a steamboat to convey supplies from New Orleans to Pine Pluff and Little Rock. He had taken the steamer to New Orleans, loaded her with a cargo of military supplies that he had purchased, and was returning to his own plantation. The cabin and berths were crowded with passengers, and so he slept on the deck, exposed to the damp air on the river. He contracted pneumonia and died soon after reaching home.

After Dr. Jordan's death, Mrs. Jordan sent nearly all of the Negroes to a plantation that she owned on the Red River, except for some old and trusted ones she retained to care for the home place. The Negro cabins were left unoccupied and were superintended by Mr. Roberts, the doctor's faithful overseer. Mrs. Jordan moved to Little Rock, leaving her mansion unoccupied.

When our regiment occupied the Jordan Place after the fall of the Arkansas Post we found enough vacant Negro cabins for each mess to occupy one. Another cabin was used for our regiment surgeon's office, and still another, containing two rooms, for our Masonic lodge room. Several other cabins were occupied by the overseer and some aged and infirm Negroes. Colonel Carter and his staff occupied the parlor on the upper floor of the two-story frame mansion, and the main room on the ground floor was our guardhouse. There was corn enough in the cribs to feed us and our horses during several months. We also found a cotton gin and a gristmill, one bale of cotton weighing one thousand pounds, and a lot of unginned cotton. So we were well-housed and cared for. As we spent much time here, the Jordan Place was the next best place to home, but most of us had to leave it frequently on scouting or picket service.

We fed our horses with corn from the well-filled cribs and took part of it to the mill and ground it into meal for bread, which sometimes was our only food. We prepared the bread in the following manner. First we seasoned the meal very highly with salt, stirring it in with a large spoon. Then we saturated the meal with boiling water, stirring till it became soft mush. Then, after covering the bottom of a hot iron oven with dry meal and greasing its sides with lard to prevent the bread from sticking, we poured in the mush. We covered the oven with a hot lid and baked the bread slowly between two fires, one under the oven, the other on its lid. The melted salt caused the mush to rise almost like light bread and gave it a delightful flavor.

Though the crippled government mare that I now rode was not fit for cavalry service, she had borne the trip from Pine Bluff tolerably well. So I hoped that she might last till I could procure an able-bodied animal.

All the sergeants of our company except William Gates, our orderly sergeant, had died or been discharged on account of physical disability, and I was elected third sergeant. The ranks of second and fourth sergeant had been dispensed with because our corporals could do the work. We were a scouting and picketing regiment and were sometimes separated into small bodies, all of which were stationed at different points on the Arkansas River, from Napoleon on the state's east line to Fort Smith near its west line. And when our headquarters was at some other point, we were sometimes cut up into detachments. Nearly always part of each detached company was retained at our regiment's headquarters and commanded by some officer. Twice, under such circumstances, I was left at regiment headquarters to command a remnant of our company and acted as captain thereof, though third sergeant was the highest military rank that I ever held.

Once, while at the Jordan Place, most of our regiment marched down toward Napoleon, and detachments were picketed at different points near the river on its southeast side. Our company picketed at the office of Dr. Rawlins, a resident physician who had evacuated ahead of the fighting with his family and his Negroes, leaving the place temporarily vacant. It was about four miles up the river from Napoleon.

While here, my messmate Dr. McFall and I went down the river to Napoleon. Nearly all its people had gone, and we saw only three elderly men. It seemed difficult to decide whether these men were Confederates or "Unionists," for they were very discreet. Yankee transports or gunboats were continually passing up and down the Mississippi, but they let the old men alone. As it happened, these men kept a boat in a slough that flowed into the Arkansas a few hundred yards above the town, and in the night, when the darkness hid them, they ferried Confederates across the Mississippi. They could locate any steamboat or gunboat nearby by the lights that were in it and then evade it in the darkness.

One of the three men kept a marble, or gravestone, store, and he told us that some days previously a Yankee war vessel had docked there for an hour or two. A member of the crew came into his store, stole a headstone, and almost succeeded in conveying it to his vessel, but the merchant intercepted him, wrested the stone from him, and restored it to its place in the store.

While here, McFall and I took a view of the broad Mississippi. We were in great danger, for at any moment a Yankee transport or gunboat might come by and discover us. After conversing with the three men in the town, we rode down the Mississippi about two miles. All along the way the levee was double, that is, in two parts. The part next to the river was about six feet higher than the other and only broad enough for footmen to walk on. But the outer, or lower, part was broad enough for horsemen to ride on. The bottom beyond the levee was an impenetrable thicket and the ground on which it stood was covered with water all the way. If an enemy were to land and divide and take the levee both behind and before us, there would be no possible chance for escape. We were on the lower part of the levee. It may have been fortunate that the high part was between us and the river, for before we had gone far, two large Yankee transports came down the river and passed us, probably not more than two hundred yards from the shore. The doors and windows of both vessels were closed, and we saw no one on board. I do not know whether anyone inside saw us, but they could have if they were looking.

About two miles below Napoleon, we saw a new log cabin below the steep bank near the river. A man was just outside, apparently very busy manipulating something. We hallooed at him and asked him some questions, which he answered briefly and evasively in a husky voice. The transports were yet in sight, and we suspected that the man may have been making signs to someone on the boats. Our curiosity had led us into great danger, and we turned and went back up the river on the outer side of the levee.

On arriving at Napoleon, Dr. McFall and I took the road to our encampment at Dr. Rawlins' place. Before long we were met by a Negro woman whom some friends had sent to warn us of danger. She was riding swiftly, and as she got within speaking distance she cried, "Hurry up and go to your company. The Yankees are coming up Boggy Bayou."

Boggy Bayou was a stream that arose in a pond near the Arkansas and flowed south. The road that led up it was a dim trail and intersected our road. As I afterward learned, a company of Yankee cavalry marching up that road came to a Confederate vedette in a thicket. The vedetter was a boy who, not recognizing the Yankees as such, ordered them to halt.

"We do not halt," they answered. "You are our prisoner."

Then they advanced and took his gun, but let him keep his horse. They made him go with them as their prisoner. They soon entered a canebrake, and the boy darted into the dense growth and escaped. He went to his comrades and reported his adventure. They sent a messenger to inform our company of the approach of the Yankees. The boy had magnified the company of Yankees into a large body, so that by the time Dr. McFall and I reached camp we found our company ready either to fight or to mount and fly.

We watched for the enemy till night, and then, Captain Alston not being present, our first lieutenant, A. D. Edwards, marched us into a thicket of tall weeds in a field, where we stood all night waiting. I had retained a steady nerve during the dangers of the day, but now I became fearful. I judged that, if a large force of the enemy should discover and attack us, the tall weeds would prevent us from distinguishing between friends and foes and we would be so confused that we could not defend ourselves and must be slaughtered. Being weary, besides, I lost courage and resolved to surrender, a thing that I had often said I would not do to save my life. We stood guard till day, however, and no enemy appeared.

During this expedition, Colonel Carter, Captain Alston, a lad named Willett, who belonged to Carter's staff, and three others had crossed the Mississippi River in the night to the state of Mississippi and stayed several days. The section that they visited was occupied by Yankee soldiers, but the citizens were loyal. This little party ran a great risk by going there, but they went cautiously from house to house and so avoided the enemy.

Their purpose was to enlist recruits, but they obtained only one. Captain Alston enlisted a man who was subject to the conscript law, but he offered as a substitute his wife's brother, a delicate sixteen-year-old lad named Jesse Lewis, who consented to serve in his place. Captain Alston accepted the lad and swore him into the service. He was a good boy and served faithfully as a soldier. Later he went with us into Missouri, but the inclemency of the weather, loss of sleep, and toilsome marches by day and night were too much for him. Before we could regain our camping ground at the Jordan Place in Arkansas he contracted pneumonia and died.

After the return of Carter and his recruiting party from Mississippi, we returned to our comfortable quarters at the Jordan Place, where we remained till about the first of April. Then we marched up the Arkansas to Pine Bluff.

March to Spring River, Arkansas, April, 1863

There were said to be 56,000 soldiers encamped near and around Pine Bluff. On the day after our arrival a man was to be shot by sentence of court-martial for deserting a third time. Every man was ordered to be present at the execution. His sentence may have been just, but I was determined not to see his execution. I had entered the army to defend my country's rights, was doing the best I could, and needed not to see a man put to death to spur me to duty. I told Lieutenant Edwards that, regardless of the consequences, I would not go out to see the man shot, and he assumed the responsibility to detail me, only me, to keep our camp while all the others went to the execution.

The prisoner had been guarded in the courthouse, and I saw him pass on the road to the place of execution. He was sick, and was hauled in a wagon, escorted by his guard. He was seated on his own coffin, and his face was buried in a handkerchief that he held with both hands. A minister of the gospel sat with him on the coffin. The procession soon passed beyond my sight, but shortly afterward I heard the report of guns very plain.

We soon learned that a body of our men, including our brigade, was soon to march to Missouri, but the condition of my government mare was such that she could not be used on such an expedition. And so it seemed that I must be left in Arkansas. I mounted the mare to ride her to water, but her loins had become so weak that she could not bear my weight, and I had to dismount hurriedly to prevent her from falling. Then our officers took a splendid mule from the teams for me to ride. This did not subject us to any inconvenience, for our trains were reduced for the expedition to one wagon for each regiment. So I was to go to Missouri.

Colonel Parsons' regiment was detached and sent to Louisiana, where it was engaged in a battle. This reduced our brigade to Burford's Nineteenth Regiment, Carter's Twenty-first Regiment, and Morgan's squadron, with Carter commanding the brigade.

We marched from Pine Bluff up to near the source of Spring River and encamped at a little town called Jackson, near the south line of Missouri. In this region Spring River is in a narrow valley which is bounded on both sides by tall, steep mountains and huge impassable rocks. Therefore our road followed the meanderings of the river, which at this point is a small creek whose water is perennial and rapid. Here, on Spring River, I first saw white women working between plow handles.

Other troops were encamped near us with General [John Sappington] Marmaduke, who was to command us all. General Marmaduke was a small man of singular appearance. His hair was yellow and his complexion yellowish; he wore a yellow cap, a yellow coat, and a yellow vest and pants; he rode a yellowish bay or sorrel horse. He was a Missourian and had been made a major general in Missouri. He was an excellent raider, but the Yankees had driven him from his native state into Arkansas.

On his first return expedition, he had advanced far into Missouri, but was retreating before an overwhelming force of the enemy. His road was through broken country in which a line of battle could not be formed. The enemy's front often attacked his rear guard, but was as often repulsed. One night, in the darkness, the enemy stealthily surrounded him, and, because their number was overpowering, escape seemed impossible. Marmaduke opened fire on those in front of him, cutting a gap, which he broadened by widening his range. Then his whole command—except half of his artillery, who kept their places and continued to fire—went through the gap. Then the artillery that had gone through the gap turned and kept the gap open by a continuous fire, and the artillery that had been left came out through the gap. When all were out, they resumed their successful retreat.[8]

This was to be Marmaduke's second expedition into his native state, and our force amounted to about five thousand men, exclusive of our wagon train. General Marmaduke organized it by dividing our force into the Missouri division, which was all Missourians, consisting of five regiments, with Colonel [Joseph O.] Shelby commanding; the Arkansas division of two brigades, one containing eight companies of Arkansians and two of Missourians, while the other, Greene's brigade, had all Missourians, with Colonel Brubage [Col. John Q. Burbridge] of Arkansas, commanding; the Texas division, containing the Texas brigade and Colonel [Colton] Greene's brigade of Missourians; and Captain [Timothy] Reves's Missourian unattached.

The Texas brigade consisted of Colonel Burford's Nineteenth Regiment, Colonel Carter's Twenty-first Regiment, and Major Morgan's squadron of two companies under Captains Von Tress and Lemons, Senior Lieutenant Colonel Watson commanding. Colonel

[8] Marmaduke's first expedition was between December 31, 1862, and January 25, 1863. See Stephen B. Oates, *Confederate Cavalry West of the River*, pp. 114–120.

Carter, acting division commander, and Colonel Burford, absent. Captain Alston also being absent, Lt. A. D. Edwards commanded Carter's Twenty-first Regiment.

After organizing his command, General Marmaduke called the officers together and told them that he expected to lead them into danger sometimes, but would always lead them out.

March to Fort Patterson, Missouri

About the eighteenth of April we departed from our encampment near Jackson on Spring River. On the nineteenth we crossed the state line into Ripley County, Missouri. Just across the line we passed a residence where some women and children stood in the door and watched us pass only a few steps from them, but made no demonstration. But after that, nearly all the residences we passed on that day were those of friends. The old ladies came out and cheered us with shouts. One of them said, "You're the first Confederate soldiers I've seen in two years."

We were just thirteen days in Missouri, and during each twenty four hours of that time we had either a battle with the enemy, an all-night march, or a soaking rain. One morning I awoke in a puddle of water. It had rained in the night, but the rain was warm, and I had been so weary from marching that I had slept soundly.

As we advanced, Carter's Twenty-first Regiment, half of [J. A.] Pratt's battery, two cannons, and Reves's unattached company of Missourians, all commanded by Lt. Col. D. C. Giddings, proceeded in advance of the rest of the command, leaving them a considerable distance to the rear of us.

I did not know why we were thus isolated till our purpose was explained by the development. When the Yankees overran Missouri, many of her citizens swore allegiance to the United States—many of them merely to save their property. Then a proportion of them were drafted to serve for a time as United States soldiers and were called the Missouri State Militia. Most of these were stationed at a place called Camp Patterson, to guard and care for military stores that were said to be valued at three million dollars. This was a rather obscure place on the Cape Girardeau and Iron Mountain Road, about forty miles east of Iron Mountain. Here they had built two two-story frame houses in which they had deposited the military stores. They had also built a wooden fort about a quarter of a mile south of their camp on a high hill that was surrounded by a dense forest of tall trees. They kept more than twenty men picketing at a "secesh" residence several miles south of their camp. The men slept in a barn in imagined security. Our job was to capture these pickets, then the fort, and lastly the camp with its occupants and military stores. It was believed that we were strong enough to accomplish our goal.

We had marched all day and all night after crossing the state line into Missouri, and before daybreak, while yet marching, we were ordered to cap our guns. This was a surprise to me and doubtless to many others. I could not cap my gun because of the uneven motion of my mule, and so I halted. I was near the rear of our regiment, and the rearmost man soon passed me, leaving me out of sight. My mule, unwilling to be left, struggled to advance, and I yet could not cap my gun. After vainly trying for about two minutes and losing some of my caps, I quit trying to control my mule, and she galloped after the regiment. Just before overtaking my comrades, I heard firing ahead. Our men had halted and entered an enclosure that surrounded a barn. So I entered it also.

The barn contained twenty-three Federal pickets from Camp Patterson, all Missourians. They had slept there, and their horses, though bridled and saddled, were running unconfined in the enclosure. The pickets had locked themselves up in the barn and were ineffectually firing over the door shutter at our men.

Captain Reves shouted, "If you don't come out, we'll set the barn on fire and burn you alive." Then they came out and ran around the barn when some of our men continued to shoot. But finally they surrendered. None of them was killed or wounded, although one escaped. Our only casualties were two men wounded, shot accidentally by their own comrades, who were shooting at the Federals.

We left our wounded men in the care of Mr. Blazedell of Company H. They stayed with a nearby family who were friends, while we continued our march toward Camp Patterson. When our two

wounded men became able to ride, they and their attendant rejoined us.

A few minutes after our departure, another body of Federal pickets
from Camp Patterson arrived to relieve those whom we had captured. They had heard the firing, and they halted at the yard gate of
the residence. The landlord, our two wounded men, and their nurse
were sitting on the porch, and the pickets asked, "What did all that
firing mean?" The landlord told them what had happened, and they
rode away at a gallop.

Piloted by Reves's company, we marched to Fort Patterson. When
within hearing of the fort, we imprudently shelled the woods with
Pratt's artillery and thus gave the enemy warning of our approach.
The fort was vacant, but they had laid several strands of telegraph
wire near it, in which the feet of our horses became entangled, but
only for a minute.

Reves's company, well aware of the entire situation, led us to the
depository at Camp Patterson. The Federals, on learning of our approach, had hastily loaded several wagons with military stores, set the
public buildings on fire, and retreated toward Iron Mountain, perhaps a day's march west, pursued by most of our men.

We left a few of our men at the depository under Lt. William
Anderson of Captain Hanner's Company G, to guard our prisoners
and to care for such goods as could be rescued from the burning
buildings. Our main body had been gone but a few minutes when
the Federal relief guard arrived. Their officer addressed Anderson's
men in a commanding voice, saying, "Surrender!", to which one of
our men replied by shooting him dead. Some of the officer's men, not
seeming to regard this killing as unmilitary, said, "Served him right.
He ought not to have been such a fool." Then they all surrendered
and became our prisoners.

Some of our men who pursued the retreating enemy pushed their
horses to overtake them. But the Federals got a considerable start,
and some time elapsed before any Texians could come up with them.
Indeed, if the Federals had all been sober, it is probable that none of
them would have been overtaken. But some of them had tapped their

whiskey barrels and imbibed too much liquor. As they rode it took effect and they became unconscious of the situation and let their horses reduce their gait to a slow walk. Some of our horses outran others, and the Texians became scattered on the Iron Mountain Road. I was one of those who pursued the enemy, but I failed to overtake them because my mule refused to push ahead.

William Gipson and I finally passed Colonel Giddings, who had halted because his horse had become exhausted. We heard firing ahead and soon began to pass the enemy's killed and wounded, scattered along the road. The faces of the slain and wounded were still red from the whiskey that they had drunk. Several of our men had dismounted to care for the wounded Federals, thus weakening our active force, but Gipson and I galloped by them.

Ten miles from Fort Patterson we came to a deep ravine whose walls were rock. It was bordered on each side by a narrow bottom whose surface also was naked rock from which the soil had been washed by freshets. Here the enemy had abandoned three wagons and their teams. Two of the wagons were on the east side of the ravine, which we occupied, while the third was across and just beyond. We took possession of the two on the east side, but would not risk our lives to cross the ravine for the other. The wagons had been loaded hurriedly, with goods piled upon them as high as they would lie, but by careful reloading we got all the goods onto one wagon, reserving the other for transportation of the wounded Federals whom we expected to pick up on our return to Camp Patterson.

We judged that the enemy were hidden in the ravine, and Lieutenant Montgomery of Branch's Company A rode to its brink to see. On his return he reported that there were only a few and proposed that we storm them.

We had about forty men present, with only three commissioned officers, Capt. Sample Howard of Company C, and Lieutenants Montgomery of Company A and A. D. Edwards of Company H. They took a vote, and the outcome was two to one against Montgomery's proposal. So we did not charge.

On the way back to Camp Patterson, we counted the killed and wounded of the enemy and found fourteen of each. The red faces of the dead had now turned black. We had not time to bury them, and so we let them lie.

As we then proceeded we loaded the empty wagon with thirteen of the wounded, all dangerously hurt. Their groans and cries as I helped put them on the wagon were repeated whenever the wagon jolted. One of the wounded prisoners was able to ride on horseback, and Sgt. George W. Lawrence, of Company H, who was in charge of the wagon, dismounted and set the prisoner on his own horse. Then he gave me charge of him. I and my prisoner then rode at leisure, and the wagon left us.

My prisoner had been shot in the back, the ball passing through his shoulder blade and lodging under the skin of the front part of his neck. Fortunately, it did not wound any organs, but made a visible lump on the front of his neck. Bad as the wound was, the man seemed in no pain during most of our ride, and he conversed freely. He told me that he lived in Pike County and that his command consisted of six hundred men. When he was wounded he was riding slowly and leisurely, unapprehensive of danger. When I reproached him for fighting his own countrymen, he said, "Don't you know that we are conscripts?"

He then asked me how many men were in our command, but I refused to tell him. I did not know but that he might soon recover his liberty, and it was my policy not to report our strength to an enemy.

Before reaching our destination, the prisoner became so weak that if we had gone much farther he would have fallen from his horse. We passed the residence where our other wounded prisoners had stopped and were being cared for by our medical staff. But I conducted my prisoner to where our captured pickets were guarded. These helped him off the horse, handled him gently, and laid him on a pallet. And here I left him.

During this engagement only one Texian was hurt, but not by the enemy. The horse of Captain Hanner of Orange County ran against a tree with him and hurt his shoulder, maiming him for several days.

Back at Camp Patterson I found that our whole command had

arrived, and, as night was near, we all soon encamped nearby. I was almost barefooted, and the next day I drew a pair of new boots from the captured goods. Some of our regiment had rescued letters from the post office before the burning building fell. They were mostly love letters from sweethearts at home to lovers in the army. One that I read said, "Father says that if the secesh are not expelled soon, he will move to Illinois."

March Toward Cape Girardeau

On the next morning we marched east from Camp Patterson. We crossed the Saint Francis River at a deep ford to a long narrow prairie that extended lengthwise north and south up and down the river. Then we passed through the south end of a town of considerable size that seemed to be unoccupied.

We marched till late in the night. Once we passed a modest cottage by the road side, where we saw an elderly man and his wife and daughter, standing at a low front-yard fence. The daughter was singing "Dixie." One of our men asked them, "Are there any seccesionists about here?"

"Yes, I'm one of them," the old gentleman replied. They had taken their stand by the fence when our front arrived, and they stood there, the girl singing "Dixie," till we all had passed.

Down the road we passed a large house in which about six persons were singing a hymn, and some men of Captain Wilson's Company I, who marched just rear of our Company H, joined in and sang with them till we were beyond hearing them.

These singings were quite cheering to us. Soon after passing the last-mentioned house, we entered the little town of Palmyra, which had recently been occupied by the Federal captain McNeill. Shortly after McNeill's arrival there, a man who lived in the vicinity and sympathized with the Federals disappeared mysteriously. McNeill caused twelve citizens who were secessionists to be arrested and imprisoned, and threatened to have them shot if the missing man was not found by a certain day. The time elapsed, and since no tidings were heard of the missing man, McNeill had the twelve men executed. On the following day, the missing man returned all right. On learning of our approach, McNeill and his company fled to some other locality.

In Palmyra, we found plenty of wood for cooking purposes and corn for our horses and mules, all of which McNeill had gathered for his own company. Then, on the next morning, we marched for Cape Girardeau on the Mississippi River.

A few miles north of Palmyra is a large creek called Whitewater River, which then was spanned by a substantial bridge. On the north side of this stream a company of Federals was guarding the bridge. Reves's company and a few more of our Missourians went ahead up the stream two or three miles to a ford, crossed it, came down upon the Federals who were guarding the bridge, and attacked them by surprise. But the Federals were game. Their horses were already saddled up, so they mounted and charged upon our men. The Confederates fired upon them and wounded their captain, besides killing two of his men and capturing their camp. The remaining Federals escaped, and four of Reves's company were dangerously wounded.

Because of a miscalculation of the time necessary for the attacking party to accomplish its route, our main force, including the Twenty-first Texas, was far behind and we marched directly to the bridge. The wounded captain and all his living men had gone, but we saw the two who were slain.

Some distance south of the bridge, we met two men who told us of the combat. A few steps farther, we met two carriages containing some ladies who had been to the scene of action to minister to our wounded men. Beyond this, we met two ambulances containing our four wounded men, who were being conveyed to the homes of friends.

The day was far spent when we left the Whitewater, and we marched several hours in the night. That night we overtook two Federals who were gently conducting their wounded captain in an ambulance drawn by a horse. We gave them the right of way, but they went slowly, and we passed them.

After our departure from Palmyra, our three divisions separated, General Marmaduke with Colonel Burbridge's division going one way, and Colonel Shelby with his division going another. Their purpose was to pull down telegraph wires and destroy bridges and other public property that the Federals could use. Colonel Carter, with the Texas brigade, Colonel Greene's brigade, and Reves's company, was to go immediately to Cape Girardeau, which was occupied by a body of Federals. Colonel Shelby's division was to join ours near Cape Girardeau, where Shelby, ranking Carter, was to be in command till Marmaduke's arrival. Meanwhile, Marmaduke ordered Shelby to make a slight demonstration against Cape Girardeau and then to retire.

On the afternoon of the day after we passed Whitewater River, we encamped at a point that, by the road, was about two and a half miles south of Cape Girardeau. Carter's division was now alone.

Demonstration at Cape Girardeau

That night Colonel Carter sent ten messengers to Cape Girardeau with a flag of truce and a written demand, in the name of Sterling Price, to the Federal commander to surrender the town and garrison by daybreak on the following morning. But Colonel Carter was fanciful. He caused his ten messengers to go wrapped in striped Texas homemade blankets and to wear broad-brimmed hats. This gave them the appearance of West Texas cowboys and was probably aimed to inspire the Federals with awe.

The Federals had blocked the road leading west from the town with three successive ditches whose embankments, which for convenience we called forts, were each held by a strong picket guard. The pickets at the first fort permitted our truce-bearers to pass to the second, but the second pickets halted them and sent the written demand into town to their commander. He sent his written reply that if we should attack he would oppose us.

Colonel Carter then sent the same men again, with a written admonition to the Federal commander to move all families from the town before daybreak. The messengers, as at first, were permitted to pass from the first fort to the second, whence the admonition was sent to the Federal commander. There was no need for a reply, and so the messengers returned and reported to Colonel Carter.

The Federal force was not as strong as Carter's division, and we could have captured it. But we could not have held it long for an overpowering force could have come on transports from both up and down the Mississippi River and recaptured the place. A steamboat lay anchored at Cape Girardeau, and it ran a short distance up the river, whistled at a boat coming down the river and about to dock, then ran down a short distance below the town, whistling again at a boat approaching from below. It repeated the performance many times, alternately running up and down the river and whistling at every halt. We could hear the whistling, but even though we believed that the Federals were receiving reinforcements this did not prevent us from making another demonstration the next day.

About sunrise on the next morning, we fell into line and marched north. Pratt's battery at first went ahead, but, in crossing a body of soft ground in which the wheels mired, a fine mare which our quartermaster had recently bought and was worked with a team of mules, fell dead from overstraining. This caused the battery to go slowly, and we passed it. We left the river bottom and proceeded a little west of north, where, on a high hill, we came onto a broad firm road. This was about a mile from the town, and on this road we went east down a steep hill toward Cape Girardeau.

Colonel Shelby had arrived with his division and gone ahead of us. Disobeying General Marmaduke's order to make a slight demonstration and retire, he resolved to take the town and the Federal garrison. The whole Federal force came out and met him at the first, or western, fort. This he attacked and, by a hard-fought battle, forced them back to the middle fort. Following them, he forced them to the third, or last, fort, which he also attacked.

Just then General Marmaduke arrived and inquired, "Colonel Shelby! What are you doing?"

"Making a slight demonstration, sir," Shelby replied.

General Marmaduke then called off the attackers, and all the Confederates retired westward.

Colonel Carter and his staff, with Greene's brigade, were far ahead of the Texas brigade, so we did not know what they were doing. While marching down the hill, we heard the firing in front of us and made quick time. Then a messenger met us, saying that our men had taken the first fort and the second, and had attacked the third. So we made double-quick time.

But soon we met one of Carter's staff, Dr. Nixon of Huntsville, Texas, and he addressed us: "Attention, Twenty-first! Steady! Halt! Steady! Right about face! Steady! Forward march! Steady! Quick time! Steady! Double-quick time! Steady!" So wondering at our un-expected check and retreat, we marched away from Cape Girardeau.

Our casualties in this engagement were thirty-seven men wounded, all of Shelby's division, and none killed. The Federal losses I never learned. We left all our wounded men with medical attendants, in houses of nearby families.

After we had left Cape Girardeau a safe distance behind, our march during that day was slow, with several halts of some minutes each. That night we encamped in the eastern outskirts of Jackson, a town ten miles west of Cape Girardeau, but our saddles and bridles remained on our horses during the night.

Retreat from Jackson, Missouri

We awoke early on the next morning. Just at daylight part of Shel-by's division mounted and departed on a road leading a little south of east, followed immediately by our whole command. Just before our regiment mounted, we saw a body of Federals marching from the west beyond the town. We afterward learned that it was General [William] Vandever's command from Iron Mountain, said to be seventy thousand strong.

As we marched, our regiment was in the extreme rear. Our line was about a mile long, but the extreme front had turned at a right angle south on another road, all marching quick time. The Federals had come nearer, though not within rifle shot. At sunrise they fired a cannon at us and the ball passed lengthwise over our line and fell beyond. We then made double-quick time and were soon in the righthand road, going south, with a thick timber concealing us from the enemy.

Sometime during our first day's retreat from Jackson we fell into the same road to Palmyra on which we had advanced. That after-noon we entered the Whitewater bottom, which was covered with dense thickets interspersed with small bodies of open ground. Here we halted to have an engagement with Vandever's force. At his own request, Major Morgan had been permitted to occupy the extreme rear, with his squadron, that he might be first to meet the enemy.

My stand was in a small open place, but there was a tree near by that I thought could shelter me from the enemy. My view was only about fifteen feet in the direction whence I expected him to advance. I soon heard firing in that direction, about twenty feet distant, but I could not tell if it was by friends or foes. The firing was brief, and some of our men came out of the thicket guarding prisoners whom they had captured. The prisoners were from Iowa and were very large men, more than six and a half feet tall. Some of them were facetious and joked us profanely.

The firing ceased and we crossed the bridge to the south side of the Whitewater River and encamped, leaving the men in our rear to cut down the bridge in order to impede the enemy's pursuit. The following morning we marched into Palmyra, but did not encamp. There we divided into many parts, each containing a regiment or more, and each part marched out of the town in a different direction and on a different road. After marching several miles, we turned and went back into the town by other roads than those on which we had gone out. This maneuver was not explained to us, but I judged that it was to lead the enemy to believe our force was much more numerous than it was. Upon re-entering the town, we encamped, but again kept the rigging on our horses.

That afternoon we heard cannonading in the direction of the Whitewater, apparently from only one gun, but we did not know whether it was our own or the enemy's artillery. Then we mounted and marched south. South of Palmyra, our road led us into a panhandle of the state of Missouri, extending south from latitude thirty-six degrees thirty minutes north, between the Mississippi and Saint Francis rivers, which separate the state of Missouri respectively from Tennessee and Arkansas. This panhandle is called the New Madrid District and embraces two or more counties. It is broken country consisting of a high ridge cleft by many deep valleys, each containing a small stream. These streams run in opposite directions, every alter-

nate one flowing east into the Mississippi River and the others west
into the Saint Francis. The ascent on each side of those valleys is very
steep, and halfway between any two of the streams is a sharp ridge.
Near the source of each stream, however, the terrain is not so steep
as to prevent the ascent or descent of loaded wagons. Our road was a
zigzag, running easterly on the top of the sharp ridge between the
valleys and their streams till it could find a ford on the one south of
it, then down a hill and across the stream, then up another hill, then
westerly to find a crossing of the next stream, then easterly again, and
so on, making many turns.

It was impossible to form a line of battle across these sharp ridges.
Consequently, our only engagements occurred during our halts, generally on a stream, when the enemy's front approached and attacked
our rear. Then the contest, being only between the front of one army
and the rear of the other, was equal. Our rear always repelled their
front and captured a few prisoners. Occasionally, they captured some
of our men, but somehow most of them escaped. Such skirmishes occurred daily. Of course a few of our men were wounded, but none
were killed.

Our Last Day in Missouri

On the forenoon of the first day of May we passed through a lane
extending south, down a gentle slope about half a mile long. It was
about thrity feet wide, limited by a tall fence on the righthand side
and a deep bluff on the left. Near the lower end of the lane, a house
stood just inside the field. As I came opposite the front yard, we
halted and two men and a woman came out. One man was lame in
his right hip and carried a hunting rifle.

"We're glad to see you," one man said. "You're the first Confederate soldiers we've seen in two years."

"But the Feds are driving us out," I replied. "Every time we halt,
their front fires upon our rear. They'll fire in five minutes."

Just as I closed this remark firing commenced at the upper end of
the lane. The lame man uttered a shriek of surprise and the three retreated toward another house on the opposite side of the field. Captain Pratt had masked his battery about eighty yards from the upper

end of the lane and was left in the extreme rear. When the enemy had nearly filled the vacant part of the lane, Pratt gave them a raking fire, putting them all to flight. We did not renew our retreat immediately, but waited several minutes while Carter sent an aide-de-camp to estimate the extent of the damage inflicted upon the enemy. He returned and reported about fifty slain, scattered along about fifty yards of the upper end of the lane. We suffered no casualty during this brief collision.

Soon after leaving this place, we passed a large field of corn, left from the preceding year. The fodder, including the tops, had been gathered, but the stumps of the stalks yet stood, each supporting several large ears.

Then we passed through an abandoned town. Its population may have been several hundred, but the businesshouses outnumbered the residences, and their numerous signs showed them all to be drinkinghouses. Though one of the oldest settlements of the state, this New Madrid District was yet sparsely inhabited and its people generally were not rich. It was a wonder that the surrounding country could support so many drinkinghouses.

South of the abandoned town our front division, all Missourians, halted in a valley beside a stream to take refreshment. The other two divisions passed, leaving them in the rear. The second division, Arkansians and Missourians, halted for a like purpose at the next stream. Then the third division, Texians and Missourians, passed, halted for a like purpose at another stream, and thus were changed from the rear to the front. Here Greene's brigade, Missourians, filed west down the stream and dismounted, but the Texas brigade, commanded by Lieutenant Colonel Giddings, filed along the road and remained on their horses. Their line extended south up the steep hill, from near the stream. They were just off the road, east of it, and faced front toward it. My place was about the middle of the front rank. Pratt's battery proceeded a little in front of the Texas brigade and halted farther up the hill.

When the enemy's front arrived at our first division, it was welcomed by a fire from the Confederates, and fell back. Then our first division resumed their retreat and passed the other two divisions, resuming the place in front. As they passed the third division, they were cheerful, and some of them were whistling "The Girl I Left Behind Me." The enemy came to our second division and a like result followed. The second division also passed the third.

The enemy came down a steep hill to ford the stream just behind the rear of the Texas brigade. They had left the road and formed on its lefthand side, where the tall copse hid them from our view. Here they fired upon us, the smoke arising above the copse where they were. Some Texians returned the fire, but I reserved mine until I could see an enemy to shoot at. Then my mule became restless and turned half around, so that I could not turn her again to the proper position. I reined her back of the line, intending to return to my place in proper position, but my view was obstructed by my comrades. The enemy was about seventy yards from me, just beyond the stream at the foot of the steep hill whose ascent we occupied. The copse hid them, but smoke rose behind it. I remained out of line, trying to catch sight of an enemy. While I was thus waiting, a ball whistled by my right ear. When the man who fired it had about had time to ram down another cartridge and fire again, another ball whistled by my ear. When about a similar time had elapsed a third ball whistled by in like manner. I was sure that an enemy had selected me and had shot at me three times.

Just as I was listening to hear a fourth ball whistle, I heard something strike my mule. Looking down, I saw a hole in her flank into which I could have thrust my thumb. I saw no blood, but evidently she was bleeding internally. The Yankee, having shot at me three times and missed, evidently shot the fourth time at my mule, which was a large mark.

Sure that my mule was mortally wounded and could not bear me up much longer, I rode through the ranks into the road, intending to dismount and walk. But the mule moved so naturally I thought she might carry me several hundred yards farther. So I decided to resume my place in the ranks. But when I tried to ride back, she could not move her hind feet, though she tried to walk with her fore feet.

Knowing that she would soon fall, I dismounted, holding my rifle in one hand and lifting my holsters from the saddle with the other. I was wearing two suits of clothes, but left my wallet on the mule with numerous small articles that were useful, not only to me, but to our whole company. My holsters were made of a strip of leather, long enough to convert each end to a scabbard for a pistol, reserving a space in the middle to lay across the front of my saddle. A hole had been made in this space through which to put the pommel of the saddle.

Just as I alighted, our regiment moved off at a canter, leaving the road and going north through a thick forest. I was badly bruised in the right hip by a fall that I had suffered more than a week previously and every step caused me much pain. I saw a man riding a stout horse, so I asked him to halt and take me up behind him. But he looked at me and passed on. Much disappointed by his slight, I made a similar request of another, but he did as the first. I then became angry and desperate and decided I would not ask another one of them for help, even to save my life.

Just as I made this resolve, the rearmost man passed me. He was Walter A. Stewart, of Company F, whose home was in Washington County, Texas. I recovered hope and called loudly "Walt Stewart!" He was riding so fast that he could not halt till he had passed me by about seventy yards. Then he turned and rode back to me.

I handed him my rifle and holsters. The hole in the leather between the two pistol scabbards was too small for the pommel of his saddle to pass through, so he laid the holsters loosely across the front part of his saddle, behind the pommel. The pain in my bruised hip was so severe that it took me about five minutes to climb onto Stewart's horse behind him. During this time, the Yankees continued shooting at us, and we heard several bullets whistle by. Our comrades had now disappeared in the forest beyond. When I was well seated behind him on his horse, he handed me my rifle, but let the holsters remain, balanced loosely on his lap. I told him I was ready to go, so he spurred his horse. As the animal made the first jump, down went my holsters. Stewart halted and asked, "What shall we do about that?"

He had already risked his life to save me, so I told him to go on and leave them, which he did. We soon overtook and passed our regiment, turning into the road that ran nearly parallel with the course we had taken. Our comrades followed, and Stewart set me down just behind Pratt's battery.

Soon afterward a comrade brought me a rigged horse and helped me mount. I rode him the remainder of that day. This comrade thought the rider of the horse had been killed or severely wounded, but he was mistaken. The owner was Jonathan Willhour, of Company C, whose home was in Lavaca County, Texas, and his horse had escaped during the battle that day.

On May 1, our front division had built a floating bridge across the Saint Francis River from a point on the Arkansas side called Chalk Bluff. Here the course of the river is southward, and on the Missouri side there was a low, dense, thickety bottom, while on the Arkansas side is an almost insurmountable bluff about seventy feet higher than the bottom on the other side. This was Chalk Bluff, and from it the step-rising ground extended about a mile and a half west. In order to cross the river, the teams were taken from the cannons, their caissons, and the wagons, and were pulled across the river by hand. Then the cavalry were dismounted and walked across on the bridge, while the horses and mules were pushed into the river to swim over.

At nightfall we arrived at this crossing at Chalk Bluff and dismounted, entrusting our horses to other comrades who would swim them across the river. Then we separated by companies into picket guards, each to guard a special point. Our Company H, commanded by Lieutenant Edwards, stood in pitchy darkness in a dense thicket. We heard a cannon fire continuously at short intervals. Thinking it was Pratt's battery intimidating the enemy, I cheered softly.

I do not know how long we stood picket, for time seemed to pass slowly, but it was probably three hours. At last we were marched back to the crossing where our comrades were still pushing horses and mules into the river. Then we crossed on the floating bridge and ascended the bluff. The last comrade who crossed on the bridge demolished it and let its timbers float down the stream. Since we could not distinguish our horses in the darkness, we proceeded a mile and a half west on foot and encamped on high ground. In the morning

Willhour regained his horse, and I was again set on foot. The enemy pursued us to the east bank of the Saint Francis River, but did not continue into Arkansas.

We had been to Missouri, a state which was already overrun by our enemies, and after a seemingly tedious hard service of thirteen days, we were back in Arkansas. But why had we gone? When we had an opportunity to rest a little, Colonel Carter explained that our national government at Richmond had learned that the Federal government at Washington, D.C., was raising a great army with which to expel all Confederate soldiers from Arkansas and then invade Texas and Louisiana. The purpose of our visit to Missouri was to provoke them to turn their attention to the defense of that state. In this we had been successful. We had not only diverted their attention from their conquest of Arkansas, Texas, and Louisiana to the defense of Missouri, but, destroying bridges and telegraph lines and tearing up railroads, we had also crippled their communication between their garrisons in Missouri.

We had at least subjected them to considerable expense, inconvenience, and confusion in Missouri, but we had not rescued that state from subjugation. General Marmaduke had previously conducted an army into Missouri and later conducted a third army thither, but all to no good result.[9]

Battle Across the Saint Francis River

On the morning of the second day of May, 1863, as we encamped on the Saint Francis River, Lt. G. W. Farris, of Company A, Twenty-first Regiment, invited me to go back to the bluff with him and about thirty others to look for Yankees. We took position on the brink of the bluff. The river here was narrow, the bottom on the east side was seventy or more feet lower than the bluff, so that the angle from perpendicular was only about twenty-two degrees, and the distance easy range for our short-range rifles. No enemy was in sight, but after

[9] According to Oates, "in terms of strategic objectives, Marmaduke's second Missouri raid was a complete failure" (*Confederate Calvary West of the River*, p. 130).

two or three minutes about two hundred rifles were turned loose upon us from enemies concealed in the bottom east of the river.

Some of our men returned the fire, but I reserved mine till I could see an enemy. Soon they moved, and at first I could see only their hats. Then they looked up, and I saw their faces under their hats. I was about to shoot one in the face when a foolish young Confederate, who was lying down to shoot, cursed me for shooting over him. His insolence startled me and I did not fire. Then the enemy ceased firing and again disappeared in the thicket.

We correctly judged that they had fallen back upon their main force, and most of our comrades returned to camp. But about eight of us remained to see if they would return. Five of us were from Colonel Carter's regiment, under Lieutenant Farris, and the other three were from Colonel Burford's regiment, under Captain Killingsworth. We separated into two squads, each to occupy a separate position, but I left Farris' squad and joined Killingsworth's so that each squad would have four men. Farris and his squad descended to the foot of the bluff near the edge of the water, where they could have a better view of the enemy if they should again approach. But Killingsworth and his squad occupied a position a little back of the bluff, where we could not have seen the enemy if they should return. I do not know why we did so, but Captain Killingsworth was our boss.

After we had waited a very short time, the enemy again turned loose their artillery upon us. From the report of their cannons, we judged them to be about two hundred yards east of the river. They overshot us, their shells passing far above our heads, but as the shells whizzed by they made a screaming noise that made me think of brush heaps flying through the air. The enemy continued to shell us for ten or fifteen minutes and then ceased.

Soon afterward about two hundred of the enemy again approached the river and fired on us, but without effect, save that Mr. Dodge, of Killingworth's squad, who had gone to the brink of the bluff to see and shoot at the enemy, was severely wounded in the hip. This was our only casualty during that day. Farris' squad, which was now on a level with the enemy, could see them better than during their first sally and so returned their fire. But this firing did not last long. They reported three more of the enemy killed, that they saw, making four killed that we knew of.

Soon after the firing ceased, a colored servant named Abram arrived with a message that our regiment would soon march and we must return to the encampment, and we did so. But the enemy did not pursue us. Their sole purpose seems to have been to drive us out of Missouri, and, having done this, Vandever's army troubled us no more.

Two Battles at Taylor's Creek, Arkansas

From our encampment on the Saint Francis River, we marched south, on the afternoon of May 2, 1863. I rode on a baggage wagon till I could buy a horse. My first attempt was with a sharp comrade who had two horses, and he swindled upon me a fine-looking horse that had a disease called "the big-head," making it unfit for hard service. After a few days, by giving much boot, I swapped it off for a more hardy horse.

Our march was not disturbed till we reached a stream called Taylor's Creek, where we encountered a body of the enemy encamped in a thickety bottom. After a short fight in which each force was obscured from the other by the thicket, we put them to flight. There were no casualties so far as we knew.

That day we encamped in an open place north of Taylor's Creek bottom, but near it. In the afternoon we discovered another body of the enemy, also encamped in the bottom. We believed them to be the same that we had fought in the morning, but we were mistaken. These were Walker's Jayhawkers, the "Fifth Kansas" Regiment, U.S. Cavalry, noted for their ruthless warfare against families and their burning of houses. Colonel Carter sent Burford's regiment and Morgan's squadron to attack them, ordering our men to retreat as soon as the fighting should become hot. But he held his own regiment in reserve and ordered us to be ready to charge when our comrades should emerge from the bottom.

These orders were strictly obeyed, but the enemy dismounted. They hid behind trees and lay down behind logs, and sent a hailstorm of bullets among us. And so we retreated. Our casualties were all from the Twenty-first Regiment. Capt. Martin M. Kenny was severely wounded; Lieutenants McGeehee and Triplett, mortally wounded; Lt. William Anderson, severely wounded, and Private Angier, killed. Also, some of our horses were killed. The enemy's casualties were only two men severely wounded, but the Federals retreated and left us in possession of the field.

After nightfall, a detachment wearing truce badges and carrying torches went in search of killed and wounded men. I was in this detachment, and we were conducted by Colonel Carter himself. During the search, Colonel Carter said to me, "I know that I erred in giving the orders. If I had conducted the whole brigade together in a general charge and had pursued the enemy, we would have captured them. But through my error, we have let them escape." I believe that his remark was correct.

The enemy had already moved their wounded men and had fled. Among our men, Captain Kenny, who commanded Company K, was shot in the neck through the breathing pipe; long after his wound had healed he could speak only in whispers. Lieutenant McGeehee was shot through the bladder, and the Yankee detachment had found him before we did. They asked him how many men we had, and he told them we had enough to avenge his death. Then they asked him if they could do anything for him. He said that he would be obliged to them for a sip of water. So they gave him a canteenful. When we found him, some of our men carried him to a nearby house, but I think he died before day. Lieutenant Triplett and Anderson were of Captain Hanner's Company G, and their homes were in Orange County, Texas. Lieutenant Triplett suffered many days and then died. At first it was believed that Lieutenant Anderson would never walk again, but he recovered and participated in subsequent battles.

Early on the next morning we went in pursuit of the enemy. A little south of Taylor's Creek bottom we passed the two wounded Federals huddled with a physician in a fence corner, with a blanket hung over them for protection against the weather. They had been left by their comrades because they were not able to travel, but we had not leisure to care for them yet. Our road crossed the grading for the

Memphis and Little Rock Railroad. Though not completed east of the White River, the railroad was running trains from Little Rock to De Valls Bluff. On account of the steep ascent of its course, it was very crooked, following the meanderings of a creek, and the grading was a ditch about eight feet deep. This ditch was spanned by a bridge that was floored with loose lumber, on which horsemen must go very slowly or they would fall, horses and men, into the ditch. Now we saw clearly the propriety of Colonel Carter's remark on the preceding night. If we had pursued the enemy, as he said, we would have captured nearly all of them, for if they had tried to make quick time across the bridge, they would have fallen into the ditch. Otherwise, they must have halted and surrendered.

We crossed the bridge slowly, most or all of us dismounting and leading our horses. We did not go far beyond, for we were sure we could not overtake the enemy without following them into Helena, where we might meet an overwhelming force. Then we countermarched to our encampment north of Taylor's Creek bottom.

On our return we halted at the place where the enemy had left the wounded men and their physician. Lieutenant Edwards dismounted and asked them who they were. One of the men answered, "A couple of wounded boys and a doctor."

"What command do you belong to?" asked Edwards.

"Fifth Kansas," the wounded man replied.

Edwards then asked them what other casualties they had suffered, and the answer was, "None that we are aware of." Edwards searched them for concealed weapons, but found none. Some of our men then carried the wounded Federals to a house, and their physician went with them.

We remained several days at our encampment on Taylor's Creek, and on a Sabbath day Colonel Carter preached at a church about three miles distant. I went out to hear him. He preached what I thought was a good sermon, in which he said, "I began to preach when I was seventeen years old and have preached ever since. I was a much better preacher then than I am now, because I was a much better man." Though he erred, Colonel Carter had the virtue of acknowledging his faults.

Encounter with an Ironclad Gunboat

We marched from Taylor's Creek south to Chiro County[10] in the southeast corner of Arkansas. One night, just at twilight, our regiment encamped in a small apple orchard on the premises of a Mr. Gaines, brother of General Gaines (a civil general and once attorney general of the state of Mississippi). But Burford's Nineteenth Regiment, Morgan's squadron, and Pratt's battery, together with a regiment and battery of Missourians, proceeded to the Mississippi River, one mile east, to lie in wait for an ironclad gunboat that was expected to pass near the west shore, going down the river. The two batteries contained four guns each, and they took their stand in a thicket back to the levee of the river.

In the apple orchard, the Twenty-first Texas had just finished cooking supper when we heard the reports of eight cannons on the river, fired in quick succession. A few minutes later other reports succeeded them. We were immediately ordered to pack up and march, which we did hurriedly and in bad order, though coolly.

We soon fell in with those who had gone to the river and were retreating, but the night was so dark that we did not recognize each other. At daylight I found myself in company with Major Lindsay of Missouri, and he hold me of their fight the night before with the gunboat.

According to Lindsay, the ironclad passed within point-blank range of our men, who were laying in ambush in a thicket on shore. But as it was followed by a wooden transport which it was guarding, they let the gunboat pass. When the transport was within range of our artillery, they fired their eight loads into it, disabling one of its side wheels so that it could not go straight but ran in a curve. The only sign of distress that our men heard was the wailing of a female who was evidently much frightened.

Anticipating that the gunboat would come back and fire upon them, our men moved to one side out of its range. It did come back and halt in close range of the point our men had just left. They heard someone aboard say, "You have fired into an unarmed transport.

---

[10] Zuber is probably referring to Chicot County.

Now try me." Then it opened fire upon our abandoned ground. Our force then retreated, but the gunboat continued to shell the bottom. We suffered no casualties, and the only damage known to have been inflicted upon the enemy was the crippling of one of the transport's wheels.

We continued our march to a point near the residence of General Gaines, where we encamped several days. During this time I was sent in command of a detachment of eight men, as a picket guard, to a point on Mason's Bayou, eight or ten miles south of our encampment. Here, for two nights and a day I kept two vedettes on guard about two hundred yards south of our camp, waiting for enemy forces who might be coming by land up the bayou. Then we were sent for, to return to camp, as our army was about to march. When we arrived, our army was gone, but by following their trail, we came upon them.

Again at the Jordan Place

After considerable marching, our regiment again arrived at the Jordan Place, about ten miles above the Arkansas Post on the Arkansas River. Colonel Parsons had returned from Louisiana with his regiment and was again in nominal command of our brigade, with Carter contesting. But only the Twenty-first Texas occupied the Jordan Place, with Parsons' and Burford's regiments, Morgan's squadron, and Pratt's battery encamping elsewhere. Again we were in the next best place to home, in the abandoned cabins, but now the houseflies were so numerous as to be distressing. Colonel Carter and his staff again occupied the Jordan mansion. Our purpose was to guard the ascent of the Arkansas River, which was the road by which the enemy must pass in order to get to Pine Bluff or Little Rock.

In July there arrived at the Jordan Place an Arkansas regiment of the army that, under General [John Clifford] Pemberton, had defended Vicksburg, Mississippi, but had been captured and paroled by the Federals under General [Nathaniel P.] Banks. General Pemberton was a Northern man by birth who had migrated south and married. As some of these men were sick, they rested a few hours in the cabins which we occupied. I conversed with several of the men, and they unanimously said that they were determined never to fight another hour for Southern rights. They said that every man of that regiment was of the same mind.

They said that during the week or more of the siege of Vicksburg, with their provisions exhausted, they had lived upon a diet of peas and the flesh of mules that they slaughtered. They said that they had mules and peas enough to last a week or longer, and were willing to continue the defense at all hazards, but Generals Pemberton and Banks had ordered their respective armies to cease firing. Both armies continued to dig ditches and to build embankments, however, with the works of the enemy converging toward those of the Confederates till the workmen of both armies were within speaking distance of each other.

The people of Missouri were about equally divided in sentiment, with one half being Confederates and the other half so-called Unionists, and the families were themselves divided. Thus the opposing generals, Pemberton and Banks, evidently by agreement, so manipulated their men that the Missouri regiments of both armies working in the ditches and on the embankments were placed within speaking distance of each other, with a father on one side and his son on the other, or a brother opposing his brother, and so with brothers-in-law, cousins, and neighbors. They all conversed together in elevated voices, and their words were repeated from regiment to regiment and company to company until soon all Pemberton's command knew the sentiments of the Missourians in both armies.

The Missourians in the Federal army asserted positively that the Confederates would surrender on the fourth day of July. On that day Pemberton visited Banks under a flag of truce and returned with a copy of stipulations of surrender, signed by Banks and himself. Thus by strategy Pemberton had induced his men to surrender. This manipulation caused Pemberton's army to lose confidence in all our officers, and with it the hope of final success.

Our Final Departure from the Jordan Place

Shortly thereafter our regiment left the Jordan Place and marched up the river to Pine Bluff. I had become disabled by a bone felon on my finger and was boarding with a citizen named Ross, three miles east of the Jordan Place. Because of this, I was permitted to travel alone at leisure. Sometime during that first day, I was seized by a severe malarial chill that continued for several hours. I was compelled to halt, just as I came to the plantation of a man named Morton, a Northerner by birth, who had come south and married a wealthy slaveholding woman.

During the war Morton had sent his family farther south for safety, but he, his overseer, and his Negroes were yet on the plantation. I dismounted and went to the front door of his mansion. I knocked, but got no answer. Then I went around to the back door. On my way I passed a Negro woman with a tin tray containing four goblets of sweet milk, by which I understood that the dinner hour had arrived. But I was too sick to care for dinner. At the back door, which was open, I met the landlord, told him my situation, and asked permission to stay till I was able to travel. He replied that he did not entertain travelers. Then I sat down on one of his stone steps and said, "I cannot go any farther. Here I will sit till I die." He then said that the overseer would entertain me and showed me a house only a few steps from the mansion that he called the overseer's house.

The overseer received me coldly. I told him I was too sick to sit up and asked for a bed. There were two beds in the room, one of which had a mosquito bar over it, but he put me on the other. By night my fever had subsided and I was able to take supper, which an Indian brought to me. The overseer, a man who slept in the good bed, and the Indian were the only persons I saw in the house, and the Indian was the only one who seemed to sympathize with me in my trouble.

On the following morning I arose early and the Indian brought breakfast to me. I offered to pay the overseer for my fare, but he declined, saying that Morton supplied the fare and never accepted pay for entertainment. Then, though still quite sick, I gladly left Mr. Morton's inhospitable premises.

Proceeding up the river, I met a man and asked where I could find the nearest physician. He told me of an excellent one who lived a short distance away, about two hundred yards east of the ferry. He said that I need not take my horse across the river, but the ferryman would take me over and back in a skiff.

When I reached the ferry, I hitched my horse and told the ferryman what I wanted and that I was not able to walk from the river to the doctor's house. Therefore, he hallooed and told the doctor that a soldier, sick with chills, was at the river and wished him to come. The doctor called back that he was coming. Then the ferryman took me across the river in a skiff. Just as we landed, the doctor arrived on horseback. He said that he was on his way to visit a patient in the country and had just mounted when he heard the ferryman's call.

The doctor gave me a supply of medicine, and I swallowed some of it immediately. Then I paid him his bill, which was very light. He said that he regretted charging soldiers, but had to in order to sustain his stock of medicines. The ferryman then took me back to the west bank of the river, and I mounted my horse and resumed my journey.

The medicine I took was too late to prevent a chill on that day, but it diminished its severity. Though it did not last long, it was succeeded by a numbing fever. I was too drowsy to ride, so I dismounted, hitched my horse, and spread my blanket on the grass beside the road. Then I lay down and fell asleep. When I awoke, the fever had subsided, though I was very weak. I then mounted my horse and rode on.

About two o'clock that afternoon I called at a mansion, owned by a man named Jack Smith. Smith and another man were sitting on the piazza. From their conversation, I inferred that the other man was a Yankee spy and Smith was a submissionist. I asked for dinner, but my principal purpose was to obtain a little rest. Smith said, "We don't eat here till sundown. Go to Charlie Brent's. He will entertain you and make no charge." So I left.

I arrived at Charlie Brent's before night, and he and his family received me kindly. I told him what Jack Smith had said, and Mrs. Brent replied, "Yes, he always sends soldiers to us."

I remained at Mr. Brent's for several days, taking medicine, during which time I made some explorations about his premises. I was surprised at the unnecessary public works thereon. His place was on a very high hill that stands on the west bank of the Arkansas River, terminating in a high bluff on the river. The levee was not suspended here, but was built on the highest part of the hill, where it probably never would be needed. Brent's houses and farm were all well back, west of the levee. He had lived there many years and had never suffered from an overflow or backwater or been threatened by such. His son-in-law, who was older than he, had a dwelling and farm back of his, on which he too had lived for many years in perfect safety. I asked Mr. Brent why a levee had been built on that high bluff, and he did not know. I could imagine but one use for it—to give work to a contractor and his employees.

A brother of Mrs. Brent's was also there. He had been captured and paroled at Vicksburg, and, like those whom I had seen at the Jordan Place, had lost hope of final success. Some of Banks's soldiers had hanged him, but others had rescued him in time to save his life. The rope had cut his neck, however, and the scar was still visible. To my surpise, he spoke well of General Banks.

While I was at Mr. Brent's, Capt. Martin M. Kenny called for an hour or two. He was the man who had been wounded in the neck in the battle at Taylor's Creek, with the ball passing through his larynx, and he could yet speak only in whispers. At this time he was much distressed because many of our soldiers desired furloughs.

At Mr. Brent's, I found two or three other Confederate soldiers who, like myself, were suffering from malarial chills, all of whom stayed till cured, and our generous landlord refused to receive any pay. He owned no Negroes, and he and his family worked on his farm to support themselves and their guests. I stayed at Mr. Brent's till my chills were cured, but my gangrenous finger was no better. I departed for Pine Bluff where our regiment was encamped.

My Final Departure from Pine Bluff, Arkansas

At Pine Bluff I visited the courthouse, in which our daily guard was stationed, and found an informal assemblage of citizens. All Confederate soldiers had been recalled from all places below Pine Bluff, and now there was no guard to prevent the enemy from coming up the river to take the town and possibly Little Rock as well. Many citizens of Pine Bluff had resolved to fly before their arrival, but others were determined to stay. The purpose of the meeting was to request the soldiers to destroy the jail so the enemy could not confine their citizens in it. They would not assume the responsibility of destroying it, lest the enemy should punish them. The meeting did not agree to adopt any policy, but it revealed the fact that many of the citizens were badly demoralized.

Captain Alston asked me about my crippled finger, and wished to see it. When I showed it to him, he said that I should get a furlough and go home till I was well. I told him that I had several times applied for one, but our surgeon had refused, saying that the army was the place to get my finger cured. I had become discouraged and thought it useless to apply to him again. Captain Alson said, "I will see him and request him to give you one." Then he left me.

A few moments later, the surgeon, Dr. J. T. Norris, came to me and inquired how my finger was. I told him I believed that it was rotting off. He wished to see it, and I showed it to him. He said, "I will give you a furlough, and you can go home and stay there till it gets well."

I said, "So much of it has rotted that it will never again be useful to me, and I think you may do better to amputate it."

He replied, "It will be a trouble to you as long as you keep it, and I advise you to have it amputated after it gets well, but, to avoid much suffering, and probably to save your life, not till then."

I was guided by his advice. He then gave me a sick man's furlough for fifteen days—just time enough to go home, but no time to stay there or come back. But he was not allowed to give a furlough for more than fifteen days, and he told me I could have my leave of absence extended every fifteen days by a written affidavit from a home physician. His former refusal to give me a sick man's furlough was, as he said, on account of many applications of well men who feigned sickness to obtain furloughs, and, to relieve himself of their importunity, he had resolved to grant no more furloughs.

Armed with my furlough, I immediately departed for home and never saw Pine Bluff again.

Again in Arkansas, 1864

In all, with numerous extensions because of the condition of my finger, my furlough lasted five months. By this time the finger had wasted away until the second phalanx was only the size of a common-sized knitting needle. Its nerves were so near the surface that it suffered a cold sensation, even on a hot day, unless it was covered by a glove. It was permanently crooked, and, as I used the bridle in this hand when riding, the slightest jerk of my horse's head hurt it severely. I was more crippled with it than I could have been without, and I resolved to have it amputated as soon as I could, as Dr. Norris had advised. When I thought my finger was nearly as well as it would ever be, I returned to our regiment in Arkansas.

While I had been away, the enemy had ascended the Arkansas River and captured Little Rock and Pine Bluff. But our troops, aware of their approach, had escaped by retreating. Our regiment, Carter's, had tried to retake Pine Bluff, but had been repulsed, losing one man, our commissary, Richard Matson of Washington County, Texas, killed. General Holmes, commander of the Confederate army in Arkansas, had retreated from Little Rock to Camden, on the Ouachita River, and established headquarters there. Our brigade was also at Camden. It was now composed of three regiments and one battalion. (Morgan's squardron had grown by accessions to a battalion.) A pontoon bridge spanned the Ouachita at this point. Parson's and Burford's regiments and Morgan's battalion were encamped on the south side of the river near the town, and Carter's regiment, Lieutenant Colonel Giddings commanding, was encamped on the north side, in a low bottom that was subject to overflow. Here I rejoined our regiment.

I found our men much discouraged by our recent misfortunes, and I also was much discouraged. I had expected to be discharged at the expiration of three years, but the conscript law was now so changed as to include all men under fifty years of age, and I expected that before I should reach that age, it would be so changed as to include all men under sixty and probably after that all under seventy years—and then possibly all under eighty years old.

So I began to fear that instead of performing my duty as a faithful volunteer soldier, I was being used as a permanent *slave* and would never again be permitted to enjoy the society of my family or to provide for them. Influenced by this fear, I prayed to God that I might be killed in the next battle. Yet I clung to the hope, though it seemed to be an unreasonable one, that we might yet achieve a final victory, again be a free people, and retire our foolish congressmen and tyrannical military officers to private life.

I had intended to have my cripped finger amputated on my arrival at the encampment, but we were in daily expectation of being ordered to march, and I feared we would not remain stationary long enough for it to heal.

General [Thomas J.] Churchill, commander of our army at the Arkansas Post when it was captured by the enemy, had been afterward exchanged and had been ordered to assume command of our brigade. Upon arriving at Camden, he addressed the officers of Parsons' and Burford's regiments, the privates south of the river also being present. But the men were strangely attached to Colonel Parsons, and they treated General Churchill with scorn. Seeing that his assumption of command would cause a general mutiny of those two regiments, the General abandoned the command and did not visit our regiment. But when the officers of our regiment learned what had been done, they held a meeting in which they prepared a letter to General Churchill, depreciating the conduct of the two other regiments and regretting his nonassumption of the command. But the General left our brigade in command of its senior colonel, William H. Parsons.

Our brigade then left Camden, and, after several marches seemingly intended just to keep us busy, we encamped two days at Lanark, a hamlet below Camden near the Ouachita River but north of it. Here Colonel Parsons harangued us, saying that we were going to Texas. There every company would be detached to go to its own county, where it would remain twenty days, ten in service to the Confederacy and ten with our respective families, after which we would return to the army somewhere. He said that our ten days of service to the Confederacy would be of incalculable value, but left us in ignorance as to what that service should be.

ᗝᕙ 7 ᕘᗢ

Campaigning in Louisiana

In Texas Again, 1864

From Lanark, Arkansas, we marched to Shreveport, Louisiana, where we encamped about ten days before marching into Texas. In Texas, each company branched off at the point nearest its home county. With most of the other companies of our regiment, our company marched under Lieutenant Colonel Giddings till we arrived in Grimes County, where we established headquarters in Wallace Prairie. Then we were divided into squads, each commanded by a lieutenant or noncommissioned officer, and each squad was ordered to march to a different section of the county.

My residence, like those of some other men of Captain Alston's company, was in the northern part of the county, and we were permitted to go home soon after entering the county. For the next twenty days the history of our squad was substantially the history of every squad in the brigade in their respective localities. Orders were sent by Colonel Parsons to the commandant of the regiment and by him to the commandants of squads. Our orders were to explore the section that was allotted to us and to arrest every man who was subject to conscription but had not yet joined the army.

I called together the men of our company whose homes were near mine, and we explored our section, which included Roan's Prairie and Anderson. We called at the residence of every man who was subject to conscription, but somehow all except one man hid themselves, leaving their families to report that they had gone to some unknown point on business. The one exception I instructed to report to the enrolling officer of the county, which he promised to do.

At the end of the first ten days, I reported our proceedings to Captain Alston at Wallace Prairie. According to reports of other squads, only one man had been arrested, and he was present. Captain Alston reported him to the county enrolling officer and let him go. We were then instructed to go home and stay ten days with our families, after which we should rejoin the company on the road to Shreveport.

Thus our service of "incalculable value" in Texas was to arrest and enlist disobedient conscripts and fill our deficient companies with them. I believe that every company of our brigade failed, as we did, thus to replenish our army. This was fortunate, for nearly all conscripted men, as well as those who enlisted to avoid conscription, were dissatisfied murmurers, whose clamor weakened the patriotism of others, engendered a mutinous spirit, and dampened zeal. As nearly all the men of our regiment had been enlisted after the passage of the first conscript law, it had been more or less demoralized from the beginning.

After staying at home ten days with my family, I again departed for the army. I started alone, but on the way I fell in with some men of Greene's brigade. We arrived at Marshall, Texas, on the eighth of April, where news had just come of a battle being fought near Mansfield, Louisiana, in which the Confederates were achieving a great victory. Some of us rode hard toward Mansfield, hoping to get there in time to participate in the battle, but we were too late.

My Ride Through the Battlefield of Pleasant Hill
and Mansfield, Louisiana, April, 1864

We could not reach Mansfield till the night of the ninth of April. I stopped at a house three miles north of town, where I found a man severely wounded in the leg from the battle on the preceding day.

On the tenth, I went through Mansfield and the ground where the battle had been fought, between Mansfield and Pleasant Hill, a distance of about fifteen miles. I did not see any of the slain or wounded men, but I met our burial party returning to Mansfield, where our army had left a hospital and small guard. Our men had buried the Federals as well as the Confederates. The dwellings along the road were uninhabited, as the people had fled from the danger of the battle. The battle had been fought mostly in the forest through which my road lay, but I saw several horses lying dead in enclosures that surrounded houses, and broad gaps in tall fences where the retreating or pursuing army had made passage, nearly all of which were on the west side of the road.

My road lay through a dense thicket where I overtook a long train of Confederate wagons from many regiments. I could not pass them in the road, so I rode in the thicket. The wagons went slowly, but the thicket so impeded my advancement that I was a long time passing each wagon.

Past noon, I overtook a Louisianian who was riding beside a wagon. He handed me a large Yankee cracker, evidently captured from the enemy. I ate the cracker, and it strengthened and encouraged me. After a long time I got into the road ahead of the train and left it far behind.

Sometimes after leaving the train I heard cannonading toward the Red River, a little north of east from me, but I continued on until late that afternoon, when I arrived at a house three miles north of Pleasant Hill. Here I found the first family at home since entering the battlefield. I saw only the man, who came out to talk to me. I asked him where I could find entertainment for the night for myself and my horse. He said that both armies had visited every house for miles around and had taken everything eatable from every place but one.

He said that the man who lived at the house, two miles away, was the overseer, and that even though both armies had visited him, neither had disturbed anything on the place.

Another soldier had fallen in with me during that day, so we went together to the overseer's house. I left my comrade to hold my horse at the stile while I went to the entrance of the dwelling. In the hall I found the overseer, his wife, and another woman. I asked for entertainment for the night, but he replied that he did not entertain travelers.

"But we are Confederate soldiers on leave of absence and in pursuit of the army," I said. "We are in great need, but we have money to pay our fare."

"I cannot accommodate you without breaking my unalterable rule," the man said firmly. "But a few nights ago, an army camped just beyond that little valley yonder. They fed their horses with corn in the ear unshucked, and probably you can find plenty of corn on those ears to feed your horses."

So I returned to the stile, where my comrade was holding my horse. We went across the little valley to the camp, where we found some corn. The shucks had been bitten open and some grain chewed off the cobs, but about half the grains yet remained. So we shelled corn onto our blankets to feed our horses.

Three young men had already encamped there, and one of them had just killed a fat young hog that had been feeding on the corn. We stayed at the camp while they went to a nearby Negro cabin to borrow a kettle, an oven, and a frying pan. The Negroes said they had been forbidden to sell, loan, or give away anything. The overseer had been listening behind the cabin and came around and told the Negroes, "Let these men have all they want, so far as you have it." The Negroes then loaned them the needed vessels and gave them a lot of meal, which they brought to the camp.

We boiled water in the kettle and dressed the hog. Then we stewed and fried some of the meat and baked bread in the oven. Our fare was sumptuous for supper that night and for breakfast the next morning, and we carried bread and meat with us for dinner that day. Before leaving the camp, the young men restored the vessels to the

Negroes and gave them half the hog and the part of the meal that remained uncooked.

On the eleventh of April, my comrade and I left our camp near the overseer's house, passed through Pleasant Hill, and then took a road leading northwest for the Red River, on which we expected to rejoin the army.

On the way we met a man who told us that the cannonading that I had heard on the preceding day came from a battle between our cavalry and a Yankee gunboat at Bayou Pierre, and that our General [Tom] Green had been killed. This was sad news to me. In 1836 General Green had served as a private soldier in the same company with me, and I claimed him as one of my personal friends. I had not seen him since January, 1839, when I was in Houston for a few days and had boarded at the same house with him. The Third Texas Congress was then sitting in Houston, and Green was a clerk in the House of Representatives.

After riding some distance farther, we met an ambulance with all its curtains fastened down so that we could not see inside. It was the cortege attending the remains of General Green. A caparisoned horse was being led by a halter fastened to the hinder part of the ambubulance, and an escort of about thirty men followed.

In the evening we arrived at the encampment of our cavalry at the west edge of the Red River bottom, across from where the Battle of Bayou Pierre had been fought. Brig. Gen. H. P. Bee of Texas had succeeded Green in command of all cavalry in the Trans-Mississippi Department. Colonel Parsons and his regiment being absent, Colonel Carter was commanding our brigade. Only part of Carter's regiment was there, and I was the only man present of Alston's Company H. Therefore I encamped temporarily with Capt. G. W. Farris' Company A, formerly Capt. A. M. Branch's company.

Near Natchitoches, Louisiana

On the twelfth of April, we left our encampment near Bayou Pierre and marched down the Red River for Natchitoches. Our road was on the high land west of the Red River bottom, and we were several days marching. Nearly all our brigade rejoined us on the way, and about three miles west of Natchitoches, our regiment, Carter's, camped at a schoolhouse with a spring, while the rest of our brigade camped nearby. The schoolhouse was a small, neat, one-story log house, newly built and well seated with plank benches. It had also been used as a house of worship, for it contained a pulpit. But part of the Yankee army had been there and had left such obscene writing in pencil on the pulpit that one of our officers said, "I believe that the blackguard who wrote that was killed in the next battle in which he fought, for I don't believe that God would let so vile a man live."

When the Federals occupied Natchitoches, they had come up by way of the Red River, but not all the way by the old channel. During a freshet in 1838, the water broke through the levee on the east side of the river four miles above Natchitoches and washed out a new channel many miles long, which reentered the old channel about ten miles above Alexandria. Ever since that event, the old channel had been navigable only in times of great swells in the stream, and commerce was carried on through the new channel. The old channel was called "Old Cane River," and the new channel the "Bon Dieu." A new town called "Grand Ecore" was built near the point at which the Bon Dieu left the old channel, and passengers and goods could be shipped up the Bon Dieu to Grand Ecore and conveyed by land four miles down the west side of Old Cane to Natchitoches. The Yankees ascended the Bon Dieu to Grand Ecore and then marched the four miles to Natchitoches. They did not burn any houses in Natchitoches, doubtless because they had some adherents there and the town was built so compactly that they could not burn some of the houses without burning all, including those of their friends.

The Federals then ascended the Red River from Natchitoches and Grand Ecore by boat to a point convenient to Pleasant Hill and marched to that town. The Battle of Pleasant Hill and Mansfield was fought on the seventh and eighth of April, after which the Federals retreated down the Red River to Grand Ecore. They were there when we encamped near Natchitoches, but they kept vedettes stationed at the north end of the town. We also kept pickets in and near the town.

After we had occupied our position a few days, the Federals, under

General Banks, marched through Natchitoches some fifteen thousand
strong. On the way our Lieutenant Colonel Morgan fell in behind
with his battalion and fired upon them, killing eight men. The Federals did not halt or return the fire, however, but proceeded at
double-quick time, crossing Old Cane River eight miles below the
town and marching down on the east side of that river. At the same
time, a Federal gunboat descended the Bon Dieu River.

On the same day, General Bee marched all the cavalry of the
Trans-Mississippi Department, except our brigade and Wood's battalion, down the same river on the west side. His personal command
was thirty thousand men.

Meanwhile, our brigade had been pursuing the enemy, and we
overtook them as they forded Old Cane River. We halted behind a
tall rail fence about one hundred yards from the river and left some
men holding our horses, six horses to each man. Then we advanced
to the river. Nine companies of Carter's regiment waded the river,
which was about waist-deep, leaving our Company H to guard the
ford so that the enemy could not recross. Captain Ware's company
from Parsons' regiment was left with us. The nine companies of our
regiment engaged the enemy, killing some, and then recrossed the
river, got on their horses, and retreated to a mansion about a mile
distant. But part of the enemy returned to the east bank of the river
and opened fire upon Ware's and Alston's companies on the west
bank. The minnie balls whistled thick among us, but did no damage.
We returned the fire, but our rifles were short range and the river
was broad, so our bullets fell into the water before reaching the
middle.

Morgan's battalion had taken position on the west bank at another
ford, about two hundred yards above us, near a mansion that was
owned by a widow. Part of the enemy came back to the bank opposite
Morgan's battalion and opened fire upon them, and Morgan's men
returned the fire. Then the enemy crossed the river, drove Morgan's
battalion back, and set fire to and burned down the widow's mansion.

Then the Federals who were opposite our two companies tried to
cross the river to charge upon us. But when their front line came near

the limit of our range, they halted in the water, knowing the range limit by the pattering of our bullets in the water.

Now the enemy's artillery had advanced and opened fire upon us. None of us was hurt, but Captain Ware ordered a retreat and we obeyed. Before we reached the tall fence, though, half of an exploded shell struck Captain Alston on the back of his head, knocking him down. He thought the blow was fatal and begged his friends to go on and not risk their lives in a futile effort to save his. But he rallied and came out without help.

Short of breath, I knew that I could not run more than a hundred yards and so I trotted. I crossed the tall fence and found Lieutenant Edwards, of Alston's company, exhausted and panting. He handed his pistol to me and said, "I can't go on and must fall into the hands of the enemy. Take my pistol and go."

Just then a rifle ball, which had passed through a crack of the rail fence, struck Edwards on the hip and knocked him down. It did not enter his flesh, but produced a large and painful bruise. I took his hand, lifted him up, and handed his pistol back to him.

I supported him as best I could in going very slowly toward our horses. I had not been the hindmost man over the fence as I had thought, for Mr. Eberle of our company overtook us and assisted me with Lieutenant Edwards.

We mounted our horses and went about a mile back to a mansion occupied by a lady who had recently become a widow. Our regiment encamped in the enclosure around the mansion.

Our recent exercise had made us very thirsty, but we obtained excellent water from a cistern in the basement of the mansion. As I was entering the basement for water, a young man who was not one of us requested me not to enter the house, for the enemy, while passing up the river, had frightened the lady and she was afraid of us. I told him we would enter only the basement, only for water.

I entered the basement, drank freely of the invigorating cold water, filled my canteen, and came out. A big crowd of soldiers stood near the door, and each of them asked me for a drink. I handed my canteen to them, and they soon emptied it.

I re-entered the basement, refilled my canteen, and again came out. Just as I came out, a young man asked me for a drink of water, but I refused him, saying that I had already given away a canteenful and must take this to my messmates. It was a dark night, but as he turned to leave, I recognized him as a special friend of mine, Mr. Robert Gary of Farris' Company A. I called him back and gave him water. I have often thanked God for directing me to do this little kindness, for about forty hours later Mr. Gray was slain in battle.

First Battle near Cloutierville, Louisiana

The next morning our brigade marched back to the ford and crossed to the east side of the river. The enemy had just marched down the river. We pursued them closely, our front guard frequently capturing some of their stragglers who fell behind their rear guard.

On their recent march up the river, the enemy had burned about two-thirds of the dwellings along the way. Now, on their downward march, they were burning most of the remaining dwellings, all the cornhouses, and some fences and were kidnapping all the Negroes they could catch. Most of the white families had fled to other parts for refuge.

Our officials at Richmond had appointed Maj. Gen. John A. Wharton, Jr., as commander of all cavalry in the Trans-Mississippi Department. He had come to assume command and was accompanied by Francis R. Lubbock, who had served on President Jefferson Davis' staff. But when Wharton arrived at Natchitoches, General Bee had marched all of the cavalry, except our brigade and Wood's battalion, down the west side of Old Cane River. So Wharton found Wood's battalion and marched it down the east side of the river, overtook us, and then assumed personal command of our brigade and the battalion.

That afternoon we crossed Old Cane River and halted about a half-mile north of a town called Clucherville [Cloutierville],[1] which

[1] Zuber is probably referring to Cloutierville, and the name will be so spelled in the text following. The skirmish near Cloutierville took place April 22–23, 1864 (The Orr Brothers, *Campaigning with Parsons' Texas Cavalry Brigade*, p. 133 n.).

is on a bend of Old Cane River on the east side, where the river changes its course from south to nearly east. When we halted, Colonel Carter, now commanding the Twenty-first Texas Cavalry, marched a northeasterly course toward a point on the river below the town. At the edge of the thick timber of the river bottom we dismounted and left men holding our horses while our main force proceeded on foot under Lieutenant Colonel Giddings.

This procedure indicated an early battle. I had temporarily exchanged guns with a man who was absent on furlough and regarded this exchange as fortunate. My hunting rifle bore up only two hundred yards, while the gun that I was now using, a Mississippi rifle, was said to bear up four hundred yards.

We soon came within sight of part of the enemy, who occupied a position near the levee on the north bank of the river. We tried to charge them, but they retreated, keeping beyond the range of our guns, the best of which bore up only four hundred yards. Their guns bore up one thousand yards, but they were poor marksmen, and even though their bullets whistled among us, they did not hurt any of us.

The enemy retreated to the levee, but, instead of crossing, they continued retreating down it toward the east. Now some of our men thought they were about to turn on us and cried out, "They're flanking us! They're flanking us!" Then nearly all retreated. Colonel Giddings did his best to call them back, and I joined him, shouting, "Come back, boys, and charge them! They're already whipped! Let's catch some of them!"

But all to no avail. Our stampede may have been fortunate, however, for we were mistaken. The Federals were not trying to flank us, but, as we afterward learned, five thousand of their men were ambushed behind the levee. Had our men obeyed Colonel Giddings and me, those who were pretending to retreat would have drawn us to within point-blank shot of the five thousand, who would have turned their rifles loose on us and would probably have killed us all.

Our men retreated in double-quick time, but I, being short of breath, trotted. I knew that if I should run, I would soon break down and be caught if pursued. The timber was thick, so my comrades were soon beyond my sight and I thought I was the hindmost man. I came to a tree whose circumference was not quite as large as that of my body.

I halted and I looked back. About four hundred yards from me were probably thirty Yankees, all in a row. Their backs were toward me, and they stood so close together that I could not see daylight between any two of them. As I rested against the tree, I looked at them through the sights of my gun. But my eyesight was now failing, and they all looked like a section of blue cloth stretched out. I was not sure whether the ball would rise or fall if shot at that distance. So I took aim at about the middle of the thorax and fired, judging that if the ball should rise it might strike one of them on the upper part of the back, or the neck, or the head, but should it fall, it would strike on the lower part of the body.

This was the only time that I ever shot at a man with the hope that my ball would reach him. I had always intended that if I should ever get a fair shot at the enemy, I would look to see if I had hit him, but now, as soon as I fired, I felt unsafe because my gun was empty and I was alone and helpless. I hastened to screen myself behind the tree again, bracing my back against it while I reloaded my gun.

While I was ramming down the load, three balls were shot at me, all at once. I did not hear the explosions, because our firing when we had all been together had deafened me. I felt two balls strike the tree behind me, as if two strong men had driven heavy axes into the tree. And I heard the other ball whistle by my right shoulder, which was exposed, since the tree was too small to shelter me completely.

If I did not shoot a man then, I never did. I wish I could know that I never did, for it is a horrible thing to take a fellow man's life, even in war when we are fighting for our rights. When I had reloaded my gun, I stepped from behind the tree to see if I had done any execution, but the enemy had disappeared. I proceeded toward our horses and heard some bullets whistle.

We all arrived safely at our horses, where Colonel Carter and his staff had halted. Then we remounted and proceeded to the point on the road that we had left. In the meantime, part of the enemy had countermarched and had assaulted our other regiments and battalions. Some Confederates were wounded and some Federals were wounded and killed. The Confederates had repulsed the enemy but had not pursued them.

Second Battle near Cloutierville, Louisiana

In the night following the first battle near Cloutierville, our regiment, which was now the front of our force, passed through the town. The moon shone brightly, and we could see that none of the houses had been burned by the enemy.

The course of our road changed, with that of the river, from nearly south to nearly east. Doubtless we marched over ground on which our regiment had done its part of the battle the preceding day. During this march the moon set and the night became very dark.

About forty-five minutes before day we all halted, and two cannon passed our front. The artillery halted a short distance in front of our regiment and opened fire upon the enemy, whom we, the cavalry, did not see. We could plainly see the direction in which the shells flew by the streaks of flame that issued from their ends. To my surprise, their course was nearly southwest, and I though that they were shot across the river. But, just where the artillery halted, the river formed an acute angle, changing its course from nearly east to nearly southwest, and the direction of our road changed with that of the river. About one thousand yards southwest of our artillery, the enemy's rear had halted. This was what our artillery was shooting at. We heard our shells explode in or near the enemy's line, but did not hear any responsive firing by the enemy. At this point, the river and the road resumed their course south. The streaks of light that issued from our shells as they flew were beautiful and exhilarating.

After firing several rounds at the enemy, the two pieces of artillery withdrew, and I saw them no more. Then we all advanced, and when our regiment had gone a little beyond the point from which our artillery had been firing, we halted again.

When daylight came I was surprised, after we had marched through a thick forest all the way from Cloutierville, at the scenery into which we had entered. We had come to what had once been a large plantation, but most of it had been turned out many years and it now looked like a Texas prairie. A thick forest, which bound it on the north and east and partly on the west, was about 200 yards away from where a mansion had once stood. In their upward march the Yankees had burned all the wooden houses on the plantation and as much as they could of its fences. A recently cultivated field, which extended south beyond our sight, was hedged about with Cherokee roses, and on the west side of this great field was a fence, near the river at the brink of the bluff. Just east of the bend of the river were the ashes of the mansion, but the body of a dairy house made of bricks was yet standing, although its roof had been burned. Around the buildings and enclosures, the fence and its palings, which had extended about 300 yards south, had also been burned. At the south end of the enclosure was a set of house logs, where the enemy had probably pulled down a house. On the north side, the gateposts at the entrance had not been burned and were yet standing.

The fire of our artillery had provoked the enemy to send back about three thousand horsemen, and they now occupied what had been the enclosure around the mansion. We had halted about 150 yards north of the gateposts, but a grove of trees obstructed our view, and we, the noncommissioned officers and privates, did not know the extent of the work before us. Therefore, under cover of the timber, Captain Farris' Company A was sent east of the enemy's rear to reconnoiter.

When daylight came I found that General Wharton was present and commanding, with Francis R. Lubbock acting as adjutant general. They had brought Wood's battalion, making our isolated force about three thousand men. While waiting for orders, I saw two men of Farris' company carrying a dead man on a blanket to a large tree at the border of the eastern forest, where I judged they intended to bury him. Later, I discovered that the dead man was my friend Robert Gary, to whom I had given a drink of water about forty hours before.

Meanwhile General Wharton determined that one of our regiments should charge the area around the mansion and, if possible, drive the enemy out of it, while the other regiments and battalions retained their present ground and supported the attacking regiment. He asked Colonel Parsons if he and his regiment would make the attack, but Parsons refused. Then General Wharton put the same question to Colonel Burford and received a similar answer. Finally he asked Colonel Carter, who replied that he would, but one company of his regiment was absent, reconnoitering.

Then Wharton asked Parsons if any company of his regiment would join Colonel Carter's regiment in the charge, and Parsons agreed that the Methodist Bulls should go. The Methodist Bulls were from Captain [William J.] Neal's company, and were said to all be members of the Methodist church, while Captain Neal and his second lieutenant, J. Fred Cox, were Methodist preachers.[2] So it was settled that the nine present companies of our regiment and Captain Neal's company should make the charge.

Colonel Carter returned to his regiment and told us what had been determined. He also said that General Paulinac [C. J. Polignac][3], with three thousand Louisiana infantry, was only three miles behind us and would keep within that distance to support us if we should be overpowered. That was the last I heard of this help until many years later, when I learned that before the charge, Gen. E. Kirby Smith had recalled Polignac and his infantry to Shreveport. We remained ignorant of their recall, and our ignorance sustained our courage.

We made the charge, with Neal's company taking the lead. On arriving at the gateposts, the men of each company dismounted and left their horses with men to hold them, then charged on foot into the area. As Neal's company entered the area, the enemy abandoned it and fled twelve hundred yards south of the wall of the brick dairy house. Neal's company then proceeded to the pile of house logs on the south side while our nine companies halted at the dairy house. Captain Alston was present, although suffering a severe headache from the blow he had gotten at the ford.

I knew our rifles would not bear up to the enemy if shot from that point, and I obtained permission from Captain Alston to go to Captain Neal's company, about three hundred yards nearer the enemy. Captain Neal's company all had long-range guns, which would bear up one thousand yards or more. But at great distances, the balls would

[2] Cox was regimental chaplain (ibid., p. 6).

[3] The correct spelling is Polignac and the name will be so spelled in the text following.

wobble and hit wide of the mark, while their force would become so spent as not to enter what they hit.

All the men were lying down, resting their guns on logs and shooting at the nearest enemies, who were about nine hundred yards away. Captain Neal was standing up, observing where the balls fell by the dust they knocked up, and advising his men where to shoot and how much to elevate their guns. No man was more cool and thoughtful in battle than he.

I stood up with Captain Neal. The enemy balls whistled among us, but only one man was hit. While Lieutenant [J. W.] Wright was taking aim, a ball struck him on the breast but did not enter. Nearly all the company rose and started toward him, but Captain Neal said, "You men attend to the enemy. I will attend to him." Then they all lay down again while the Captain put a patch on the Lieutenant's bruise.

I stayed with this company about ten minutes and fired one shot at the enemy. But Captain Neal, who was watching for the fall of my ball, said that it did not go halfway to them. So I returned to my own company at the dairy house.

The enemy's artillery was now sending its shells over us. I had gone about seventy yards from Neal's company when Lieutenant William Anderson, of Captain Hanner's Company G, who was about seventy yards beyond me, called, "Zuber, tell that company that the order is to fall back."

I turned and repeated the order to Captain Neal, who barely had time to repeat it to his company before they all sprang up and fell back in double-quick time and soon passed me. Since I was short of breath, I trotted and was soon left out of sight.

Every man had left the brick dairy house. When I arrived at the gateposts some of the horses had been killed, but a few had been left hitched to the gateposts. Only two of the horse holders were present, each holding two horses. One of these was a young man who was lying flat on his stomach, under a horse's belly and between its feet, calling aloud for his brother, Ruf. But Ruf had departed in a hurry, not waiting to mount his horse. The other horse holder was Oswald Jones, of our Company H, who was seated on the ground, holding

his own horse and mine. Just as I arrived, two men came up, supporting Mortimer Gibony, who was severely wounded in a hip. All their
horses were hitched to posts. Gibony's companions lifted him onto
his horse, mounted their own, and the three left.

Jones said, "Zuber, I'm glad you've come." He handed my bridle
rein to me, mounted his horse, and away he went. My joints were
stiff, and I could not mount quickly, but I finally departed too.

Our men were not frightened, but, knowing that the enemy's guns
ranged a thousand yards, while ours ranged only four hundred yards,
and that their number was many times greater than ours, we pru-
dently left the field. They pursued us into the area from which we had
driven them, but finally halted, although their cannonballs and shells
continued to fly over our heads.

Once mounted, I saw that our men had retired through open
ground toward the thick timber north of us and some of them had
entered it. So I followed. They were marching back toward Cloutierville in disorder. Those who had mounted quickest or had run fastest
arrived first, and late arrivals were falling into line while the lines
were moving. The commandants of regiments and battalions had
formed as they arrived, without halting: the commandant of Wood's
battalion first, Parsons of the Twelfth Texas following, then Burford
of the Nineteenth, next Carter of the Twenty-first, and last, Morgan
of his battalion. Officers rode on the south side of the line, directing
the men where to fall in. "Wood's in the front!" "The Twelfth
ahead!" "The Nineteenth here!" "The Twenty-first behind!" "Morgan's in the rear!" And officers of each battalion or regiment were
riding likewise, directing men to their respective companies. "Company A ahead!" "Company F ahead!" "Here is Company B!"
"Company E behind!" As each man approached his place, his company and those to the rear of it would slow up to make room for him.
Thus we formed while marching.

Meanwhile the enemy's artillery was sending its cannonballs and
shells over our heads, cutting down branches of trees, which fell close
but injured no one. We were literally bringing order out of chaos,
probably due to General Wharton's experience, skill, and fine judgment. But behind Wharton, the providence of God directed us, and

that, doubtless, in answer to prayer. Yes, I prayed, and so did others.
I always prayed before a battle, after a battle, during a battle, and at
other times.

We continued to march westerly till the enemy lost our bearings
and ceased firing. Then we fell into the road on which we had advanced from Cloutierville and countermarched to the scene of our
recent engagement. The Federals had abandoned the enclosure that
they had retaken and had resumed their march south, down Old
Cane River, and we resumed our pursuit of them. In the meantime
we heard the sound of artillery far away in the south, which assured
us that General Bee's forces had engaged the enemy's front.

In this battle our losses were Robert Gary and Jonathan Willhour,
killed; Mortimer Gibony, severely wounded; and Lieutenant Wright,
bruised by a spent minnie ball. Earlier in the battle, after Lieutenant
Edwards, of Company H, had been knocked down and bruised on
one hip by a spent minnie ball, he had laid a pillow across his saddle
to sit on when riding. During our charge in the second battle, he
halted with the horse holders at the gateposts, and stood with four
horses, two on each side of him. When the enemy's artillery opened
fire on us, a ball or shell passed through all four horses killing them.
When they fell, Edwards fell between them and they pressed him so
tightly that he could scarcely breathe. Finally, two of the horse
holders extricated him and helped him onto his horse.

On our march down the river, I saw one newly made grave, just
beyond the hedge, a short distance below the temporary encampment
of the enemy, and I assumed that they had lost only one man.

Battle of Monette's Ferry

From the field of our second battle near Cloutierville, Old Cane
River flows south about ten miles. In all this distance, its channel is
bounded on either side by an almost perpendicular bluff, about
seventy feet high, which no army could ascend. Our road lay almost
on the brink of the bluff on the east side, and as we marched we
could plainly see the channel of the river, except in a few short bends.

The Bon Dieu River flows parallel with Old Cane, about a mile
east of it, and along the whole ten miles, immediately west of the Bon

Dieu, is an impassable marsh, or quagmire, in which a man's whole body would sink. At the end of ten miles, the channel of Old Cane, which at this point is shallow and dry, abruptly changes its course eastward and unites with the Bon Dieu. The space between Old Cane River and the marsh was then a succession of cottonfields or corn-fields, which were separated by Cherokee-rose hedges.

Our road changed its course eastward with that of Old Cane River, and some distance below the bend it again changed its course south-ward and crossed Old Cane at a dry ford. This ford was called "Monette's Ferry" because, in 1838, prior to the formation of the new channel, this ford had not been dry.

Banks's Federal army, consisting of fifteen thousand men—cavalry, infantry, artillerymen, and teamsters—was marching south, closely strung along seven or eight miles of road between our second battle-ground near Cloutierville and Monette's Ferry, and their accompany-ing gunboats kept opposite the army on the Bon Dieu. Wharton's personal command of three thousand cavalry was yet with us. (For convenience, I designated our pursuing force as "Wharton's personal command," though I am not sure that Wharton was still with us. I did not see him to recognize him after our second battle near Cloutier-ville.) Polignac's three thousand infantry were believed to be only three miles behind Wharton's cavalry, ready to support them in case of emergency. Bee's thirty thousand cavalry and artillery, covering miles of road, had marched down Old Cane on the west side, till their front ranks reached Monette's Ferry.

Banks's Federal army, accompanied by a multitude of Negroes of all ages whom they had enticed or forced from the plantations the soldiers had destroyed, was flanked on each side by impassable nat-ural barriers—two bluffs on the right and a marsh on the left. The front of Bee's thirty thousand cavalry and artillery faced them and Wharton's three thousand cavalry pursued them closely. There was not room between Old Cane River and the marsh for the divisions all to form at once, and only the front ranks and rearguard could engage the Confederates. Thus, they were so surrounded by natural barriers and Confederates that they could not get out.

Bee had arrived at Monette's Ferry before Banks and his army, and he sent four regiments of cavalry and the Val Verde battery of six cannons across the dry ford to the north or east side of Old Cane to meet the Federals, promising that he would follow with the rest of his cavalry to hurl the enemy back. The Federals advanced, and our regiments and battery opened fire, compelling them to halt. The enemy returned the fire, and a battle ensued in which we lost some valuable men. Yet our regiments and battery maintained their ground and resisted the enemy's attempts to advance.

Now Banks was in a desperate condition. He knew that Bee was in front of him, with twice his number of men. If he should try to cross the river at the ford, his army would be cut to pieces, but natural barriers made it impossible to retreat laterally. Also, Wharton's personal company, three thousand strong, was ready to ambush and defeat him should he try to retreat north. Thus hopelessly situated, he evidently intended to surrender, for he burned his wagons and freight. (Soon afterward I saw the debris, including his wagon irons, which were not combustible. The ashes covered about two acres of ground.)

In the meantime, still expecting the promised aid, yet on the verge of victory, our four regiments and battery received a dispatch from General Bee, ordering them to unhitch the horses from the artillery and, with the horses, to recross the river, leaving the artillery behind. But the artillerymen said that those cannons had cost the Confederacy too many precious lives to be given up. So they all recrossed the river, taking the cannons with them. Then General Bee, with his thirty thousand men, fell back up the river, leaving the way open for Banks's forces to escape, which they did, thus permitting Banks to be in communication again with his gunboats on the Bon Dieu. Whereupon Bee, having let the enemy escape, returned and marched his thirty thousand men in pursuit. But why chase the bird after letting it out of its cage?

Wharton's command had followed Banks to Monette's Ferry, and as we rode past their burned wagons and freight we found two blind old Negro women, whom the Federals had left behind. They had two wagon sheets to protect them against the scorching sun, but little to eat or drink.

Not knowing that the women were blind, I said, "You ought to have stayed with your master and mistress, then you would not be suffering here."

"We couldn't help ourselves," one replied. "Dey jest took us up in der arms and put us in de wagon, and drove on wid us. Dey was mighty good to us till dey got in trouble. Den dey jest put us out and left us." We could not do anything for the women, but had to pass on to the dry ford, where we crossed Old Cane River and joined General Bee in pursuit of the enemy.

Sometime later, General Bee published a paper, signed by almost all commandants of Texas brigades or regiments who participated in the affair. That paper, instead of casting the responsibility upon General Smith, where I believe it belongs, said that General Bee was overpowered by Banks at Monette's Ferry and was compelled to do as he did. But their statement conflicts with what I saw and what I learned from reliable men who participated in the events.

Banks's command was the Nineteenth Corps of the United States Army, which later joined Sherman's devastating raid through Georgia. It was said that Sherman could not have made the raid without his help. If so, we lost our cause by letting Banks escape at Monette's Ferry in 1864.

Operations About Alexandria, Louisiana

From Monette's Ferry we marched south along the Red River toward Alexandria. Along most of our route our road lay on high land, near the west edge of the Red River bottom. The Yankees had previously burned nearly all dwellings and now were amusing themselves by burning all the cornhouses. Our front ranks skirmished with their rear guard every day, but my regiment, being near the middle, did not participate in the skirmishes. At a point probably about twenty miles northwest of Alexandria, we crossed a stream on a small embankment called a "dirt bridge" and entered into the Red River bottom. This dirt bridge and the channel it crossed were a great curiosity. The bridge was built over a broad spring, from which water flowed in opposite directions, north and south. Both streams were reinforced by numerous other springs and small branches, thus becoming two large creeks. One was called Bayou Coti and flowed northeast through the bottom, discharging into the Red River some miles above Alexandria. The other was called Bayou Rapides, and it flowed southeast through the bottom, discharging into the Red River some miles below Alexandria.

The Yankees now possessed Alexandria and had burned part of it. My regiment crossed the dirt bridge and marched to a point some four or five miles northwest of Alexandria, where we encamped on Bayou Rapides. From this point, which we called our "cook camp," we skirmished with bodies of the enemy who came out scouting from Alexandria, while detailed men kept the camp, with our baggage and provisions, cooked our meals, and sent them to us by couriers.

About the thirtieth of April, we encountered a body of Federal cavalry on a plantation and tried to engage them. They fled, mostly on level ground, while we, trying to go directly toward them, had to cross some high cotton ridges in pursuit and could not go as fast as they. So they kept beyond gunshot of us and continued to increase their distance. In their flight they set fire to a large mansion, and before we could reach it the flames were beyond control. Then they entered the forest and disappeared.

My horse was a spirited animal, but in jumping obliquely across the cotton ridges he strained some of his limbs and became temporarily unfit for service. So I had to return to our cook camp to doctor him and give him rest.

On arriving at the camp, I bathed in the Bayou Rapides. The water was very cold, and shortly afterwards I was attacked with a severe spell of pneumonia. I shall always remember the kindness of my comrade Isaiah Robinson, who gathered moss and put it under me for a bed, and did other work to try to make me easy. Before night, I became delirious, and do not distinctly remember anything that occurred during the next twenty-six days.

Sick—May and June, 1864

The enemy retired from Alexandria and went down the Red River. Then the Confederates occupied the town. A hospital was established in the bottom, somewhere above Alexandria, and I was removed to it. Dr. Thomas Petty, of Brenham, Texas, who had been assistant surgeon of the Twenty-first Texas Cavalry, was our hospital physician.

Our cavalry pursued the enemy down the Red River and were defeated in a battle on Yellow Bayou. The enemy then crossed the Atchafalaya (a bayou which flows south out of the Red River a short distance above its mouth) and proceeded down the east side. A small body of our cavalry followed, but the enemy turned and came back up the bayou. Our men fled from them and recrossed the bayou by swimming. Several of them drowned. Our commanding officers believed the Federals were coming back to retake Alexandria and sent a dispatch to Dr. Petty, ordering him to retreat into the piney woods. He was told to take those sick and wounded men who were able to go and to leave the rest with their nurses at the hospital. But Dr. Petty would not leave any of us. He put those who were not able to ride on horseback into ambulances and took us all to the residence of Michel Paul, a French Creole who lived in the woods about forty miles northwest of Alexandria, near Hindston post office.

Dr. Petty stayed with us for several days and then returned to the army, leaving a comrade named Forehand as my nurse. Mr. Forehand was a good and sympathetic man but could not handle me without hurting me severely, and he requested to be relieved.

A big Irishman took his place. He was cruel, negligent, and insulting. He permitted a blister plaster on my left side to eat deep into the flesh, to become a wad, and finally to become buried under the cuticle. The doctor had instructed that at first I should be allowed a teaspoonful of water once in each hour, but my Irish nurse continued to allow me only this long afterward. I became intolerably thirsty, and my lungs became so dry that I could not cough up the phlegm. I kept begging for more water, which he refused to give me for a time. Finally, he set a vessel of water and a dipper by me, cursed me, and told me to drink my death. I drank freely. I coughed up much phlegm, my pain subsided, and I fell asleep and slept about twelve hours.

When I awoke, I was free from pain but so weak that I could not walk. I felt as if I were in another state of existence. The house, its furniture, and all the people except my Irish nurse semed strange to me. I did not even recognize the young woman, Miss Sidney Paul, who had brought all my meals to me since my arrival. I could remember nothing distinctly except my agonizing pain, my thirst for water, and the relief that it gave me when I got it. I did not know where I was or the name of my landlord. A wounded comrade had died in my room, but I did not know it.

I inquired what the month and day was, and was surprised on learning that it was the twenty-sixth of May. I consulted my diary, remembering that I had made my last entry therein on the day I had been taken sick, and found it to be the thirtieth of April. I was told of the recent movements of our army and those of our enemies, including our defeat at Yellow Bayou, all which was new to me.

After a few days a messenger arrived and ordered my Irish nurse to return to our regiment, which was encamped on the west bank of the Red River, four miles above Alexandria. I resolved to go along, and since I could not mount my horse, my nurse lifted me up. A convalescent comrade named Long also went with us.

On the way we crossed the Boeuf River. Its source was below the road on which we had gone to Mr. Paul's, but its numerous springs and tributary branches swelled it suddenly to a river, which looked large enough to be navigated. There was neither ferry nor bridge, but it was spanned by a succession of hewn logs, spliced together, which served as a floating bridge for men on foot. The Irishman and Long swam our horses across the river and carried our wallets and horse rigging over on the floating logs. I was too weak to walk on the logs, but I "cooned" them by crawling across on my hands and knees. We camped that night on the east bank of the Boeuf and arrived at the encampment on the west bank of the Red River before noon the following day.

Our regiment was preparing to march that day for Brenham, Texas. I now no longer wished to remain in the army, for I knew of no prospect for effecting anything desirable in Texas. Our regiment surgeon, Dr. Norris, gave me a sick man's furlough and a passport to travel at ease to Brenham. He told me that so long as I was disabled I could apply to him once every thirty days and receive a new furlough.

I immediately departed for home, but, from necessity, I stayed near our regiment till a short time after we entered Texas. I could mount my horse by making him jump his forefeet over a log, so that they were on one side and his hind feet on the other. Then I could climb on the log and mount from it. But when no log or stump was present, I had to be lifted on or off my horse, and if no help was near I waited till someone came along.

On the first evening I stopped a short time before night, to be sure of getting entertainment. I was yet in the Red River bottom, and the landlord, whose name was Ennis, called a servant to help me off my horse and care for him, while he invited me in and treated me hospitably. On the next morning, at daybreak, a servant girl awakened me with my breakfast. I asked for my bill, but was told that there was no charge. Then a servant brought my horse, ready for me to mount. He lifted me up and I departed.

During my ride from Alexandria to Burr's ferry on the Sabine River, I kept with our regiment. We arrived there before night, and the regiment camped on the Louisiana side of the river. However, I called at the residence of Mr. Burr, owner of the ferry, and applied for entertainment. Burr, a widower, was out, but his daughter received me. She said that her father never received soldiers, but her husband was an unwilling conscript in the Confederate army, and, for his sake, she would not turn me away. I learned that her father was a Yankee, born and reared in some Northern state, and that they both were unionists. At dusk Mr. Burr came in. He was sour and reticent, but he did not send me away. I endured my unpleasant situation patiently, and in the morning Mr. Burr charged me with a big bill for my fare.

We crossed the Sabine River into Texas and I felt almost as if I were home. Some distance west of the Sabine, our road forked and the regiment took the lefthand, or lower, route, via Cold Spring, Montgomery, and Hempstead, to Brenham, while I took the righthand, or upper, route, via Moscow and Huntsville, to my home in Grimes County. When I reached there, I found my dear family well. We had a joyful meeting, but it was marred by my feebleness and the gloomy prospect for our country

About the first day of July I went to Brenham to have my furlough renewed. Dr. Norris gave me a new one for thirty days. When I started home from Brenham, I managed to mount my horse from the ground for the first time since my attack of pneumonia.

Back Home Again

At home I found the people demoralized. In my section they had not been very patriotic from the first, and now they had lost interest in our cause and wished for peace on any terms. I heard many say, "I wish the war would end one way or the other." But I wished it to end one way, not the other.

Most of our people would sign any petition presented to them for the detail of men from the army to perform "needed work for the public," whether such work were needed or not, and whether the men applying for the details were capable of performing it or not. Sometimes their motive really was to get the work done, but most often people signed these petitions to relieve men from army service. Details were thus procured for applicants who professed to be school-teachers, carpenters, cabinetmakers, saddlers, shoemakers, and tanners. And almost any man who had hides in a tan trough, or vat, could be detailed as a tanner.

The details became so numerous that our enrolling officers finally refused to recognize any, and made prisoners of those who held them, thus subjecting many worthy men to great indignity. They even annoyed some who were home on sick furlough. This I understood to be the condition throughout the Trans-Mississippi Department.

Soon after I arrived home, sick, I became afflicted with rheumatism. I decided to teach school and applied to Lieutentant Colonel Giddings for a permanent detailment as a teacher. If he should approve my application, it would be forwarded to Galveston for General [John B.] Magruder's approval and then returned to me. I did not wait for this, however, but commenced teaching. Also, as the election of our civil officers was drawing near, I became a candidate for the office of county commissioner.

According to state law at that time, our counties were divided into militia captains' districts, called "beats," their numbers being in proportion to the size and population of each county. Each beat was entitled to two justices of the peace and one constable. The conscript law having absorbed our militia companies, the beats had ceased to be militia districts, but they continued as judicial districts for justices of the peace. Every county was entitled to four county commissioners, who, with the county chief justice (county judge), constituted our county court. These commissioners were elected collectively by the voters of the county at large, but no two of them could reside in one beat. I attended the election at the courthouse in Anderson, Grimes County, and was elected county commissioner.[1]

General [J. G.] Walker was now superintendent of the enrolling officers of the state. Therefore, immediately after the adjournment of the first session of our county court, I visited General Walker's deputy. His deportment was stiff, and his responses were few, brief, and cold. I explained my situation, telling him frankly that I had become disabled for army service and had procured by election as

---

[1] In his *Ancestry and Kindred of W. P. Zuber, Texas Veteran* (1905), Zuber says that he was county commissioner of Precinct 2, Grimes County, from 1876 to 1878.

county commissioner to be relieved of such service. I requested him to protect me against annoyance by enrolling officers.

"How far from here do you live?" he asked.

"Thirteen miles," I answered.

"Then I believe that you are able to do army service," he said. "Otherwise, you could not have come here."

Soon after this I received my application for detailment as a schoolteacher, with the following endorsement: "Approved. I do not believe that he will ever again be able to perform army service; but I believe he will be useful as a schoolteacher." It was signed "D. C. Giddings, Lt. Col. 21st Reg., Texas Cavalry." But below the signature was the notation: "Disapproved, J. B. Magruder, Major General Commanding, Department of Texas." It now seemed certain that I would be annoyed by enrolling officers, as were nearly all details and petty officers, and I was in continuous dread of such annoyance. But time proved I was an exception to the rule.

Our Last Encampment on the Little Brazos

I learned that our regiment, Twenty-first Texas Cavalry had been recalled to Texas and was encamped in Wallace Prairie, Grimes County, so I visited them. I found that Colonel Carter, who had long been trying to supplant Colonel Parsons as senior colonel of the brigade, had finally succeeded, after a delay of more than a year by authorities at Richmond.[2] But, knowing that Parsons' and Burford's regiments would mutiny if he should assume command of the brigade, he had his regiment transferred to Gen. Walter P. Lane's brigade. Colonel Carter and Lieutenant Colonel Giddings were absent, leaving Major Chenoweth in temporary command of the regiment. Captain Alston was also absent, and Lieutenant Edwards was in command of his company.

[2] For a brief note on the Carter-Parsons problem see William Steele to S. S. Anderson, June 5, 1864, *The War of the Rebellion: A Compilation of the Official Records of the Union and Confederate Armies,* 1st series, vol. xxxiv, p. 628.

To my chagrin, I found the men of our regiment broken in spirit and utterly ineffective. They had learned of General Lee's surrender at Appomattox and expected soon to hear that Gen. Joseph E. Johnston, in Georgia, had also surrendered. They had lost hope, expecting the conscript law to hold them in service indefinitely.

I was much distressed by our reverses, but had a faint hope that the soldiers of the Trans-Mississippi Department might yet rally and save the Confederacy. It pained me to find our regiment disheartened, and I resolved that after returning home and arranging my affairs I would rejoin our company and stay with it till we either succeeded or the last glimmer of hope expired. Although unfit for service, I also hoped that my example might inspire some of my comrades with hope, courage, and energy.

After arranging some home affairs, I returned to our regiment in Wallace Prairie. It was ready to march to the encampment of Gen. Walter P. Lane, to whose brigade we had been transferred. Colonel Carter was yet absent, and I never saw him again, but Lieutenant Colonel Giddings was present and commanding. Captain Alston was absent on a court-martial in Parsons' brigade, somewhere on the Brazos above Bryan, and I never saw him again either. But Lieutenant Edwards was still commanding our company, and I reported to him for duty.

We marched through Navasota to Millican, which was then the northern terminus of the Houston and Texas Central Railway. Work on the road had been suspended at this point due to the war. From Millican, we proceeded to Bryan, and thence ten miles west to the San Antonio crossing of the Little Brazos, three miles east of Moseley's ferry on the Brazos. The space between the Brazos and the Little Brazos was bottom land. It was then mostly uncultivated. Here we encamped near the east bank of the Little Brazos, about two furlongs from the encampment of Madison's regiment, in which General Lane had his headquarters. This was our last encampment.

We had no chaplain, but there was in Capt. M. Kenny's Company K a Methodist preacher named J. L. Angel, who was very modest. A petition was sent to Colonel Giddings, signed by nearly all the men in the regiment, requesting him to appoint Mr. Angel chaplain of the regiment. Colonel Giddings replied substantially as follows: "By the last edition of our regulations, I have no right to take a man from the ranks and make him a noncombatant, but I hereby detail Rev. J. L. Angel to act as chaplain for this regiment, subject to a recall at any time by the commandant of Company K."

Mr. Angel accepted the detailment and held a religious service in our regiment on the next Sunday, which was our last Sabbath before the "breakup."

I was yet badly crippled in the little finger of my left hand. On my request, our surgeon, Dr. Norris, amputated the finger at the middle of the first phalanx. This was his last surgical operation in the army.

While here at our last encampment, we received a full supply of sabers and short rifles for cavalry service. A full supply of clothing had also been sent, but the wagons on which it was coming were robbed. These supplies had long been in Shreveport, in charge of Gen. E. Kirby Smith, but had not been sent to us. The guns and sabers could be useful at home, whither we soon carried them. General Smith also had charge of a supply of pistols and money, but I do not know what became of that.

From here, Lieutenant Colonel Giddings retired to his home in Brenham, leaving Major Chenoweth in command of the regiment. I applied to Lieutenant Edwards for a discharge, which application I took to Major Chenoweth. He signed it, and then I took the paper to General Lane. But General Lane declined to sign, saying that he did not have authority to discharge the men.

Our Masonic lodge held one meeting here, granted demits to all its members, and surrendered its dispensation to the Grand Lodge of Texas.

News of the surrender of Gen. Joseph H. Johnston in Georgia and that of Gen. Dick Taylor, and of the capture of President Jefferson Davis, his family, and his cabinet all came in quick succession and confirmed the men of our regiment in their resignation to "submit to the inevitable." About half of them went home, but in due respect to our Confederate government, the rest of us waited for formal permission to leave. As we waited from day to day, our mail carriers displayed wonderful fidelity, continuing to bring our mail with the regularity of clockwork, though our government paper with which they were paid had become utterly worthless.

After the "Breakup"

Major Chenoweth became weary of waiting for us to take absence without leave, and finally he ordered, "Pack Up! Saddle Up! Mount! Fall into line! Forward! March!" We obeyed, not knowing what we were about to do, with the major taking the lead toward Bryan. I was nearly the rearmost man, but gradually the major dropped back till he became the rearmost. Then he dropped completely out of sight and I did not see him again for a year or two.

We were now marching east, without a leader, and the road was our only guide. But our men gradually left the line, like the major, and disappeared, until I was left alone. I passed through Bryan, and several miles southwest of town called at a house and found a man named Johnson, his wife, and two young men who were returning home from the army. They all expressed great joy at the termination of the war.

President Abraham Lincoln was dead and Vice-President Andrew Johnson had succeeded him to fill out his unexpired term. Johnson was a Tennessean, and the last Southern man who had been elected to the vice-presidency. But he was affiliated with the Abolition, or so-called Republican, party, and we Southerners did not expect any justice to be administered by him. He surprised us, however, by issuing his "amnesty" proclamation, which provided that all persons who had participated in or supported the late "rebellion," and all who did not own property of the value of twenty thousand dollars or more, or more than one hundred bales of cotton, should be restored to all rights of citizenship by swearing to obey and support the Constitution and laws of the United States, including the Thirteenth Amendment to the Constitution. The chief justice or county judge of each county was authorized to administer the oath to the citizens after taking it himself. All laws or parts of laws that conflicted with the laws of the United States were declared null and void. After taking the required oath, the existing officers of the seceded states were to continue performing the functions of their respective offices till their successors should be duly elected or appointed. Also, the seceded states should, as soon as practical, reorganize and resume their former functions in the Union.

Thus we were to resume quietly our original position in the United States, the only exceptions being that our Negroes were free and no one of us could possess property of more value than twenty thousand dollars or more than one hundred bales of cotton. Very few of us in Grimes County were concerned with the second exception, however. The conditions were comparatively mild as the dictates of a conqueror and the misfortune of being conquered made it necessary that we should accept them in good faith, which we did.

Our county chief justice, Dr. George M. Patrick, having himself taken the oath, administered it to the ex-Confederate soldiers and officeholders of the county, including myself. We then proceeded to elect state, district, county, and beat officers. [In 1866] J. W. Throckmorton was elected governor of the state of Texas, Anthony M. Branch of Walker County was chosen as representative to Congress, and John R. Kennard of Grimes County was elected district judge. Dr. Patrick was reelected chief justice of Grimes County, while four county commissioners were elected, as well as two magistrates and one constable for each beat. Governor Throckmorton had been an avowed Unionist, and was one of seven members of the Convention of 1861 who refused to sign the Ordinance of Secession. But he had always behaved as a loyal citizen. Congressman Branch had been a captain in the Confederate army and a representative in the Confederate Congress. Judge Kennard had been a major in the Confederate army, and Judge Patrick had filled the office of chief justice during every term but one since the organization of the county in 1845.

We were now restored to the United States, and considered that the war was ended. But a majority of the federal congress repudiated President Johnson's clemency and determined that the South should be "reconciled," that is, that her people must be punished. Two members, John A. Logan and James A. Garfield, said that President Jefferson Davis and General Robert E. Lee should be put to death. Representative Branch went to Washington, D.C., to present his credentials, but was rejected. Congress ignored our governor, our legislature, all our state and county officers, and their official acts. It elected Colbert Caldwell judge of the district to replace Judge Kennard. Caldwell never held court, and the district was deprived of the administration of justice. Then E. M. Pease was appointed provisional governor and Throckmorton had to retire to private life.

I was yet too feeble to make a living by manual labor, and so I rented out my farm and took a school on the site of the present village of Bedias, in Grimes County, which I taught from the first day of November, 1865, till Christmas, 1866.

The United States Congress next appointed for each county a "bureau agent" to settle differences between white persons and "freedmen." Judicial authority was given to these agents, and they administered "law" without the assistance or restraint of juries. There was no appeal from their decisions. Most of these bureau agents had been lieutenants in the Federal army, and many of their decisions seemed to be favorable to Negroes and adverse to the white people, regardless of law or equity. Lieutenant Reiland, who was bureau agent for Grimes County, tried to administer justice equitably, however, and one of his acts was to administer the amnesty oath to me and others to whom Judge Patrick had already administered it.

The Federal colonel commanding the post at Millican reached the climax of injustice when he built a stockade in the vicinity of Millican. Its floor was twenty feet above the ground, surrounded by a tall balustrade, and it had no roof. He often arrested citizens without informing them of the offense they were arrested for. They were imprisoned in the stockade, exposed to all sorts of weather, and guarded by soldiers who stood around it on the ground below.

During 1867, yellow fever broke out in Huntsville, destroying one-third of its inhabitants, including many comrades of the Twenty-first Regiment. Among them was A. M. Branch, the rejected congressman from Texas.

The plague commenced in a valley and slowly climbed a steep hill into the heart of the town. Last of all, it attacked the penitentiary, and destroyed many of the guards and convicts. The officers and guards could have left the institution without violating any law, for Governor Pease had leased it to a Northern syndicate who refused to assume its duties until the plague ceased. But the men stayed on. Those who survived were nursed, unguarded, by fellow convicts, and all stayed at their posts except for four convalescent convicts who escaped while their guards and nurses were sticken.

One of those stricken was Colonel Gillaspie, who had been my captain in the Texas army and had fought at San Jacinto in 1836. He had been the first superintendent of the penitentiary and, being a brick mason by trade, he had built it, with convict labor, in 1846. Gillaspie and his wife and son died of the plague.

I returned to my farm and made a crop that year. I made two bales of cotton, but could not sell it till I made an affidavit that I had taken the amnesty oath. Thus I had to take the oath twice, and then swear that I had taken it.

Military Government

After General Ulysses S. Grant became President of the United States [in 1869,] it was decided that the South must be completely humbled. Accordingly, a general of the United States Army was appointed military governor of Texas.

Congress also decreed that no appointee to office in a state that had seceded should assume the duties of his office till he had taken what was called the "ironclad oath," that is, *he should swear that he had not willingly favored or supported any rebellion or conspiracy against the government of the United States, or given aid or support to her enemies.*

In consequence of this provision, the South was flooded with adventurers from the North, who came in search of position. These were termed "carpetbaggers," indicating that they brought nothing but their gripsacks, called carpetbags. Also, some Southern men who had willingly served the Confederacy took the ironclad oath to obtain office or position, and they were called "scalawags." These carpetbaggers and scalawags organized a secret political society called the "Loyal League," and they would not support any man for office who did not belong to their society, or who had not been nominated for office by the league. Thus, nearly all higher offices went to scalawags and carpetbaggers, while the lower offices went to Negroes, nearly all of whom were totally illiterate.

In 1868, with my health not restored, I again rented out my farm and taught school, this time in a neighborhood called Goshen, ten miles southwest of Huntsville. During that year, there was some excitement in the vicinity when piles of shavings and some boxes of matches were found under two stores. The immediate conclusion was that someone intended to burn the town. Certain actions of the bureau agent, named Butler, I believe, seemed to indicate that he had incited some Negroes to commit the supposed arson. Butler had told the Negroes that he would not permit any freedman to vote at a popular election unless he had first joined the Loyal League. Some of those who had joined were on their way to one of the League meetings, but professed to be going to a religious meeting and thus induced another Negro, who was not a Loyal Leaguer, to go with them. When he did not have the password, they accused him of being a spy and beat him severely. On being interrogated as to why they did so, they said that Butler had so instructed them. The white people became alarmed when the combustibles were found, and the premises were guarded all night by sentinels, but no further evidence of arson was found.

Bureau Agent Butler also tried to humiliate the white Democrats by sending Negroes to arrest a white man for an alleged offense. In order to counteract Butler's influence, the white people gave a barbecue dinner in a beautiful grove, to which they invited all white men and colored persons of both sexes. It was attended by about four hundred white men and about fifteen hundred Negroes. I was present, but did not partake of the dinner. Two sumptuous tables were spread, one for white men and the other for Negroes. Many speeches were delivered by both whites and Negroes.

Capt. Lew Hightower was master of ceremonies and principal orator. He invited each colored gentleman to conduct his lady to the table and thence to her seat. Most of the speakers censured Butler, who did not attend the meeting, for his alleged deception and tyranny and for his attempt to array the freedman against the white people. They professed gratitude to the freed people for the faithful service and protection they had given the white families during the war. They said that every free man had the right to vote as he pleased, "irrespective of race, color, or former condition of slavery," and also the right to affiliate himself with any political party that he chose. The colored orators professed obedience to the laws and love for the white people of the South, who had always been their best friends. Afterward, many freedmen became Democrats, and there were no more signs of arson.

In 1869 I returned from Goshen to Prairie Plains and taught the Prairie Plains school, renting a house nearby for myself and my family. I had rented my farm to a Negro named Sam, as I could not get a white tenant. I soon learned that the Negroes were expecting the federal government to appropriate all lands belonging to former secessionists and give the lands to the Negroes, and that many Negroes were already choosing the places they expected to occupy. My tenant, Sam, had decided that my farm would be his permanent home, and tried to avoid paying his rent. He also took the privilege of moving some of my fences, without permission. So I notified him that as soon as he should gather his crop, I must resume possession of my farm.

After this I tried to rent the land to other freedmen, but Sam was a popular Baptist preacher and so they refused, saying they did not want to dispossess Sam. Then I decided to reoccupy my farm myself, and he finally gave it up, but only after much praying that God would hasten the time when the land should be distributed to the freedmen.

In the autumn of 1869, I gave up my school and returned to my farm. I found that it needed to be enlarged and my rail fences needed repairing, so I tried to hire Negroes to make the rails. Three-fourths of a mile north of me was a plantation with many freedmen and their families, and, since their crops were laid by, I tried to hire them to make the rails. But they would not at first work for money. Their landlord had advanced them a year's provision, which they had wasted. Therefore, when these were gone and the Negroes were threatened with starvation, they reluctantly agreed to make my rails, for which I paid them in beef.

About two miles south of me was the house in which they held religious meetings, with preaching morning and night on Sunday, and prayer meeting one night in midweek. My house was between their quarters and their place of worship, but I had fenced in part of their path, a dim byway, so they went partly around my enclosure going to and from the church by day or night. They would ride through a brushy thicket nearby, making a great noise that much disturbed me and my family. But we had to endure it.

The Negroes of our vicinity knew that I was an honest and trustful man, and seemed to have confidence in me. At one of their local Loyal League meetings, they resolved to endorse me, without my knowledge or consent, to their county Loyal League convention for any office that I should desire, if I would join the League. But I respectfully declined their offer.

The military governor ordered an election, to be held at each county seat and to continue for four successive days. He appointed a presiding officer, who in turn appointed judges and clerks—all Republicans, of course. But every political party was to have an agent present, whose duty it was to object to illegal voters. Every voter was to be registered previous to the first day of the election, and for the purpose, a board of registrars, all Republicans, was appointed to register the voters.

When some colored voters were turned down in Grimes County because they were not legal voters, they made application a second time and in some cases were accepted. One instance was that of a smooth-faced colored boy named Tom. My brother-in-law, J. R. Edwards, was present when Tom applied for registration. Edwards objected, telling the board that the boy was only seventeen years old, and that the reason he knew this was that Tom had been born on his premises. So the board did not register him then, but later he returned and was registered, as their records proved. It was also believed that they registered some freedmen twice and refused to register many Democrats who were legally entitled to vote.

In August, 1870, the Twelfth Legislature passed the General Pension Act, which was approved by Governor Edmund J. Davis. It provided that every soldier who had served three months or more in the Texas army, commencing before the first day of July, 1836, and who had been honorably discharged should be entitled to an annual pension during his natural life of $250. Each pensioner who had been permanently disabled by wounds received in the war for Texas independence would get an annual pension of $500 during his natural life.

In order to collect this money, the applicant should present affidavits of himself and his witnesses to the state treasurer, declaring that he had performed the required service. He would then be issued a "pension certificate," which stated that the holder was entitled to the pension, and the amount he was to receive. Then, at the proper time and place, with evidence of his continued existence, the treasurer should pay the specified sum to the pensioner.[3]

But I judged that the act was dictated by policy. It was known that nearly all the pensioners were Democrats and had either participated in the Confederate army or sympathized with the Confederates during the war and, of course, were opposed to the tyrannical acts of the administration. I believed, therefore, that the real purpose of the act was to win over their influence to the dominant party. Nevertheless, I knew the act to be just, and determined to accept my part of the pension, but not to surrender my principles.

Accordingly, I secured the affidavits of Ben W. Robinson and Jonathan Collard, who had served with me during the San Jacinto campaign in 1836, and then I visited Austin.

The railroad northwest from Hempstead had been built to a point between Brenham and Austin. I went that far by railway and then on by stagecoach to the capital. I arrived there on the night of December 31, 1870, and took temporary board and lodging at the Avenue Hotel. Austin was then a small town, the population sparse and scattered, with most of its territory uninhabited.

The next morning, January 1, 1871, I went out to see the city and to look for a place to stay. I found that the entire space north of the

---

[3] H. P. N. Gammel, ed., *The Laws of Texas, 1822–1897*, VI, 292–293.

Capitol was an unsettled prairie, destitute of houses except for a private boardinghouse about a hundred yards away, operated by a Mrs. McCall.[4] I was directed there by Captain Freeman, who had commanded a company in the Twenty-first Regiment. The fare at this house was very good and Mrs. McCall was an excellent hostess. She had more than a hundred boarders. Her son, John D. McCall, later became mayor of Austin.

After breakfasting at Mrs. McCall's, I went to the Capitol, where I found almost a hundred veterans of the Texas Revolution who had come to prove their right as pensioners. Since that war, most of us had migrated to all settled parts of Texas and beyond, and very few had corresponded with one another. Consequently we thought that only about thirty of us were yet living, and now we greeted our old comrades as if they had arisen from their graves.

I presented my affidavits to Judge A. A. Bledsoe, at the comptroller's office, but he said that he and the Governor had agreed to guard against fraud by demanding additional evidence from the General Land Office, showing that we had received land for our service in the Texas army. So I went to the Land Office, and the chief clerk gave me a certificate stating that the records showed that as a soldier who served during the Battle of San Jacinto, I had received 640 acres of land.

Next I returned to the comptroller's office and presented this certificate, for which the comptroller gave me a pension certificate, stating my service and that I was entitled to an annual pension of $250. Now all I had to do was to present evidence of my continued existence, and he would issue to me a warrant on the state treasurer for $250, to be paid on or after the first day of January of each year during my natural life.[5]

But when I asked for my treasury warrant, the comptroller said that the legislature had appropriated only ten thousand dollars with which to pay the first year. Also, since the time between the date of

[4] Mrs. A. P. McCall lived at the southeast corner of Congress Avenue and Walnut Street (*Austin City Directory*, 1872).
[5] The *Texas Almanac for 1872* carried a list of pensioners who had been certified up to December 1, 1871. Zuber was among those named (p. 155).

the Pension Act, August 13, and the first day of January was only a fraction of a year, he and the governor had agreed to pay only $96 that year to the first applicants, knowing that the appropriation would be exhausted before half of the known pensioners could be paid. I appreciated the smallness of the appropriation, being sure that the legislature, like myself, had underestimated the number of veterans yet living. So I accepted the $96, even though it was not enough to pay me for the trouble and expense of going so far to get it.

This was the third day of January, and I was now ready to go home. The stagecoach would not leave till four o'clock the next morning, however, so I went into a room in the basement of the Capitol, where there was a comfortable fire, to warm myself. Many of my comrades had already gone home, but a few yet remained, and these were now talking over old times and enjoying the warm fire.

All were middle-aged men, except for one young man, and I thought they were all pensioners. One of them was a stranger who stared at me but did not speak. Some of my comrades lauded the legislators profusely for their liberality in granting us the pension, but I said that, considering their character, they probably were actuated by policy. Also, I said that I did not believe that the Governor was capable of an intentionally generous act toward us, as nearly all of us had been secessionists.

As soon as I finished, the young man said to the stranger who had stared at me, "Come, Governor, it is time for us to go upstairs." And the two departed.

If I had known that the Governor was present, I would not have said what I did. But I did not regret it, for I thought that he ought to know what self-respecting citizens thought of his administration. I now expected he might take revenge upon me; but, as it developed, I fear he may have taken it wholesale on all the veterans.

A few days later, when the legislature met again, both Governor Davis and Comptroller Bledsoe recommended that the Pension Act be repealed, as the number of pensioners so far exceeded what had been expected that it would bankrupt the state to pay them. The argument was valid, but it was an exercise of bad faith in the voluntary promise of the state and inconsistent, coming from Governor Davis, who, with his legislature, was exceedingly prodigal of public money and credit. The bill to repeal the Pension Act failed, for want of a majority of both branches of the legislature. But they also failed to make further appropriations for the payment. Thus the Pension Act remained unrepealed, but inoperative, till January, 1873.

At four o'clock on the morning of January 4, 1871, I departed for home. I went by stagecoach to the temporary terminus of the railroad, thence by railroad to Navasota, and thence on foot, twenty-seven miles, to Prairie Plains.

I worked very hard that year, but made a sorry crop. The weather was very changeable, alternating between flood and drought, so that I could not anticipate what it would be. My plantings of cotton were all at the wrong times, and I could not have a stand to come up. Twice the hot drought parched my seeds in the ground, and twice drenching rains packed the soil around the seeds and they rotted. I became greatly discouraged and sought for some other occupation than farming.

In the autumn of that year we had a general alarm throughout the state over an expected insurrection of the Negroes. They had been much disappointed on learning that the land, horses, cattle, and other stock of their former owners would not be seized and distributed among them. Some of them had even said it would have been better if they had not been set free, than to be free and homeless.

In November a report was circulated that a large body of Negroes was coming from the southern counties to burn the town of Bryan and a hundred or so excited white men armed themselves and rode down the road. Just south of the town they met about a thousand Negroes, all armed with six-shooters. The white men fired and the Negroes turned about and fled down the road in great confusion. The white men pursued them for several miles, continuing to fire, but finally the Negroes left the road and fled west to the Brazos bottom. The white men then returned to Bryan to help guard against any further attack, but no attack was made.

No white man was hurt, but the bodies of about fifty slain Negroes still armed with six-shooters, were counted in the road. No legal investigation was held of this affair, and no Negro would acknowledge that he had participated in it. About fifty Negroes of Grimes County were known to have been absent from home during this time, but later they would not tell where they had been.

A few days later, Governor Davis got a locomotive and three railroad passenger cars and, with part of his staff and a large number of Negroes, proceeded via Chapel Hill, Hempstead, Navasota, Bryan, Calvert, Bremond, and other towns to Groesbeck, in Limestone County, which was then the northern terminus of the Houston and Texas Central Railway. At Bremond they halted an hour or two while several men of the governor's staff explored the town, each with an arm linked in that of a Negro. At Groesbeck, the Governor held a brief consultation with a scalawag named [A.] Zadeck, who was mayor of the town. Then the Governor and his staff returned to Austin, leaving some of their Negro associates behind.

A Mr. [D. C.] Applewhite, an auctioneer from Houston, had gone with his wife to visit relatives in the older states, and a day or two after the Governor and his staff left Groesbeck, Applewhite and his wife arrived at the stage stand there, on their return home. Mayor Zadeck inquired if Applewhite was armed, and he replied that he was, since the law permitted travelers to go armed at that time. Zadeck then went over to some Negro policemen and whispered something. The Negroes ran toward Applewhite, but he fled through a storehouse into another street.

The Negroes followed Applewhite, so he halted and cried, "I surrender!" But someone shot him in the back and killed him.[6] Then the Negroes all fled. The entire town was instantly ablaze with indignation. The young men were eager to punish Zadeck, but the older men restrained them. Because of this disturbance, Governor Davis put Limestone County under martial law. After a long delay, Zadeck was brought to trial, and all the facts were proved. But the judge was also a scalawag and, with his obedient jury, caused Zadeck to be acquitted.

The murder of Applewhite aroused general indignation through-

[6] Applewhite was killed on September 30, 1871, by Mitchell Cotton, one of the Negro state police (W. C. Nunn, *Texas under the Carpetbaggers*, pp. 87–92).

out the state, and almost all newspapers condemned it severely. This brought out the Governor's militia, and, aided by the federal guards who yet infested the state, they gutted many of the presses. The murder also added to the general sense of insecurity that prevailed throughout the state and, very soon after, a report was circulated that the Negroes were conspiring to rise simultaneously on a certain night and kill all the white people. Its origin and spread were a mystery. Messengers were sent from house to house to warn every white family of the supposed danger, and families hastily assembled at convenient points for mutual protection. But no assault was made, and no Negro professed to know of the supposed conspiracy.

On the night set for the supposed uprising, some Negroes assembled near Prairie Plains for religious worship at their church and a number of armed white men appeared. Finding that the Negroes were not armed, the white men explained the cause of their visit and told them to disperse and go to their respective homes, which they immediately did. For several days thereafter, the white men kept watch over the Negroes by hunting with them, each white man alone with one Negro, but finally we were satisfied that no conspiracy existed.

In 1873, after my oldest daughter died, I sold my farm and livestock and moved with my family to Bremond, where I was a Bible agent. Then we moved to Owensville, about twelve miles east of Bremond. I found wood cheap and water free, and it was nearly like living in the country. Grass was bountiful, so I bought some milch cows, and we made our own milk and butter.

At Owensville I extended one of my trips south into the northern part of Brazos County, where I found a vacancy at a school for a session of five months. I accepted the job and dropped my book agency. In my article of agreement I promised to make it a free school, if possible. Otherwise, my patrons were to pay me at the rate of two dollars per month for each pupil subscribed. But I had been an ardent secessionist and was now an ardent states-right Democrat, and the existing powers were opposed to permitting any but radical Republicans to teach. Furthermore, the supervisor of this school district was an ignorant Negro, living in Houston, who did his work by having special deputies examine each applicant.

I engaged board and lodging with my friend John Walker, who was a former messmate from the army at San Jacinto. Then I went home and arranged to keep my family at Owensville, while I rode every Sunday evening down to John Walker's and every Friday evening back to Owensville. On Saturdays, however, I often rode to Bryan, eight miles south of my school, to try to procure an examination. But no person in the district was authorized to examine teachers except the Negro supervisor at Houston, and he, being incompetent, could act only through his special deputies.

When my term had nearly expired, a Republican named Mc-Carty said that he would examine me and send his report to the board of education in Austin. So, without a moment of drilling, I sat down and promptly answered every question he put to me for the next hour and a half, except for the last one. McCarty then closed his book and said he would refer my case to the board of education. Then he unceremoniously departed. McCarty did not assign me to any class of teachers, nor recommend any salary for me, and so I failed to be recognized as a public teacher.

The Texas Veterans Association

In June, 1872, at the Democratic State Convention at Corsicana, five veterans of the San Jacinto army met and passed resolutions requesting all veterans of the Texas Revolution to meet at the State Fair in Houston in March, 1873 to organize permanently. They also elected Col. John M. Swisher, who was not present, as temporary secretary of the general association to be formed. In all, their minutes covered one page of foolscap paper.

They mailed these minutes to Colonel Swisher, requesting that he publish them and call all veterans together to the appointed time and place. But Colonel Swisher did not perform his duty. In spite of this, some of the veterans met at the Navarro County Fair in Corsicana in September, 1872. This meeting was the embryo of the Texas Veterans Association.

Andrew McMillan, who resided two miles from Owensville, was a veteran of the San Jacinto army, and he and I visited the fair. We went to Calvert and took a late train, and, before we reached Corsicana, there were thirteen veterans in the car. We arrived in the night, and took entertainment at Miller's Hotel.

On the next morning, I found that of the veterans present, I had known only two during the San Jacinto campaign, William F. Williams of Falls County and Andrew McMillan, who had come with me. Each of us needed to be introduced by some man who was known to be a veteran soldier. McMillan had been sick during nearly all of the campaign and had formed but few acquaintances, but Williams was well known in the army. So I figured that he could vouch for me. But Williams did not recognize me, because on that campaign I had been a lad not quite sixteen years old. And so I began to remind him of things that had happened so long ago.

"You served in Capt. James Gillaspie's company?" I asked.

"So I did," said Williams.

"And I served in Capt. James Gillaspie's company."

"I knew every man in Gillaspie's company," said Williams.

"Then you knew me," I answered.

"No," said Williams. "I did not."

"I was one of the four young boys in the company."

"I knew three or four young boys in that company," said Williams.

"They were Bill Kennard, Sam Wiley, Alphonso Steele, and Bill Zuber," I said.

"I knew Kennard, Wiley, and Steele," said Williams. "But not Zuber."

"I will make you know me," I replied. "Do you remember the day on which the army marched from Donoho's near Groce's, to McCarley's on Spring Creek?"

"Yes, I remember," said Williams.

"You were on the rear guard that day."

"Yes, I was."

"Your guard had to rest very often to avoid crowding up on the army, which was in front of you."

"So we did."

"On such occasions, your guard rested at ease, lying down on the grass which skirted the road."

"So we did."

"On that guard was a lad whose dress was peculiar, and he was a little homesick and sad. He had large teeth, and you tried to cheer him by calling him 'the pretty little man with a mouthful of bones.' "

"Oh, yes! I remember that incident as if it had just happened, though I have not thought of it from that moment till this."

"A few days after the Battle of San Jacinto, when the army marched five miles up Buffalo Bayou and encamped, your men encamped in an isolated place in a thicket, about a hundred yards north of the general encampment."

"So we did."

"You boiled some shelled corn in a pot, and when it had cooled, you ate it with spoons. While you were eating it, I straggled to your camp and you hailed. 'Hello! Kentuck! How do you feel?' 'I'm sick.' 'Can we do anything for you?' you inquired. 'Yes,' I said. 'I think a dose of that boiled corn would cure me.' You said, 'Welcome! Help yourself.' Then one of your messmates said, 'Williams, who is that you are inviting to make free?' You said, 'Oh, it's one of my boys.' "

"I remember that, too, as clearly as if it just happened."

"Again, while we were marching west, after the Battle of San Jacinto, and had crossed the Brazos to the west edge of the bottom, many men of Gillaspie's company became sick. So the captain got permission from General Rusk to remain there for a few days and rest, after which we were to overtake the army."

"Yes, I know that to be true."

"You and Arnold's first lieutenant, Edwards, had been left behind, and you were pursuing the army on horseback when we arrived at our camp."

"I remember that."

"I was putting down some dough in a large Dutch oven to bake a loaf of bread. You said you had not tasted bread for a week, so I told you to wait till I baked it and I would divide with you both. So you waited, sitting on your horses. When it was baked, I divided the loaf into two halves, and one into quarters, and gave one quarter to you and the other to Edwards. Then you thanked me and departed."

"I remember all that. Don't tell me any more, for I now know you as well as any man in that army. You are a genuine soldier of the San Jacinto army."

About ten o'clock that morning other veterans arrived at the hotel, among whom was my friend Alphonso Steele, and there were now about thirty veterans of the Texas Revolution present. We organized by electing Capt. George B. Erath president, and Gen. Jerome B. Robertson secretary, both of whom were Democrats. Captain Erath was now quite old, very weak physically, and nearly blind, but his mental faculties were sound and fresh. General Robertson was also advanced in years, but still in the vigor of manhood. After transacting some business, which required only a few minutes of time, we resolved to meet at the State Fair at Houston in March, 1873, and to request all veterans of the Texas Revolution to meet with us.

I did not attend the meeting in Houston, but a large number of veterans did. They were bid welcome by citizens and then were entertained at the Market House, after which they were invited to meet at the State Fair in Houston in March each year thereafter, as long as any of us should live.

The veterans formed and adopted a constitution and organized by electing Col. Francis W. Johnson president, Capt. P. B. Dexter secretary, and Mr. Moses Austin Bryan assistant secretary. Mr. Bryan, who was a nephew of General Stephen F. Austin and had been his private secretary in the army in 1835, was first nominated for secretary, but he declined the honor as he did not live on a railroad and could not transmit and receive letters promptly. (He lived in Independence, Washington County, which then had no railroad.) But Mr. Bryan was the secretary in fact, as Captain Dexter did not do the writing. After that he was elected secretary during each of the next thirteen years, at the end of which time he was excused from further service on his own request.

The Association continued to meet at the State Fair at Houston from 1873 through 1878, when we received an invitation from citizens of Galveston to meet in their city on San Jacinto Day, April 21,

1879. Thenceforth, we met annually on that day, wherever we were invited, and were always entertained without charge. Besides this, the railroads annually tendered to us free passage to and from our place of meeting.

In 1880, the meeting was held at San Antonio, and it was the first time that I had met with them since the preliminary meeting in Corsicana in 1872.

No More Wars

In the fall of 1872 I had made two trips west in search of a permanent home, the first time going as far as Waco and Valley Mills, and the second time to Grandbury. I returned through Johnson, Hill, and Limestone counties, but the price of land had risen so that I did not feel able to purchase it.

Near Christmas that year, I paid one thousand dollars for two hundred acres of land, partly improved, about three and one-half miles northeast of Hearne. I lived there two years. The first years I farmed, but the second year I taught school on Heads Prairie, several miles from home. Hence, I had to board. In the fall of 1874 I sold my farm in Robertson County and purchased a farm of one hundred acres in the northern part of Grimes County, near Iola, in Anderson Prairie, where I lived for about twelve years.

In 1886 I sold this land to my two sons, D. C. and J. A. Zuber, in return for which they were to take care of me and my wife for the rest of our lives, though neither of us was then an invalid, and I was able to help supply our wants.

During the next twenty years, my wife and I lived with first one and then another of our children. Part of that time we lived in a small cottage which my son-in-law, Mr. Mize, erected for us a few hundred yards from their residence.

In 1904 my wife died, and two years later Mr. Mize decided to move to Austin. Therefore I went to the Capitol in search of something to do. Mr. [C. E.] Gilbert, then state superintendent of public grounds and buildings, insisted that I become the guide in the Senate Chamber, to explain certain pictures in the room, such as "The

Battle of San Jacinto." I gladly accepted, since I was acquainted with the subjects of that picture, and I took great pleasure in explaining it to many visitors.

The legislature has kindly honored me with this place in the Senate Chamber from term to term, up to the present, 1913, which honor I shall gratefully appreciate while I live. I love them all and wish them a long and useful life. Now, I am very feeble in body, but my mind is remarkably good, and I trust will continue so. I am near my ninety-third year, though my life seems short. All of my old comrades have passed away, and I, the last survivor, am yet spared. I give God the praise.

APPENDIX A

An Escape from the Alamo

This account is taken from W. P. Zuber's article on the escape of Moses Rose as published in the 1873 edition of *The Texas Almanac*. Those portions which are enclosed in brackets were not in the original account, but are quoted from another account by W. P. Zuber published in Mrs. Anna M. J. (Hardwick) Pennybacker's *History of Texas for Schools*, 1895.

PRAIRIE PLAINS, GRIMES COUNTY, TEXAS

MAY 7*th*, 1877

Editor Texas Almanac:

I regard the following account worthy of preservation, as it enhances a report of the last scene in the Alamo that has ever [sic] been made known to the survivors of those who fell in that fortress.

Moses Rose, a native of France, was an early immigrant to Texas, and resided in Nacogdoches, where my father, Mr. Abraham Zuber, made his acquaintance in 1827. I believe that he never married. My father regarded and treated him as a friend, and I have often heard him say that he believed Rose to be a man of strict veracity. In 1830, I saw him several times at my father's residence, in what is now San Augustine County [District of Aes]. He was then about forty-five years old, and spoke very broken English.

[He had been a soldier in Napoleon's army in the invasion of Russia and the retreat from Moscow. . . . Mr. Frost Thorn, of Nacogdoches, employed him as a messenger between that town and Natchitoches,

Louisiana. Said Thorn generally kept four wagons running between the two towns, carrying cotton and other produce to Natchitoches and returning with goods from Nacogdoches. He arranged with settlers on the road to repair his wagons and supply his teamsters with provender and provisions, on short credit. Rose's duty was to bear the money and pay the debts thus contracted. At the same time, he carried the mail between the two towns on private contract, there being no government mail on this route. Hence, I infer that he was trustworthy. . . . He was a close observer and had a retentive memory.]

Rose was a warm friend of Col. James Bowie, and accompanied or followed him to the Alamo in the fall of 1835, and continued with him till within three days of the fall of the fort.

During the last five days and nights of his stay, the enemy bombarded the fort almost incessantly, and several times advanced to the wall, and the men within were so constantly engaged that they ate and slept only at short intervals, while one body of the enemy was retiring to be relieved by another, yet they had not sustained a single loss.

The following is the substance of Rose's account of his escape and the circumstances connected therewith, as he related them to my parents, and they related them to me:

About two hours before sunset, on the third day of March, 1836, the bombardment suddenly ceased, and the enemy withdrew an unusual distance. Taking advantage of that opportunity, Col. Travis paraded all of his effective men in a single file; and, taking his position in front of the centre, he stood for some moments apparently speechless from emotion. Then, nerving himself for the occasion, he addressed them substantially as follows:

MY BRAVE COMPANIONS—Stern necessity compels me to employ the few moments afforded by this probably brief cessation of conflict in making known to you the most interesting, yet the most solemn, melancholy, and unwelcome fact that perishing humanity can realize. But how shall I find language to prepare you for its reception? I cannot do so. All that I can say to this purpose is, be prepared for the worst. I must come to the point. Our fate is sealed. Within a very few days—perhaps a very few hours—we must all be in eternity. This is our destiny, and we cannot avoid it. This is our *certain* doom.

I have deceived you long by the promise of help. But I crave your pardon, hoping that after hearing my explanation, you will not only regard my conduct as pardonable, but heartily sympathize with me in my extreme necessity. In deceiving you, I also deceived myself, having been first deceived [sic] by others.

I have continually received the strongest assurances of help from home. Every letter from the Council and every one that I have seen from individuals at home, has teemed with assurances that our people were ready, willing, and anxious to come to our relief; and that within a very short time we might confidently expect recruits enough to repel any force that would be brought against us. These assurances I received as facts. They inspired me with the greatest confidence that our little band would be made the nucleus of an army of sufficient magnitude to repel our foes, and to enforce peace on our own terms. In the honest and simple confidence of my heart, I have transmitted to you these promises of help, and my confident hopes of success.—But the promised help has not come and our hopes are not to be realized.

I have evidently confided too much in the promises of our friends. But let us not be in haste to censure them. The enemy has invaded our territory much earlier than we anticipated; and their present approach is a matter of surprise. Our friends were evidently not informed of our perilous condition in time to save us. Doubtless they would have been here by the time they expected any considerable force of the enemy. When they find a Mexican army in their midst, I hope they will show themselves true to their cause.

My calls on Col. Fannin remain unanswered, and my messengers have not returned. The probabilities are that his whole command has fallen into the hands of the enemy, or been cut to pieces, and that our couriers have been cut off.

I trust that I have now explained my conduct to your satisfaction and that you do not censure me for my course.

I must again refer to the assurances of help from home. *They are what deceived me, and they caused me to deceive you.* Relying upon those assurances, I determined to remain within these walls until the promised help should arrive, stoutly resisting all assaults from without. Upon the same reliance, I retained you here, regarding the increasing force of our assailants with contempt, till they outnumbered us more than twenty to one, and escape became impossible. For the same reason, I scorned their demand of a surrender at discretion and defied their threat to put every one of us to the sword, if the fort should be taken by storm.

I must now speak of our present situation. Here we are, surrounded by an army that could almost eat us for breakfast, from whose arms our lives are, for the present, protected by these stone walls. We have no hope for help, for no force that we could ever reasonably have expected, could cut its way through the strong ranks of these Mexicans. We dare not surrender; for, should we do so, that black flag, now waving in our sight, as well as the merciless character of our enemies, admonishes us of what would be our doom. We cannot cut our way out through the enemy's ranks; for, in attempting that, we should all be slain in less than ten minutes. Nothing remains then, but to stay within this fort, and fight to the last moment. In this case, we must, sooner or later, all be slain; for I am sure that Santa Anna is determined to storm the fort and take it, even at the greatest cost of the lives of his own men.

Then we must die! Our speedy dissolution is a fixed and inevitable fact.—Our business is, not to make a fruitless effort to save our lives, but to choose the manner of our death. But three modes are presented to us. Let us choose that by which we may best serve our country. Shall we surrender, and be deliberately shot, without taking the life of a single enemy? Shall we try to cut our way out through the Mexican ranks, and be butchered before we can kill twenty of our adversaries? I am opposed to either method; for in either case, we could but lose our lives, without benefiting our friends at home—our fathers and mothers, our brothers and sisters, our wives and little ones. The Mexican army is strong enough to march through the country, and exterminate its inhabitants, and our countrymen are not able to oppose them in open field. My choice, then, is to remain in this fort, to resist every assault, and to sell our lives as dearly as possible.

Then let us band together as brothers, and vow to die together. Let us resolve to withstand our adversaries to the last; and, at each advance, to kill as many of them as possible. And when, at last, they shall storm our fortress, let us kill them as they come! kill them as they scale our walls! kill them as they leap within! kill them as they raise their weapons, and as they use them! kill them as they kill our companions! and continue to kill them as long as one of us shall remain alive!

By this policy, I trust that we shall so weaken our enemies that our countrymen at home can meet them on fair terms, cut them up, expel them from the country, and thus establish their own independence, and secure prosperity and happiness to our families and our country. And, *be assured*, our memory will be gratefully cherished by posterity, till all history shall be erased, and all noble deeds shall be forgotten.

But I leave every man to his own choice. Should any man prefer to surrender, and be tied and shot; or to attempt an escape through the Mexican ranks, and be killed before he can run a hundred yards, he is at liberty to do so.

My own choice is to stay in this fort, and die for my country, fighting as long as breath shall remain in my body. *This I will do, even if you leave me alone.* Do as you think best—but no man can die with me without affording me comfort in the moment of death.

Colonel Travis then drew his sword and with its point traced a line upon the ground extending from the right to the left of the file. Then, resuming his position in front of the center, he said, "I now want every man who is determined to stay here and die with me to come across this line. Who will be the first? March!"

The first respondent was Tapley Holland, who leaped the line at a bound, exclaiming, "I am ready to die for my country!" His example was instantly followed by every man in the file, with the exception of Rose. Manifest enthusiasm was universal and tremendous. Every sick man that could walk arose from his bunk and tottered across the line. Col. Bowie, who could not leave his bed, said, "Boys, I am not able to go to you, but I wish some of you would be so kind as to remove my cot over there." Four men instantly ran to the cot and, each lifting a corner, carried it across the line. Then every sick man that could not walk made the same request, and had his bunk removed in like manner.

Rose, too, was deeply affected, but differently from his companions. He stood till every man but himself had crossed the line. A consciousness of the real situation overpowered him. He sank upon the ground, covered his face, and yielded to his own reflections. For a time he was unconscious of what was transpiring around him. A bright idea came to his relief; he spoke the Mexic[a]n dialect very fluently, and could he once get safely out of the fort he might easily pass for a Mexican and effect an escape. He looked over the area of the fort; every sick man's berth was at its wonted place; every effective soldier was at his post, as if waiting orders; he felt as if dreaming.

He directed a searching glance at the cot of Col. Bowie. There lay his gallant friend. Col. David Crockett was leaning over the cot, conversing with its occupant in an undertone. After a few seconds Bowie looked at Rose and said, "You seem not to be willing to die with us, Rose." "No," said Rose, "I am not prepared to die, and shall not do so if I can avoid it." Then Crockett also looked at him, and said,

"You may as well conclude to die with us, old man, for escape is impossible."

Rose made no reply, but looked up at the top of the wall. "I have often done worse than to climb that wall," he thought. Suiting the action to the thought he sprang up, seized his wallet of unwashed clothes, and ascended the wall. Standing on its top, he looked down within to take a last view of his dying friends. They were all now in motion, but what they were doing he heeded not. Overpowered by his feelings he looked away and saw them no more.

Looking down without, he was amazed at the scene of death that met his gaze. From the wall to a considerable distance beyond the ground was literally covered with slaughtered Mexicans and pools of blood.

He viewed this horrid scene but a moment. He threw down his wallet and leaped after it; he alighted on his feet, but the momentum of the spring threw him sprawling upon his stomach in a puddle of blood. After several seconds he recovered his breath, he arose and took up his wallet; it had fallen open and several garments had rolled out upon the blood. He hurriedly thrust them back, without trying to cleanse them of the coagulated blood which adhered to them. Then, throwing the wallet across his shoulders he walked rapidly away.

He took the road which led down the river around a bend to the ford, and through the town by the church. He waded the river at the ford and passed through the town. He saw no person in town, but the doors were all closed, and San Antonio appeared as a deserted city.

After passing through town he turned down the river. A stillness as of death prevailed. When he had gone about a quarter of a mile below the town his ears were saluted by the thunder of the bombardment, which was then renewed. That thunder continued to remind him that his friends were true to their cause, by a continual roar, with but slight intervals, until a little before sunrise on the morning of the sixth, when it ceased and he heard it no more.

At twilight he recrossed the river on a footlog about three miles below the town. He then directed his course eastwardly towards the Guadalupe river, carefully bearing to the right to avoid the Gonzales road.

On the night of the third he traveled all night, but made but little progress as his way was interrupted by large tracts of cactus or prickly pear which constantly gored him with thorns and forced him out of his course. On the morning of the fourth he was in a wretched plight for traveling, for his legs were full of thorns and very sore. The thorns were very painful, and continued to work deeper into the flesh till they produced chronic sores, which are supposed to have terminated his life.

Profiting by experience, he traveled no more at night, but on the two evenings following he made his bed on the soft mesquite grass. On the sixth of March he crossed the Guadalupe by rolling a seasoned log into the water and paddling across with his hands. He afterwards crossed the Colorado in the same manner.

[After ascending a high bluff—the east bank of the Guadalupe—he found himself at a deserted house, at which he found plenty of provisions and cooking vessels. There he took his first nourishment after leaving the Alamo. Travel had caused the thorns to work so deep in that flesh that he could not bear the pain of pulling them out, and he had become lame. There he rested two or three days, hoping that his lameness would subside, but it rather grew worse. Thenceforth he traveled on roads, subsisting, except in the instance to be noted, on provisions which he found in deserted houses. The families were retreating before the threatened advance of the enemy, and between the Guadalupe and Colorado every family on his route had left home. Between the Colorado and the Brazos he found only one family at home. With them he stayed during a considerable time; but probably from want of knowledge or skill, they did nothing to relieve his sore legs.]

He continued his journey toilsomely, tediously and painfully for several weeks, in which time he encountered many hardships and dangers which for want of space can not be inserted here. He finally arrived at the residence of my father on Lake Creek, in what is now Grimes County.

My parents had seen, in the Telegraph and Texas Register, a partial list of those who had fallen at the Alamo, and in it had observed the name of Rose. Having not heard of his escape, they had no doubt that he had died with his companions. On his arrival, my father recognized him instantly, and exclaimed, "My God! Rose, is this you, or is it your ghost?" "This is Rose, and not a ghost," was the reply.

My mother caused her washing servant to open Rose's wallet, in her presence, and found some of the garments glued together with the blood in which they had fallen when thrown from the Alamo.

My parents also examined his legs, and by the use of forceps extracted an incredible number of cactus thorns, some of them an inch and a half in length, each of which drew out a lump of flesh and was followed by a stream of blood. Salve [which my mother made] was applied to his sores and they soon began to heal.

Rose remained at my father's between two and three weeks, during which time his sores improved rapidly, and he hoped soon to be well. He then left for home. We had reliable information of him but once after his departure. He had arrived at his home in Nacogdoches, but traveling on foot had caused his legs to inflame anew, and his sores had grown so much worse that his friends thought that he could not live many months. That was the last that we heard of him.

During his stay at my father's Rose related to my parents an account of what transpired in the Alamo before he left it, of his escape, and of what befell him afterwards, and at their request he rehearsed it several times (till my mother could have repeated it as well as he). Most of the minutia[e] here recorded were elicited by particular inquiries. In the following June I returned home from the Texas army, and my parents several times rehearsed the whole account to me. . . .

[I admired the sentiments of Travis' speech even as they had come to me third-handed, and . . . I regretted the apparent impossibility of the speech being preserved for posterity. In 1871 I determined to commit it to paper and try by rearrangement of its disconnected parts to restore its form as a speech. I had enjoyed a slight personal acquaintance with Colonel Travis, had heard repetitions of some of his remarks as a lawyer before the courts, and had read printed copies of some of his dispatches from the Alamo. After refreshing my memory by repeated conversations with my mother, I wrote the sentiments of the speech in what I imagined to be Travis' style, but was careful not to change the sense. I devoted several weeks of time to successive rewritings and transpositions of the parts of that speech. This done, I was surprised at the geometrical neatness with which the parts fitted together.]

Of course it is not pretended that Col. Travis' speech is reported literally, but the ideas are precisely those he advanced, and most of the language is also nearly the same.

Hoping that this letter may meet your approval and be interesting to your readers, I am, gentlemen, most respectfully, your humble correspondent,

                                                                    W. P. ZUBER

I have carefully examined the foregoing letter of my son, William P. Zuber, and feel that I can endorse it with the greatest propriety. The arrival of Moses Rose at our residence, his condition when he came, what transpired during his stay, and the tidings that we afterwards heard of him, are all correctly stated. The part which purports to be Rose's statement of what he saw and heard in the Alamo, of his escape, and of what befell him afterwards is precisely the substance of what Rose stated to my husband and myself.

MARY ANN ZUBER

APPENDIX B

Historiography of the Account of Moses Rose and the Line That Travis Drew

BY LLERENA FRIEND

In May of 1871, W. P. Zuber sent to the editor of the *Texas Almanac* a manuscript entitled "An Escape from the Alamo." The article appeared in the *Almanac* for 1873. In his conclusion Zuber wrote: "Of course it is not pretended that Col. Travis' speech is reported literally, but the ideas are precisely those he advanced, and most of the language is almost nearly the same."[1]

Among those who were excited and inspired by the story of the Travis challenge and line of March 3, 1836, was Sidney Lanier, a visitor in Texas. He recounted the dramatic episode in his "San Antonio de Bexar," also published in 1873.[2] In 1874, in New York, the United States Publishing Company issued James M. Morphis' *History of Texas from Its Discovery and Settlement*, including "An Escape from the Alamo" as

[1] *Texas Almanac for 1873,* p. 84.
[2] William Corner, in 1890, used the Lanier material in his *San Antonio de Bexar, a Guide and History.*

it had apeared in the *Almanac.* In his footnote, Morphis stated that
he took "this account of Mr. Rose, *cum grano salis,* but it may be true."[3]

There must have been some official questioning of the accuracy of the
Zuber account. On September 14, 1877, Zuber wrote to Adj. Gen. William
Steele that he had himself composed the Travis speech in an effort
to show that Travis had explained to his men the actual situation at the
Alamo and had offered them the choice of risking the chances of surrender
or escape.[4]

Homer S. Thrall's *Pictorial History of Texas,* published in 1879, discredited
the Zuber story but erred in saying that in 1860 Rose himself
published the story of his escape. Thrall stated categorically: "This tale
is incredible, since he reported large pools of blood in the ditch, close
to the wall, when no Mexican had then approached within rifle shot."[5]

Thrall's *Pictorial History* had wide circulation, but it could not compare
in distribution or appeal with Anna M. J. (Hardwick) Pennybacker's
*A New History of Texas for Schools, also for General Reading
and for Teachers Preparing for Examination,* published by the author,
a teacher at Tyler, Texas, in 1888. That book was to go through six
future editions, and, although the last three revisions, in 1907, 1912,
and 1924, omitted the story of Moses Rose and Travis' last speech, for
the generations who learned their Texas history from Pennybacker, the
line drawn by Travis' sword made a lasting imprint.

In her 1888 *History,* Mrs. Pennybacker explained how Rose's escape
preserved the story of the Travis stand, which she described as an "imaginary
speech" written by "some unknown author."[6]

In 1894, the annual meeting of the Texas Veterans Association was
held in Waco. Dr. Rufus C. Burleson's address of welcome to the old
soldiers and their families included a mention of the Travis Speech and
of the line Travis drew. When Mrs. Georgia J. Burleson compiled *The
Life and Writings of Rufus C. Burleson,* 1901, one of the chapters was
titled "Mrs. Dickenson, the Heroine of the Alamo" and another "The
Siege and Fall of the Alamo." Mrs. Dickenson, said Burleson, "has often

[3] James M. Morphis, *A History of Texas from Its Discovery and Settlement,*
pp. 179–184.

[4] As explained by Walter Lord, *A Time to Stand,* pp. 201–204.

[5] Homer S. Thrall, *A Pictorial History of Texas from the Earliest of European
Adventures to A.D. 1879,* p. 242.

[6] Anna M. J. (Mrs. Percy V.) Pennybacker, *A New History of Texas for
Schools* (1888), pp. 71–74, 73 n., and 75 n.

told men of that solemn hour when the heroic Travis drew a long line with his sword."[7]

In 1894 Mrs. Pennybacker was working on a revision of her book. Evidently she had learned the name of the author of "An Escape from the Alamo" and addressed some questions to him. In preparation of her revisions it had become her custom to address many inquiries to the State Library, to public officials who could bring her up to date on state matters, to faculty members of Texas A. & M., to The University of Texas, and to Texas veterans. On January 2, 1895, W. P. Zuber wrote Mrs. Pennybacker of his admiration of her history book. He said he had detected a mistake, and he would make notes for its correction as soon as he had time. On March 13 he undertook to reply to three of her questions: Why did not more men come sooner to Travis' aid? What did Zuber think of Governor Smith and the Council? Why was the date of Travis' speech March 3 instead of March 4? Incidentally, he confided that he too was preparing a historical work on Texas veterans and enclosed two manuscripts: a twelve-page history of the Texas Veterans Association and an account of Rose's escape marked "For Private Consideration."[8]

The 1895 edition of *A New History for Texas Schools* gave the account of Travis' speech and identified its source in a footnote: "Captain W. P. Zuber, a Texas veteran tried and true, is the author of the following version of Travis' speech. He writes: "This does not claim to be a literal reproduction, but it is substantially what Travis said!' " For authentication, Mrs. Pennybacker added that Guy M. Bryan, nephew of Stephen F. Austin, said that Zuber "writes clearly, logically, truthfully, and conscientiously." As supplementary reading for her chapter on the Texas Revolution, she included "An Account of the Adventures of Moses Rose, Who Escaped from the Alamo."[9]

In a letter to Z. T. Fulmore, one of his fellow contributors to the *Quarterly of the Texas State Historical Association*, Zuber described his almost paternal solicitude for the Pennybacker *History*. The corrections he had offered and the items he had supplied were "solicited by the authoress," whom he had never seen. He had declined any payment be-

---

[7] Mrs. Georgia J. Burleson, comp., *The Life and Writings of Rufus C. Burleson*, pp. 736–740, 815–817.

[8] W. P. Zuber to Mrs. Pennybacker, January 2, 1895, March 9, 1895, March 13, 1895, Pennybacker Papers, The University of Texas Archives, Austin.

[9] Pennybacker, *New History of Texas* (1895), pp. 139–140, 183–188.

cause the privilege of helping in a small way to educate the children of
Texas he regarded as ample compensation.[10]

The Pennybacker revisions in 1898 and 1900 followed the 1895 edition in presenting the story of the Rose escape and the Travis speech.
By the time the 1907 edition was published the situation had changed.

Zuber was one of the earliest members of the Texas State Historical
Association and contributed articles to the first two volumes of its *Quarterly* in July, 1897, October, 1898, and January, 1899. In the fall of
1900, the *Quarterly*'s editor, Professor George P. Garrison of the history
department of The University of Texas, invited Zuber to be in Austin
for the next meeting of the Texas Veterans Association.[11] Zuber was
present for the reunion in Austin in April, 1901, and asked as a point of
personal privilege that he be allowed to read a statement relative to
Moses Rose's escape from the Alamo. That statement was printed in
the *Quarterly* for July, 1901, as "The Escape of Rose from the Alamo."
He had asked to speak in self-defense, as he had been informed that his
account published in 1873 had been contradicted. Because that contra-
diction, however unreliable, had made an impression on well-meaning
persons, he felt called upon to elaborate. He had no anxiety about questions of his veracity.[12]

For the next issue of the *Quarterly*—that of October, 1901—Zuber
had some contributions for the section "Notes and Fragments," one of
them being further defense of his story of Rose's escape, and one being
a correction of Mrs. Adele B. Looscan's article, "Decimation of the Mier
Prisoners." As a result, Garrison received some "Notes written to the
editor." Mrs. Looscan observed that she might have known her error
would not escape the observant eye of Mr. Zuber and that she could but
admire "the old gentleman's painstaking accuracy of statement and his
remarkable fund of information." In a different vein, H. A. McArdle
volunteered for the *Quarterly* a four-thousand-word article, "Imposters
of the Alamo," to include Rose and Madame Candelaria.[13]

[10] Zuber to Z. T. Fulmore, November 9, 1899, Fulmore Papers, The University of Texas Archives, Austin.

[11] Zuber to George P. Garrison, November 29, 1900, Garrison Papers, The University of Texas Archives, Austin.

[12] W. P. Zuber, "The Escape of Rose from the Alamo," *Quarterly of the Texas
State Historical Association*, 5, no. 1 (July, 1901), 1–11.

[13] Adele B. Looscan to G. P. Garrison, October 21, 1901; H. A. McArdle to
Garrison, November 28, 1901, Garrison Papers.

Zuber's next article, in the *Quarterly* for January, 1902, was entitled "Last Messenger from the Alamo," to counter a speech made by Mrs. Looscan for the Daughters of the Republic of Texas. Zuber emphasized the time of John W. Smith's departure from the Alamo because of its bearing on the reality of Travis' speech as Zuber had reported it.[14] Zuber and his wife attended the Veterans Association meeting at Lampasas in April, 1902. On May 15, he wrote Garrison that at the Lampasas meeting Eugene C. Barker had kindly suggested that "for the satisfaction of many investigators of Texas history, it would be proper for me to explain why I did not publish Rose's Escape from the Alamo earlier than the year 1873."[15] Because he recognized the propriety of the Barker suggestion, Zuber sent with his letter his jusification for the delay. The explanation appeared in the *Quarterly* for July, 1902. His account of the Rose escape, he said, was written as incidental to and proof of his version of the substance of Travis' last speech to his comrades. That speech, as recounted by Rose to Zuber's parents and by them to Zuber, he rewrote and transposed again and again. Summing up, he said: "Prior to 1871, I did not believe that the substance of Colonel Travis's last speech could be rescued from oblivion." When he had rescued the gist and spirit, he sent the manuscript to the editor of the *Almanac*. T. P. Buffington of Anderson wrote to Zuber early in 1903 requesting facts concerning some of the original Texas settlers. The Zuber answer, in true Zuber style, runs to seventeen pages of typescript. It includes the statement: "Travis drew a line. Tapley Holland was the first man to cross it."[16]

In 1907, 1912, and 1924 the Pennybacker *History for Texas Schools* carried the Travis letter of February 24, 1836, printed and in facsimile, but there was no mention of Rose or his story. This followed the pattern set by G. P. Garrison in *Texas: A Contest of Civilizations*, published by Houghton Mifflin in 1903. In 1912 came the first book to rival the Pennybacker for use in the Texas schools. This was *A School History of Texas* by Eugene C. Barker, Charles Shirley Potts, and Charles W. Ramsdell. On page 120 a footnote stated: "Captain W. P. Zuber, a

[14] W. P. Zuber, "The Last Messenger from the Alamo," *Quarterly of the Texas State Historical Association*, 5, no. 3 (January, 1902), 263–266.

[15] Zuber to Garrison, May 15, 1902, Garrison Papers.

[16] Zuber to T. P. Buffington, June 26, 1903, typescript in L. W. Kemp notes to Zuber, The University of Texas Archives, Austin.

prominent member of the Texas Veterans' Association, says that his mother used to tell him that a man named Rose came to her house, and telling her of Travis' speech, said that he took advantage of the permission to escape. But we must be very sure of our facts in history before accepting them, and in this case we cannot be sure that Rose was telling the truth."

The years passed; research went on in Texas history. In 1930 Ruby Mixon worked on a biography of Travis and earnestly sought an answer. She found that the accounts of the last seventy-two hours of Travis' life were based upon legend, fact, and fiction so confused as to "constitute a veritable Gordian knot." After painstaking analysis, she decided that no one could say positively whether the account of the Travis line was true or false.[17]

Amelia Williams wrote a dissertation with the title "A Critical Study of the Siege of the Alamo and of the Personnel of Its Defenders." She relegated the Moses Rose story to a footnote with the conclusion: "Historians have been divided in their opinion concerning this story, the most careful students having discredited it. At best they consider it a legend, plausible perhaps, but almost certainly the creation of a vivid imagination."[18]

And visitors to the Alamo continue to ask: "Where did Travis stand when he drew the line?" In 1939 the Texas Folklore Society's annual publication was called *In the Shadow of History*. Its first section, called "Rose and the Alamo," contained three articles: "The Line That Travis Drew," by J. Frank Dobie; "An Escape from the Alamo," by W. P. Zuber; and "A Vindication of Rose and His Story," by R. B. Blake. Dobie traced the treatment of the story in Texas histories, and Blake recorded evidence to prove that Rose did escape from the Alamo and was a credible witness. On March 31, 1940, Dobie's weekly article in the *Dallas News* also bore the title "The Line That Travis Drew." Dobie alluded to the Blake vindication of the Rose story and to Rufus Burleson's account of Mrs. Dickenson and her story of the long line, and the Bowie cry of "Boys, do take me over." His own conclusion was: "The

[17] Ruby Mixon, "William Barrett Travis, His Life and Letters," M.A. thesis, The University of Texas (1930), pp. 258–270.

[18] Amelia Williams, "A Critical Study of the Siege of the Alamo and of the Personnel of Its Defenders," *Southwestern Historical Quarterly*, 37 (1933), 31.n.

old story, the cherished story, the heroic story of the line that Travis drew seems to me vindicated sufficiently for credence. The mere absence of documentary proof never repudiated it anyhow." An editorial in the *Wichita Times* for April 7, 1940, summed up the Dobie article: "This new evidence does not give the story absolute confirmation, but it should be comforting to those who want so much to believe. Probably there never will be definitive proof of either the truth or falsity of the story; but those who want to believe have good basis for believing, and they will greatly outnumber the scholarly doubters."

Among the scholarly doubters was Claude Elliott, who reviewed *In the Shadow of History* for the *Southwestern Historical Quarterly.* For his money, the Dobie and Blake articles both properly belonged only in the shadow of history, even if they did give historical evidence. There might be proof that Rose had lived and was fairly reliable, but, in Elliott's opinion, "in spite of all this the fertile imagination of W. P. Zuber, to whom we are solely indebted for the Rose story, must be dealt with."[19]

Elliott was at one time president of the Texas State Historical Association, as was Dr. P. I. Nixon of San Antonio. The Program for the Fiesta de San Jacinto for 1947 featured a biographical sketch and painting of Tapley Holland. Dr. Nixon wrote the biography and quoted Sidney Lanier's description of March 3, 1836, as "one of the most pathetic days of time," noting that the first to respond to Travis was Tapley Holland. The Warren Hunter painting depicts Holland stepping across the line.

George Sessions Perry wrote in 1952 of the line that Travis drew and said of Rose: "He knew that he was in the midst of a great, almost religious experience and that he was befouling it. He sank to the ground and sat on his feet and trembled. But he belonged on a certain side of the line and he remained there. Soon, then, the men boosted him over the wall so that he could run away, and they felt cleansed and ready to fight."[20]

In 1959 came Ramsey Yelvington's *A Cloud of Witnesses: The Drama of the Alamo.* Interpreting the story with poetic license, Yelvington depicts the men swayed by Travis' ardor:

[19] Claude Elliott, review of *In the Shadow of History, Southwestern Historical Quarterly,* 47 (April, 1940), 532–533.
[20] George Sessions Perry, *Texas, a World in Itself,* pp. 277–279.

Here I draw a blood-red line
For you to cross
Or stay behind.
Who will be first
To follow me,
To throw down his life
For Liberty?

And Satan, disguised as a colonist, steps front stage to say: "And now may I have just a moment to explain why I didn't cross over the line? Because, like all myths and legends that spring up without corroboration from the most unlikely situations, this scene never happened. It's rank fiction. It's pure myth. There was never any line to cross over!"[21]

When Lon Tinkle wrote his gripping story of the days preceding the glory of the Alamo, he also had to choose between the line or no line. His conclusion was that the Rose story is "of all the incomplete and un-proved stories about the Alamo, the most dramatic and most plausible. Whether one is to believe it depends upon one's willingness to listen to a single voice giving evidence no one else can verify."[22]

Then came Walter Lord's *A Time to Stand* and the question about the Alamo, never to be satisfactorily answered: Did Travis draw a line? Lord doubts that he did, but admits that there is room to speculate and opines that every good Texan can follow J. K. Beretta's advice: "Is there any proof that Travis didn't draw the line? If not, then let us believe it."[23]

But every now and again the story is published anew. In *Texas Parade*, October, 1968, Elinor Horwitz, without documentation but with com-pleteness, recounts the story, with the original title of 1873: "Escape from the Alamo."

And then there is John Wayne's extravaganza called *The Alamo*. Apparently it votes for the line and against Rose. The news release for the movie gives the tenth day of the siege as the moment of truth when Travis at last assembled his men in the courtyard and gave them the choice of staying with him to the end or of escaping over the wall. And the script runs: "To the last man they chose to stay."

[21] Ramsey Yelvington, *A Cloud of Witnesses*, pp. 72–73.
[22] Lon Tinkle, *13 Days to Glory: The Siege of the Alamo*, p. 179.
[23] Walter Lord, *A Time to Stand*, pp. 201–204.

BIBLIOGRAPHY

COMPILED BY LLERENA FRIEND

Works by Zuber

Any Zuber bibliography, of printed or manuscript materials, will be fragmentary. He wrote too much to too many people over too long a time for there to be any possibility of assembling all his letters—or the essays on assorted topics in Texas history that frequently accompanied the letters. He said that he kept a diary. One diary he ruined by spilling ink on it; at least one was lost; but where are the others? He submitted articles to the *Texas Almanac* and to various Texas newspapers, but only fugitive pieces can be located or dated. Various diaries and personal memoranda are said still to be in existence, but these are not in the Austin collections or in the possession of the Zuber family. The following listing, then, is limited to suggested reference material readily available.

PUBLISHED WORKS

1860. "The Baggage-Guard Detached to Protect the Sick and Baggage at the Time of the Battle of San Jacinto." In *Texas Almanac for 1861*, pp. 58–60. Galveston: W. and D. Richardson.

1872. "An Escape from the Alamo." In *Texas Almanac for 1873*, pp. 80–85. Galveston: Richardson, Belo and Co.

1882. "The Burning of the Bodies of the Heroes of the Alamo. Now First Published. First Account of the Massacre of the Alamo, March 6, 1836. Most Horrible Recital on Record. Bodies of the Texas Heroes Burned in a Heap. How Santa Anna Thrust his Sword through the Dead Body of Travis. Col. Bowie's Tongue Cut Out, and the Living Body Thrown into the Flames." *Houston Post*, March 1.

Reprinted in A. J. Sowell, *Rangers and Pioneers of Texas with a Concise Account of the Early Settlements, Hardships, Massacres, Battles and Wars, by Which Texas Was Rescued from the Rules of the Savage and Consecrated to the Empire of Civilization,* pp. 146–150. N.p., 1884.

    Also reprinted by Edward G. Rohrbough as "How Jim Bowie Died." Published in *In the Shadow of History,* pp. 48–52. Texas Folklore Society Publication, 15. Austin, 1939.

1885. "Address to the People of Texas in Relation to Greer County Matters." *Dallas Herald,* October 8.

1890. "Response to Address of Welcome."   In *Proceedings of the Texas Veterans Association,* pp. 2–7. Austin.

1896. "To Miss Betty Ballinger . . . and Miss Carrie F. Kemp . . ." In *Proceedings of the Texas Veterans Association,* p. 17. Austin.

1897. "Thompson's Clandestine Passage around Nacogdoches," *Quarterly of the Texas State Historical Association,* 1, no. 1 (July), 68–70.

1898. "The Murder of the Taylors by the Indians." *Quarterly of the Texas State Historical Association,* 2, no. 2 (October), 177–178.

1899. "Captain Adolphus Sterne." *Quarterly of the Texas State Historical Association,* 2, no. 3 (January), 211–216.

1899. "To Hon. F. R. Lubbock [In re death of William E. Kennard]." In *Proceedings of the Texas Veterans Association,* p. 10. Austin.

1900. "Declaration of Texas Independence." *Galveston News,* June 24.

1901. "The Escape of Rose from the Alamo." *Quarterly of the Texas State Historical Association,* 5, no. 1 (July), 1–11.

1901. "The Escape of Rose from the Alamo." *Quarterly of the Texas State Historical Association,* 5, no. 2 (October), 164.

1901. "The Number of Decimated Mier Prisoners." *Quarterly of the Texas State Historical Association,* 5, no. 2 (October), 165–168.

1902. "The Last Messenger from the Alamo." *Quarterly of the Texas State Historical Association,* 5, no. 3 (January), 263–266.

1902. "Rose's Escape from the Alamo." *Quarterly of the Texas State Historical Association,* 6, no. 1 (July), 67–69.

1904[?]. "An Autobiography of W. P. Zuber of Iola, Grimes County, Texas, Who Has Prepared a Series of Stories Which Will Appear in Issues of the Sunday Post." *Houston Post,* n.d.

1904. "Founder of Two Texas Towns. The Interesting Life of Judge John P. Coles." *Houston Post,* March 20.

1904. "The Story of John R. Harris." *Houston Post,* April 3.

1905. *Ancestry and Kindred of W. P. Zuber, Texas Veteran.* Iola, Texas.

1939. "An Escape from the Alamo." In Section 1, "Rose and the Al-

amo," in *In the Shadow of History*. Texas Folklore Society Publication, 15. Austin.
1939. "W. P. Zuber to Charlie Jeffries, August 18, 1904." Published as
"Inventing Stories about the Alamo," in *In the Shadow of History*,
Texas Folklore Society Publication, 15. Austin.
1959. "Heroes of Texas." Printed in *The Texas Grand Lodge Magazine*
(May), pp. 180–181.
A poem composed in 1842 while Zuber was on the expedition to
repeal the Vasquez invasion. The poem and the notes were preserved
by A. A. Johnson, Jr., of Waco, one of Zuber's grandsons.
1961. Letter to Mrs. J. S. Anderson of Orange, Texas, postmarked Iola,
Grimes County, December 14, 1899. Published by *Zest Magazine*,
Houston Chronicle, April 2, 1961, as presented by Garland Roark.

MANUSCRIPTS

Compilations, Memorials, Articles, Essays

1874. Memorial of William P. Zuber on the Subject of Pensions to the
Honorable Legislature of the State of Texas. Memorials and Petitions.
Texas State Archives, Austin.
1881. The Funeral in the Alamo. Sent to A. W. Spaight, Commissioner
of Insurance, Statistics, and History. Filed under "Alamo" in Biog-
graphical and Historical Material. Texas State Archives, Austin.
This appeared as "The Burning of the Bodies of the Heroes of the
Alamo . . ." in the *Houston Post*, March 1, 1882.
1881. The Victims of Santa Anna's Cruelty. Sent to A. W. Spaight,
Commissioner of Insurance, Statistics and History. A manuscript titled
A Victim of Santa Anna's Tyranny is bound as Book XI of the Zuber
Collection, Texas State Archives, Austin.
1882. Memorial of William P. Zuber, a Texas Veteran, on the Subject
of Pensions. To the Honorable Legislature of the State of Texas Soon
to Assemble. Memorials and Petitions, Texas State Archives, Austin.
1886–1904. Biographies of Texas Veterans. Data for 130 biographies.
Zuber Papers. The University of Texas Archives, Austin.
The manuscript was acquired in 1947 by The University of Texas
Library from T. P. Buffington through L. W. Kemp.
1895. Outline History of the Texas Veterans Association. Pennybacker
Collection. The University of Texas Archives, Austin.
Twelve-page manuscript sent to Mrs. Percy V. Pennybacker.

1899[?] Sketch of William Joel Bryan.
     Tribute to W. E. Kennard.
     Biography of W. P. Zuber.
         Three articles in Lester Bugbee File entitled Biographical Sketches
     of Some Noted Texans. Bugbee Collection. The University of Texas
     Archives, Austin.

1900. A Sermon on Christian Riches. Dated Iola, Texas, December,
     1900. Bound as Book X in Zuber Collection. Texas State Archives,
     Austin.

1900. A Biography of P. H. Bell. In Vol. VIII, Veterans Biographies.
     Zuber Papers. The University of Texas Archives, Austin.

1910–1913. Eighty Years in Texas: Reminiscences of a Texas Veteran
     from 1830 to 1910. Nine bound volumes. Zuber Collection, Texas
     State Archives, Austin.

n.d. The Controverted Colony.
     Sketch of Jesse Grimes.
         Manuscripts sent to Z. T. Fulmore. Fulmore Collection, The Uni-
     versity of Texas Archives, Austin.

n.d. Dixon Manac, a Half-Breed Creek Indian. Bound in Book IX (pp.
     839–851) of the Zuber Collection, Texas State Archives, Austin.

Letters

April 5 and April 15, 1881. To A. W. Spaight. Two letters. Biographical
     and Historical Material. Texas State Archives, Austin.

December 21, 1888. To Moses Austin Bryan. Zuber Papers. The Uni-
     versity of Texas Archives, Austin.

August 19, 1889; September 14, 1889; September 23, 1889; November
     26, 1889; December 11, 1889; February 15, 1890; March 6, 1890;
     March 15, 1890; March 17, 1890; March 18, 1890; March 22, 1890;
     March 30, 1890; May 1, 1890; May 12, 1890; July 4, 1890; July 5,
     1890; August 12, 1890; September 20, 1890; December 1, 1890; Janu-
     ary 1, 1891; June 22, 1891; August 1, 1891; September 2, 1891; May
     28, 1892; April 14, 1894; June 8, 1898. To Guy M. Bryan. Zuber
     Papers. The University of Texas Archives, Austin.

January 2, 1895; March 9, 1895; March 12, 1895; March 13, 1895;
     April 8, 1895. To Mrs. Percy V. Pennybacker. Pennybacker Papers,
     The University of Texas Archives, Austin.

February 22, 1899. To Lester G. Bugbee. Bugbee Collection. The Uni-
     versity of Texas Archives, Austin.

September 27, 1899; November 9, 1899; November 10, 1899. To Z. T. Fulmore. Fulmore Papers, The University of Texas Archives, Austin.

November 29, 1900; September 7, 1901; September 9, 1901; December 10, 1901; May 15, 1902; July 9, 1903. To George P. Garrison. Garrison Papers, The University of Texas Archives, Austin.

June 26, 1903. To T. P. Buffington. Typescript filed with L. W. Kemp notes on Zuber. The University of Texas Archives, Austin.

August 17, 1904. To C. C. Jeffries. Typescript sent from Jeffries to E. W. Winkler in 1923. Zuber Papers. The University of Texas Archives, Austin.

Works Concerning Zuber

1882. Texas Department of Insurance, Statistics, and History. *Annual Report of the Commission for 1881*. Galveston: A. H. Belo & Company, Printers.

1910. "Monument to Hood's Brigade Dedicated." *Confederate Veteran*, XVIII (December), 563.

1911. Kirkpatrick, Elenita T. "Sole Survivor of the Army of the Texas Republic." *Texas Magazine*, 5, no. 1 (November), 53–54.

1912. "Sole Survivor of Battle of San Jacinto." *San Antonio Express*, December 8.

1913. "Hero of San Jacinto. W. P. Zuber Expires." *Austin Statesman*, September 23.

1930. Blair, E. L. *Early History of Grimes County*, pp. 164–171.
"Memoirs of Zuber," so called by E. L. Blair in his *Early History of Grimes County*, may be the history of Montgomery County that Zuber planned to write. (See letter from Zuber to Guy M. Bryan, June 28, 1898.) Blair describes the Memoirs as "in the nature of a history of the town of Anderson and vicinity." The manuscript was dated July, 1903, and in 1929 was in the possession of T. P. Buffington of Anderson, Texas.

1932. "Where Patriots Rest—Texas State Cemetery." *Confederate Veteran*, XI. (March), 95.

Other Pertinent Reference Material

Austin City Directory, 1872.

Bancroft, H. H. *History of the North Mexican States and Texas*. San Francisco: The History Company, 1889.

Barker, Eugene C., Charles S. Potts, and Charles W. Ramsdell. *A School History of Texas*. Evanston, Ill.: Row, Peterson & Co., 1928. First published 1912.

Bayard, Ralph. *Lone-Star Vanguard: The Catholic Re-Occupation of Texas, 1838–1848*. St. Louis: Vincentian Press, 1945.

Blake, R. B. "A Vindication of Rose and His Story," in Section 1, "Rose and the Alamo," in *In the Shadow of History*. Texas Folklore Society Publication, 15. Austin, 1930.

Blessington, Joseph P. *The Campaigns of Walker's Texas Division*. Brasada Reprint Series. Austin: Pemberton Press, 1968.

"Brief Sketches of Survivors of the Texas Revolution." *Texas Almanac for 1872*. Galveston: W. and D. Richardson, 1871.

Burleson, Mrs. Georgia J., comp. *The Life and Writings of Rufus C. Burleson*. N.p., 1901.

Corner, William. *San Antonio de Bexar, a Guide and History*. San Antonio, 1890.

Crocket, George Louis. *Two Centuries in East Texas*. Dallas: Southwest Press, 1932.

Delgado, Pedro. "Mexican Account of the Battle of San Jacinto." A translation from the Spanish of Pedro Delgado. *Texas Almanac for 1870*, pp. 41–53. Galveston: Richardson and Co., 1869. *Texas Almanac for 1873*. Galveston: Richardson, Belo and Co., 1872.

Dobie, J. Frank. "The Line That Travis Drew," in Section 1, "Rose and the Alamo," in *The Shadow of History*. Texas Folklore Society Publication, 15. Austin, 1939.

Elliott, Claude. Review of *In the Shadow of History*. *Southwestern Historical Quarterly*, 47 (April, 1940), 532–533.

Gammel, H. P. N., *The Laws of Texas, 1822–1897*. 10 vols. Austin: Gammel Book Co., 1898.

Garrison, George P. *Texas: A Contest of Civilizations*. Boston: Houghton Mifflin Co., 1903.

Gray, William Fairfax. *From Virginia to Texas, 1835*. Houston: Gray, Dillaye and Co., 1909. Reprinted, Houston: Fletcher Young Publishing Co., 1965.

The Handbook of Texas. 2 vols. Austin: Texas State Historical Association, 1952.

Hodge, F. W. *Handbook of American Indians North of Mexico*. Washington, D.C.: Government Printing Office, 1912.

Horwitz, Elinor. "Escape from the Alamo." *Texas Parade*, October, 1968.

Houston, Sam. *Writings of Sam Houston, 1813–1863*. 8 vols. New York: Plenum Publishing Corp., 1961.

Kemp, L. W. *The Signers of the Texas Declaration of Independence*. Houston: Anson Jones Press, 1944.

Looscan, Adele B. Letter to G. P. Garrison, October 21, 1901. Garrison Papers. The University of Texas Archives, Austin.

Lord, Walter. *A Time to Stand*. New York: Harper & Brothers, 1961.

McArdle, H. A. Letter to G. P. Garrison, November 28, 1901. Garrison Papers. The University of Texas Archives, Austin.

Mixon, Ruby. "William Barret Travis, His Life and Letters." Master's thesis, The University of Texas, 1930.

Morphis, James M. *A History of Texas from Its Discovery and Settlement*. New York: U.S. Publishing Co., 1874.

Nunn, W. C. *Texas under the Carpetbaggers*. Austin: University of Texas Press, 1962.

Oates, Stephen B. *Confederate Cavalry West of the River*. Austin: University of Texas Press, 1961.

The Orr Brothers. *Campaigning with Parsons' Texas Cavalry Brigade CSA*. Ed. by John Q. Anderson. Hillsborough, Texas: Hill Junior College Press, 1967.

Parsons, W. H. *The Brief and Condensed History of Parsons' Texas Cavalry Brigade, 1861–1865*. 1883. Reprinted, Waco, Texas, 1962.

Pennybacker, Anna M. J. (Mrs. Percy V). *A New History of Texas for Schools*. Especially the 1888 and 1895 editions. Tyler, Texas, 1888–1924.

Perry, George Sessions. *Texas, a World in Itself*. New York: Grosset & Dunlap, Inc., 1952.

Rowe, Edna. "The Disturbances at Anahuac in 1832." *Quarterly of the Texas State Historical Association*, 6 (1902–1903).

Smith, Ralph J. *Reminiscences of the Civil War and Other Sketches*. San Marcos, Texas, 1911. Reprinted, Waco, Texas: W. M. Morrison, 1962.

Thrall, Homer S. *A Pictorial History of Texas from the Earliest Visits of European Adventurers to A.D. 1879*. St. Louis: Thompson & Co., 1879.

Tinkle, Lon. *13 Days to Glory: The Siege of the Alamo*. New York: McGraw-Hill, Inc., 1958.

The War of the Rebellion: A Compilation of the Official Records of the Union and Confederate Armies. Four series, 128 vols. Washington D.C.: U.S. War Department, 1880–1901.

Williams, Amelia. "A Critical Study of the Siege of the Alamo and of the Personnel of its Defenders." *Southwestern Historical Quarterly*, 37 (1933), 31 n.

Yelvington, Ramsey. *A Cloud of Witnesses: The Drama of the Alamo*. Austin: University of Texas Press, 1959.

INDEX

Abolition Party: 228

Aes, District of. SEE San Augustine County, Texas

Agua Dulce River: encampment on, 64–65

Aguirre, Captain ———: at Battle of San Jacinto, 88–89, 91

Alamo, the: Mexican forces at, 43; reports on fall of, 52–54; destruction of Texan command at, 99 n.; Zuber's account of Moses Rose's escape from, 100 n., 248–254; mentioned, 111

Alexandria, Louisiana: 203, 217, 218

Almonte, Colonel Juan Nepomuceno: in Battle of San Jacinto, 82, 91, 92

Alston, Captain John R.: commands company of Carter's Lancers, 134, 135; and furloughs for Zuber, 136, 195; in battle of Shell Creek, 150; enlists recruits, 164, 165; and conscripts, 199; wounded, 205; in attack on plantation, 211; mentioned, 146, 168, 225, 226. SEE ALSO Alston's company

Alston's company: in Carter's Brigade, 137, 156; Zuber in, 137; in Parsons' Texas Cavalry, 141 n.; on Old Cane River, 204; mentioned, 156, 169, 171, 183, 198, 202, 204, 212

Alto, Texas: Carter's Brigade at, 138

Alto Miro, Texas: militia company at, 111, 113

American Civil War: Zuber designates as Confederate War, 132–133; termination of, 225–229

American Revolution: participation in, of Zuber's ancestors, 8, 9–10, 11–12

amnesty oath: required of Confederate supporters, 228, 229, 230, 231

Anahuac, Texas: Mexican evacuation of, 26, 33; siege of, 33

Anderson, Lieutenant William: 170, 187, 212

Anderson, Texas: 111, 199

Anderson Prairie, Texas: 245

Angel, J. L.: 226–227

Angier, Private ———: 187

annexation of Texas: 117–118

Applewhite, D. C.: murder of, 239–240

Archer, Branch T.: calls out militia to fight Indians, 107–108; proclamation of, questioned, 107, 110

Arkansas: strategy of Federals in, 184; mentioned, 178

Arkansas division: in expedition to Missouri, 167

Arkansas Post: Confederate command at, 141; threatened by Union forces, 154; fall of, 155; mentioned, 190

Arkansas River: Confederate guard of, 190; levee on, 193–194; mentioned, 154, 155, 160

army, Texas. SEE Cavalry, specific units; militia, Texas; Texas division

Arnold, Henrick: 111, 112

Ashford, Lieutenant John B.: 135, 137

Atchafalaya River: 219

Attoyac River: as border of the "Redlands," 22

Austin, John: 33

Austin, Stephen F.: in Harrisburgh, 30–31; Zuber correspondence on, 31 n.; mentioned, 74, 244, 257

Austin, Texas: meeting at, regarding statehood, 117; Zuber in, 235, 245; mentioned, 241

Austin's Colony: Zuber family in, 21, 25, 34–36; early hardships in, 35–36

Autrey, Mr. ———: Zuber at house of, 154–155; and Zuber's horse, 157, 159

Avenue Hotel (Austin): Zuber at, 235

ayuntamiento: in San Antonio, 112

den, 196; in Texas, 198; at Cloutierville, 207; and Zuber's teaching,
225; appoints chaplain, 226–227;
retires from service, 227; mentioned,
171, 180, 224, 226
Gilbert, C. E.: and Zuber's position as
guide, 245
Gillaspie, James C.: in Bennett's company, 49, 54; becomes captain, 73;
company of, 80; in Somervell expedition, 113; as colonel, 134, 135;
commands regiment, Carter's Brigade, 137; at Alto, 138; and conversion of Carter's Brigade into infantry regiments, 141; dies in
Huntsville, 231; mentioned, 242, 243
Gillaspie's company: 80
Gipson, William: 171
"Girl I Left Behind Me, The" (song):
181
Goliad, Texas: battle of, reported,
61–62; massacre of Texans at, 68–
70; escape from, 69–70; burial of
Fannin's command at, 98
Gonzales, Texas: battle of, 40; retreat
from, 54–56; encampment at, 114
Goodbread, John: in Runaway
Scrape, 100–101
Goshen, Texas: Zuber teaches school
at, 128, 232; arson at, 232; dinner
at, 232–233
Grandbury, Texas: 245
Grand Encore, Louisiana: 203
Grant, Ulysses S.: 231
Grass Fight, the: 42
Green, General Tom: death of,
mourned by Zuber, 202
Greene, Colonel Colton: 167. SEE
ALSO Greene's brigade
Greene's brigade: in expedition to
Missouri, 167; at Cape Girardeau,
176; mentioned, 180, 199
Grimes, Jesse: 48
Grimes County, Texas: Zuber in, xii,
xiii, 34–36, 221, 245; defense
against Indians in, 106; as part of
Montgomery County, 108; cavalry
regiment in, 198; demoralization in,
223–224; postwar elections in, 229;
and property limitations, 229; bu-
reau agent in, 230; Moses Rose in,
253
Groce's plantation: encampment at,
72–77, 242
Groesbeck, Texas: Governor Davis in,
239; Applewhite murder in, 239
Groves, Rev. John: army at house of,

146–148; threatened by Federals,
147
gunboat: ironclad, on Mississippi
River, 189–190; on Bayou Pierre,
202; on Bon Dieu River, 204, 215

Hall, William: 31
Hanner, Captain ———: 170, 172,
212
Hanner's company: 170
Harper, Andrew J.: 116
Harrelson, Colonel ———: 148
Harris, David: 25, 26–27, 82
Harris, DeWitt Clinton: 27
Harris, Jane: 27
Harris, John R.: 25, 27
Harris, William P.: 25, 29
Harris brothers: economic activities
of, 26
Harrisburg[h], Texas: spelling of
town's name, 25; Zuber family in,
25–31; location of, 25; mills in, 26;
as navigation center, 26, 27; Texas
ad interim government at, 27; yel-
low fever in, 29; threatened by
Mexican troops, 75–76; Texas army
marches to, 79–81; burning of, 81,
82–83
Hawes, General James Morrison: and
command of Twelfth Texas Cav-
alry, 153, 156
Heads Prairie, Texas: 245
Hearne, Texas: 245
Hébert, General Paul Octave: 135
Helena, Arkansas: exchange of prison-
ers at, 152; mentioned, 146, 147,
148, 150, 188
Hempstead, Texas: 128, 134, 135,
221, 235, 239
Henderson, J. P.: 119
Hicks Station, Arkansas: 154
Highsmith, Captain Malcijah Benja-
min: 157
Hightower, Captain Lew: 232–233
Hill, Isaac Lafayette: 40, 75
Hill, Parley: 149
Hill, Rev. Robert: 122
Hill County, Texas: 245
Hoard, Rev. Jesse: 122, 123
Hockley, George W.: joins military
company, 72–73; instructs Zuber on
guard duty, 77–79
Hollis, David: 108
Holmes, General Theophilus Hunter:
orders dismounting of cavalry, 142;
orders march to Arkansas Post, 154;
retreats to Camden, 196

Printed and bound by CPI Group (UK) Ltd, Croydon, CR0 4YY

09/06/2025

14685838-0001